Purple Passages

CONTEMPORARY NORTH AMERICAN POETRY SERIES

Series Editors Alan Golding, Lynn Keller, and Adalaide Morris

Purple Passages

Pound, Eliot, Zukofsky, Olson, Creeley, and the Ends of Patriarchal Poetry

RACHEL BLAU DUPLESSIS

University of Iowa Press, Iowa City

UNIVERSITY OF IOWA PRESS, IOWA CITY 52242

Copyright © 2012 by the University of Iowa Press

www.uiowapress.org

Printed in the United States of America

Design by Teresa W. Wingfield

The University of Iowa Press is a member of Green Press Initiative and is committed to preserving natural resources.

Printed on acid-free paper

Library of Congress Cataloging-in-Publication Data
DuPlessis, Rachel Blau.
Purple passages : Pound, Eliot, Zukofsky, Olson, Creeley, and the ends of patriarchal poetry / Rachel Blau DuPlessis.
p. cm.—(Contemporary North American poetry series)
Includes bibliographical references and index.
ISBN-13: 978-1-60938-084-7, ISBN-10: 1-60938-084-3 (pbk)
ISBN-13: 978-1-60938-094-6, ISBN-10: 1-60938-094-0 (ebook)
1. American poetry—20th century—History and criticism. 2. Masculinity in literature.
3. Patriarchy in literature. 4. Literature and society—United States—History—20th century.
5. Gender identity in literature. I. Title.
PS323.5.D87 2012
811'.509353—dc23   2011036872

Contents

Acknowledgments

The majority of this book was drafted during my academic year appointment in 2008–2009 as a Fellow of the National Humanities Center (NHC), enabled by a one-semester fellowship from a Temple University Study Leave and by the generosity of Dean Teresa Scott Soufas at Temple University's College of Liberal Arts, allowing me to take the full year appointment to the NHC. The hospitality and working conditions provided by the NHC are legendary. I am grateful for the research and library assistance particularly of Josiah Mark Drewry, then associate librarian for interlibrary loan and reference, National Humanities Center Library, to whom I came with some amusing and crucial queries. I am also grateful to Jonathan Culler, Michael Davidson, and Susan Stanford Friedman for their willingness to recommend this project to the NHC in the first place. I feel quite beholden to Peter Middleton, Libbie Rifkin, and (again) Michael Davidson for their exemplary work on sex-gender materials and poets' affiliations, a subject that I also broach here, despite—and because of—their contributions. My mistakes remain always, perhaps even insistently, my own.

I thank the University of Iowa Press for general encouragement, for welcoming interest, and for help in the form of two intellectually generous and incisive readers' reports that I tried to follow as best I could. Joe Parsons, Charlotte Wright, and others at the Press were enthusiastic and clearheaded in every way, as were designer Teresa W. Wingfield and copy editor Kathy Burford Lewis. I owe warm and happy thanks to Conna Clark, Philadelphia Museum of Art, for her crucial assistance with the art on the cover of this book, *Physical Culture* (1913) by Francis Picabia.

The appearances of these materials at conferences or in periodicals and anthologies were a consistent prod to the project. Papers and essays often have been considerably revised for these chapters.

One source for chapter 1 is the anthology piece written for Natalya Lusty and Julian Murphet's *Modernism and Masculinity* (Cambridge University Press, forthcoming), an article usefully commissioned while I was writing this book. I also drew on "Manifesting Literary Feminisms: Gender Buttons," a plenary at the conference Manifesting Australian Literary

Feminisms: Nexus and Faultlines, Centre for Women's Studies and Gender Research, School of Political and Social Inquiry, Monash University, Melbourne, Victoria, Australia, 13–14 December 2007. It was later published in a special issue of *Australian Literary Studies* 24.3–4 (October/November 2009): 20–38. Many thanks particularly to Ann Vickery.

Some of the material on Eliot in chapter 2 also occurs in "T. S. Eliot and Gender," in *T. S. Eliot in Context*, edited by Jason Harding (Cambridge University Press, 2011). A bit of the analysis also appears in "Singing Schools," an essay prepared for a forthcoming anthology edited by Jeffrey C. Robinson and Julie Carr.

Chapter 3 benefited from comments by Bob Perelman and Peter Quartermain in fall 2010. The chapter contains material from a review for *Contemporary Literature*; an essay written for the University of Sussex Conference on the Long Poem, Brighton, England, 16–17 May 2008; and material about textual practices from "Midrashic Sensibilities: Secular Judaism and Radical Poetics: A Personal Essay in Several Chapters," in *Radical Poetics and Secular Jewish Culture*, edited by Stephen Paul Miller and Daniel Morris (University of Alabama Press, 2010).

An early version of chapter 4 (and the seed for this book) was presented in 1996 at the National Poetry Foundation conference on the 1950s held in Orono, Maine. It was subsequently delivered at a conference in Athens, Greece (2002), at the University of Arizona (2003), and at the University of Florida, Gainesville (2004). A version treating only Ginsberg and Olson was published in *The Periphery Viewing the World*, edited by Christina Dokou, Efterpi Mitsi, and Bessie Mitsikopoulou (Selected Papers from the Fourth International Conference of the Hellenic Association for the Study of English in 2004). Some words on "Howl" also appear in the 2011 *Oxford Handbook of Modern and Contemporary American Poetry*, edited by Cary Nelson. I would like to extend thanks to Peter Quartermain for an unflinching reading of this chapter in summer 2006 and to Libbie Rifkin for seriously encouraging me to publish this article in full—a provocation to the book itself. This was published in *Jacket Magazine* 31 (http://jacketmagazine.com/31/duplessis-manhood.html).

The material in chapter 5 has not been previously published.

Part of chapter 6 was delivered at the Charles Olson Centenary Conference, Simon Fraser University, Vancouver, B.C., as a plenary lecture on 5 June 2010.

Part of chapter 7 is based on but redacts "The Hole: Death, Sexual Difference, and Gender Contradictions in Creeley's Poetry," in *Form,*

Power and Person in Robert Creeley's Life and Work, edited by Stephen Fredman and Steve McCaffery (University of Iowa Press, 2010). This article was also published in *Jacket Magazine* 36 (August 2008) (http://jacketmagazine.com/36). It was originally delivered at the Robert Creeley conference in 2006 at the State University of New York–Buffalo.

Thanks to all the editors and conference organizers noted above.

Among the friends and helper figures cited above (Michael Davidson, Bob Perelman, Peter Quartermain, Libbie Rifkin, and Ann Vickery), I would also like to mention Charles Bernstein, Stephen Collis, Joseph Donahue, Clayton Eshleman, Ben Friedlander, Alan Golding, Lynn Keller, Peter Middleton, Adalaide Morris, Peter Nicholls, Marjorie Perloff, Mark Scroggins, Sharon Thesen, John Tranter, and Barrett Watten, who all contributed something distinctive to this project or to my thinking about it.

I am grateful to the following publishers for permission to quote from the works cited: Robert Creeley, *The Collected Poems of Robert Creeley, 1945–1975*, copyright © 1982 by the Regents of the University of California, published by the University of California Press, reprinted by permission of the publisher; Robert Creeley, *The Collected Poems of Robert Creeley, 1975–2005*, copyright © 2006 by the Estate of Robert Creeley, published by the University of California Press, reprinted by permission of the publisher; Charles Olson and Frances Boldereff, *Charles Olson and Frances Boldereff: A Modern Correspondence*, Ralph Maud and Sharon Thesen, eds., Middletown, CT: Wesleyan University Press, copyright © 1999, reprinted by permission of the publisher; Ezra Pound, *The Cantos of Ezra Pound*, copyright © 1934, 1937, 1940, 1948, 1950, 1956, 1959, 1962, 1963, 1965, 1966, 1968, 1970, and 1971 by Ezra Pound, reprinted by permission of New Directions Publishing Corporation; Ezra Pound, "Canto CXVI," from *The Cantos of Ezra Pound*, copyright © 1968 by Ezra Pound, reprinted by permission of New Directions Publishing Corp; Ezra Pound, *Pound/Zukofsky*, copyright © 1981, 1987 by the Trustees of the Ezra Pound Literary Property Trust, reprinted by permission of New Directions Publishing Corporation; Gertrude Stein, "Patriarchal Poetry," permission granted by the Estate of Gertrude Stein through its Literary Executor, Mr. Stanford Gann, Jr., of Levin & Gann, P.A.; Louis Zukofsky, *Pound/Zukofsky*, copyright © 1981, 1987 by Paul Zukofsky, reprinted by permission of New Directions Publishing Corporation.

Part One

One

Manifesting Literary Feminism

*"Masculinity" [. . .] is best understood as transcending the personal, as
a heterogeneous set of ideas, constructed around assumptions of social
power, which are lived out and reinforced, or perhaps denied and challenged, in multiple and diverse ways within a whole social system in
which relations of authority, work, and domestic life are organized, in
the main, along hierarchical gender lines.*

LYNNE SEGAL, *Slow Motion*

Patriarchal poetry a choice.

GERTRUDE STEIN, "PATRIARCHAL POETRY"

1. Dear Reader: An Epistle

There are no genderless subjects in any relationship structuring
literary culture: not in production, dissemination, or reception; not in
objects, discourses, or practices; not in reading experiences or in interpretations. This book—analytic, invested, affectual—discusses masculinity and maleness in poetry as marked and constructed social subject
positions framed within a cultural poetics of gender. It investigates male
poetic power and how it constitutes and sustains itself in richly emotion-
laden interactions. Indeed, these poets' ideas and actions—about masculinity, the feminine, the effeminate, the erotic—were continuously
articulated and loomed large in their self-creation as writers, in literary
bonding, and in its deployment. Contentious male-male dyads, one characteristic formation of this period, and the sex-gender regimes in which
male poets acted and self-presented have recently come under scrutiny
by significant critical work rejecting the notion that aspects of the male
poetic career were natural manifestations of masculine subjectivity.[1] Assumptions about maleness and varieties of masculinity help construct
consequential models for institutions of poetic practice. *Purple Passages*
asks, among other questions, how particular twentieth-century male
poets—those with allegiances to the Pound tradition—faced challenges
posed both by modernist feminisms and by male-male eroticism. The

short answer? Unevenly. The dynamism of "virile thought" intercepted the trajectories both of female cultural coequality and co-temporality and of gay civic and erotic claims (Hulme 1955, 69). That is a loosely social statement and is one track within this book. Another track involves the question that Judith Butler asks in *Undoing Gender*: is the patriarchal order of sexual difference and power relations so imbedded in the "symbolic" that it is ineligible "for social intervention" (Butler 2004, 213)? Rejecting the postulate of fixed hierarchic genders means that one should "trace the moments where the binary system of gender is disputed and challenged, where the coherence of the categories are [*sic*] put into question, and where the very social life of gender turns out to be malleable and transformable" (Butler 2004, 216). This book traces some of these debates and contradictions by discussing male poets who are strongly invested in the patriarchal order.

In *The World, the Text, and the Critic*, Edward Said proposes both a "situated" text and a critic; in that spirit, this critic and book try to be "skeptical, secular, reflectively open to its [her/his] own failings" but not "value-free" (Said 1983, 26). The book also takes up the gap that Said sketches in modernism between "filiation" and "affiliation"—their interchange, their tensions, the passages between them (Said 1983, 23–24). Filiation is organic, hierarchic, and paternal, a "quasi-religious authority" or covenant; affiliation is that "new form of relationship," perpetually yearned for in all evocations of "newness"—"collegiality, professional respect, post-familial," worldly (and possibly idealized by Said) (Said 1983, 16, 20). The propulsions for the shift, the motor of any changes from and in filiative and affiliative relationships in modernism, are, in my view, hard-won, hard-fought alterations in the civic, political, and sexual status of women and sexual nonconformists.[2] In these poets' male-male relationships and in their relationships with female colleagues (somewhat less discussed here), the strains, incompleteness, and tensions of this fraught passage back and forth between these formations are explored. It becomes clearer that there is no one-way passage as Said perhaps had hoped; we will all have to negotiate repeated ways of making passages that struggle with the binary system of gender and with the ideologies that support its practices.

Both Michael Davidson and Libbie Rifkin have examined the "structural function of exclusion" of women and of the feminine "at the core of both [male] authorial identity formation and avant-garde institution building" (Rifkin 2000, 7); Andrew Mossin has signaled the importance of "male subjectivity" to the careers of these poets (Mossin 2010). While one can summarize the mechanisms through which maleness and its cultural resistances are generated—"overdetermination of male bonding" and at times "exaggerated masculine [personae]"—the exact cultural acts, practices, and choices that constructed this outcome need specifying (Watten 1999, 154, 151). These emerge in apparently affiliative poetic institutions of self- and cultural production, like editing, mentoring/ protégé bonds, declaring allegiance and continuing allegiance (in manifestos and works), muse/user relations, and acts of leading, cooperating, grouping, and following. My chapters discuss these mechanisms and institutions, emphasizing the moments of choice and articulation when all this (or some of it) was visibly in flux and might have had different outcomes. For example, one might have cultural omnivorousness but without sexism. Some of these specific, individuated cultural choices had a defining general impact in the struggles between filiation and affiliation. I want this book, then, to deliver a sense of contingency. "Patriarchal poetry a choice" is the leitmotiv (Stein [1927] 1980, 143).

Purple Passages places "gender, the apparatus of poesis, and power-oriented production and reception centrally in play" by examining "ideologies and social situations of poetry as a mode of practice" (DuPlessis 2006, 136). The book claims Gayle Rubin's focal concept "sex/gender system" for the cultural realm and calls upon the related definition offered by Teresa de Lauretis: "The sex-gender system . . . is both a sociocultural construct and a semiotic apparatus, a system of representation"; it is also historical, imbedded in personal subjectivity and general ideology, and the site of multiple contradictions (Rubin 1975, 159; de Lauretis 1987, 5). To extend the critical analysis of gender to males may seem (to some critics) to lose the sociocultural rectification of the status of women possible with a relatively monogendered feminism. Without such analysis, however, masculinity remains unmarked, unchangeable, and apparently "neutral."

Many styles and modes of maleness are available in any given historical period, and these are often exaggerated and framed by representation. Perhaps as fallout from the "affective revolutions" of the late eighteenth and nineteenth centuries, poetry as an idea in long modernity manifests a liberatory, sublime, erotic, transgressive, and pan-gendered aura (Craciun 2008, 155–156). Yet sometimes this liberatory narrative includes a *rappel à l'ordre*, symptomatically in the sex-gender realm. Thereupon rigid masculinist claims compensate for the sense, out of romanticism and the decadent, that poetry and the poetic career are feminized or queered in some way. These responses from "virile thought" are contradictory. Are these zones dangerous and to be avoided or perhaps so tempting that they must be warded off? May they be cured/answered with the (physical, mystical, political?) energies of maleness reaffirmed? Is the vitalist life force so dear to early modernists the property only of males? No surprise, then, that in Anglo-American and international twentieth-century poetries (modernist and just after), metaphors and opinions about gender and sexuality intermingled dramatically with questions of poetics and then got remixed with major social changes within modernity.

Consistent from romanticisms through modernisms (as one historical "unit" of modes of maleness) is a male-imperial potential for ranging across and deploying a variety of sex-gender stances: liberated sexuality, machine masculinity, homosociality, heterosexuality, hypermasculinity, feminine-poeticalness, queerness of one sort or another, antibourgeois transgressive maleness, dandyish indifference—freely ranging among and appropriating from these conflicting stances but not always interrogating them. One sees this vividly in Ezra Pound's chameleon spectrum of early personae: from an adherent of muscular Christianity ("Ballad of the Goody Fere") to hypermasculine bombastic leader ("Sestina: Altaforte"), sexy red-blooded male ("The Condolence"), troubadour with sensibilities ("Dance Figure"; "The House of Splendour"; "Apparuit"), modern satirist ("Tenzone"; "Salutation the Second"), decadent sympathizer ("Hugh Selwyn Mauberley"), feminist male ("Commission"), and urbane nonfeminist male ("Portrait d'une Femme").[3] Using Gertrude Stein's cheerful if vague term, I call this catholic and contradictory *imperium* of possibilities by the name "patriarchal poetry." Staking claims to this imperial range is central to experimental poetry by men.

As Barbara Johnson reminds us about Charles Baudelaire, the poetic career is constructed of "male privilege"—of which one part is "the right to play femininity," separating the feminine from women, who may, of course, not particularly want it (Johnson 1998, 127; see also Huyssen 1986, 45). This privilege extends to male claims on any and all possible sex-gender positions in poetry. This does not mean that men necessarily support females in their literary careers or view females as having an equal possibility of deploying such multiple subject positions—sometimes quite the opposite. This literary stance can go hand in hand with misogynist attitudes as well as with male-affirmative frankness: the imperative to "dance the dance of the phallus" not only is joyously self-assertive but can also be a naturalizing claim of political hegemony (Pound [1926] 1950, 86).

At the heart of modernist maleness and poetic practices are multiple contradictions and imperial urgencies, gender ideas both progressive and defensive. Gender relations are, as Cary Nelson proposed, "both symptom and subject"; the sex-gender system is a topic of debate and multiple representations on its own and "a stand in for other anxieties about cultural" and political life (Nelson 1996, 325). The eros of poesis—the ruthless and desirous bonds involved in poetry as a social and cultural practice—is a powerful obliterator of fixed and normative gender ideas; yet, at the same time, conventional sex-gender ideas and practices are hegemonic and emphatically policed. Deviance and errancy were (and are) legally, socially, economically, and politically punished, if also central to tempting subcultures.[4] Many male strategies in the artistic world result from this contradiction—aggressive macho behaviors, homosocial bonding in artistic groups, the claiming and hoarding of cultural power, problematic sexual exploitation, seductive behaviors in the aura of poetic groups, and insistence on women as culturally weak, as static ideals or static degradations (both being historically immobile roles). All these positions have implications for the nature of poetry and its practices; the claim that "real authentic [poetic] culture" remains the "prerogative of men" was a still-active if contested position in modernism (Huyssen 1986, 47).

This book examines some modernist, objectivist, and projectivist poets in the eros-laden dyads that have been vital (if sometimes temporary) bonding in their poetic careers, with their intense fluctuations between filiation and affiliation (Said 1983, 16–20). I take "dyad" from the formative, mirroring, generative, powerful (and language-bearing) relationship of the mother-child dyad and apply that suggestive term to adult friendship, colleagueship, and comradeship as affiliations invested with aesthetic and emotional nurturance but also with familial (filiative) tensions.[5] To write of even a two-person relationship in the making of literary texts, careers, and projects weans criticism away from a "genius" model (yet preserves the affect, arousals, and sublimity of that model) and moves to the study of cultural interactions and their outcomes. This book assumes that the growth of a poet's mind is social and continual, formed in yearning, in desires for mastery and power, in exposures of vulnerability and ruthlessness—that is, in eros. All this motivates my title color; purple is an imperial or regal color, the color of power, as well as a passionate, suffusing color, related to the erotic.[6]

In early modernist Anglophone writing an impresario emerged: Ezra Pound (1885–1972), who proposed stylistic and formal experimentalisms, embodied a vitalist pro-sex stance, and finally wagered his career and the outcome of his major poem of cultural analysis and critique on a real-world dictatorship, supposed to embody ethical and economic "paradise" (Bush 1991, 71–80). Pound's charisma, grasp, and problematic were at issue straight through the century, first with his own modernist peers, William Carlos Williams (1883–1963), Mina Loy (1882–1966), and T. S. Eliot (1888–1965), and later with two writers directly and thoroughly touched by his example, Louis Zukofsky (1908–1978) and Charles Olson (1910–1970). Both of these wrote long poems whose ambition was precisely Poundian—or, more precisely, both wanted to remake Pound politically yet remain within his aesthetic tradition of critique, a particularly fraught problem for claims of gender mastery, for genealogical mindsets, and for the implicit patrilineal metaphors of lines of descent that are commonplace in artistic circles.[7] Moreover, both Olson and Zukofsky were constantly compared to Pound as underlings, junior versions, and epigones. Both had to deal with the impact of that assumption, not the least in a continual annoyance, self-scrutiny, and resistance. Both handled this situation with their own gender metaphors, their own gender regimes; these, particularly their constructions of manhood, are studied here. So are Robert Creeley (1926–2005), John Wieners (1934–2002), Allen Ginsberg (1926–1997), and others who sometimes registered their situation as being in a "company." These poets invented poetic and relational strategies to negotiate their positions within the magnetic and tempting system of patriarchal gender relations. So this book is not about "men in feminism" but about men faced with feminism and with shifting gender relations, a situation that, in this period, often produced its own antibody but also its own omnivorous claims.[8]

Structures of patriarch/epigone, major/minor, synoptic/sycophantic, strong/weak, and other such cultural binaries are (or can imply) gender-inflected structures of feeling. These binaries may map women as lesser, men as greater in the cultural realm, but they also structure male-male relations.[9] This is despite the affirmation of a lateral, homosocial, affiliative "company." That is Creeley's often (yet not necessarily) male-oriented term, one curiously evoking corporate business terminology, both to appropriate it and to torque it but also to gain its hegemonic evocation.[10] One of those binaries is male gender-neutrality and universality, female gender-specificity and particularity. Hence it is difficult to see maleness constantly constructed, reaffirmed, and (possibly) self-different. The ideologies of masculinity have diverse manifestations and representations, diverse narratives. These are always historically in motion or have multiple dynamic elements. One may have degrees of adhesion to ideas/ideals of masculinity; a person's ideas and actions and texts might change over the course of a life or even within different relationships at the same time.

Poetry is the most marginal of modes "in a society in which masculinity is identified with action, enterprise, and progress—within the realms of business, industry, science, and law"; the professionalization of writing and literary criticism in the twentieth century favored fiction and journalistic popularizing (Huyssen 1986, 45). The masculinity of modernist canonical poetry has the further need to struggle against the perceived "femininity" of poetry as a mode of practice. Thereupon emerges the modernist cliché par excellence: a certain kind of aesthetic elegance and investigative intelligence "went with" heterosexual, homosocial maleness; a certain kind of middle-brow and mimetic, inadequate modernist-realism and/or sentimentalism "went with" femaleness; an overreaching unbalanced exaggeration, errant playfulness, and unbalanced sensibility "went with" gayness. This is of course ridiculous were one to give any comprehensive overview of practitioners (and has been called out as an inaccurate view of the field by any number of critics), but such clichéd framing structures are always vital—and viral. It is more accurate to say that a centralizing cultural masculinity appropriated many of these positions into "patriarchal poetry" as an imperial claim over all deployable subject positions.

Prescriptive, simplistic ethical positions about art, sexuality, and gender gained cultural traction in early modernism. In *The New Laokoon* (1910) by Irving Babbitt, a harbinger of many modernist manifestos, any predominance of the feminine in art constituted "a corruption" of sanity and balance.[11] Masculinist modernism affirms a concealed moralism in response to erosions of male hegemony hardly attributable to females or to homosexuals (many economic, political, and material forces overdetermine social change) but symptomatically focused upon them. Naming something "feminine/effeminate," like calling something "primitive," was both a temptation and a call to male power to gear up gender, sexual, and ethnic border-patrols.

In a generalizing overview of some specific United States cultural histories up to about 1920 (materials plausibly absorbed within the early lifetimes of many of these poets), Michael S. Kimmel tracks three "patterns of [white] men's response" to the "crisis" engendered by immigrants, changes in male work, but most particularly "women's struggles to enter the public arena" (Kimmel 2005, xi). While "crisis" is a rhetorical rather than historical marker, Kimmel's three patterns are uncannily replicated, in a different tonality, among the poets I have chosen. Some see masculinity as a "relentless test" often demanding a physical response—Pound's increasing phallicism might be one example, Olson's phenomenology of the male body another. A second response is outright "exclusion"—resistance to female participation and a related set of exclusions via a suspect Semiticizing; here representations of Judaic culture intermingled with sex-gender, in Olson, Eliot, and, differently, both Zukofsky and Pound. A third strategy for Kimmel's American men is the escape to a "homosocial world, whether mythic or real" (Kimmel 2005, xi). This strategy is visible in Creeley, Wieners, Olson, and Ginsberg.

Does this book mark the declaration of a new era? It does appear as if a masculinist regime—that "gendered nation" of poetry—may be self-consciously eroding, albeit with geologic slowness (Enloe 1993, 245). It therefore seemed appropriate to help it in its (historically determined, teleological?—or is this only illusory?) shift. One analytic tactic here is this: male-based power and regimes of gender-enforcement must be made visible and strange in their virulent—or even in their charming— manifestations, an estrangement effect that I have sought in this book by the socially investigative, assiduous myopia of close reading.[12] This seems a very idiomatic application of Victor Shklovsky's oft-cited goal of "defamiliarization" or "making strange" (Shklovsky 1989, 17). Things *were* this way, these chapters keep on saying, but they did not have to be. The constant message is that there were and are choices. Any regime can change—can be changed. Although discursive and aesthetic choices are not directly linked to one's personal gender and sexuality (even if one could "identify" these fully), various poets still have made claims that do explicitly, metaphorically, or actively talk about masculinity in relation to their work. I track some bizarre and elucidating moments, examining how these patterns and choices have shaped people and are shaped by them in poems, letters, and oeuvres. But omnivorous "patriarchalness" can still propose encyclopedic and pleasurable cultural mastery. Postpatriarchal culture or nonhierarchic uses of mastery occur not by fiat but

by analysis. This book disaggregates masculinities and separates patriarchalness from the Patriarchs. To do so, however, it must trek through
masculinity as a real set of coordinates/contradictions and not as an invisible and neutral universal. This emphasis on existential, social choice
is not meant as a direct answer to more psychoanalytic claims but simply
to imply that these are always socially mediated.

2. The Gender of Poetics

Purple Passages—on poetic power and its eros—is situated in
early modernism through the early contemporary, when male poets
self-consciously deployed and investigated maleness and tried to contain and/or appropriate femaleness, the effete, and the feminine. One
result was that many male poets had difficulty accepting female artists
(and sometimes conventionally "feminized" men like gays and Jews) as
coequal—in their difference—and coeval, difficulty living in a multi-
gendered world of practice. They showed considerable ambivalence to
any nonhierarchical sex-gender artistic universe. This outcome is an artifact, constructed and reconstructed, neither a natural inevitability nor
the result of permanent, essentialist attitudes. My analysis focuses on
moments in the careers of these poets when this outcome was in debate,
when the male writers tried out the possibility of a gender coequal poetic
culture. The chapters concern repeated if different moments, visible in
literary relationships and texts, when the nature of the sex-gender system in specific poetic communities was contested, even if that contestation collapsed. The book isolates these moments of ideological choice
and cultural agency. My emphasis falls on contradictions and their outcomes; the goal is to foreground struggles, not to exculpate sexism.

Because this book approaches poetry as a social institution of practice, it does not discuss poems exclusively but also treats other texts intimately generative of and expressive within the poetic career. Letters,
unfinished drafts, manifestos, essays, and prose declarations offer evidence of debates, contradictions, and outcomes in masculinity. Method-
ologically, this necessitates a close reading ethos with a commitment to
uncovering the inflection of social materials and ideologies, mainly concerning gender and sexuality, not simply in the text as content but in the
text as formal trace—as metaphor, as allusion, as genre, as diction.

Documents in poetics and letters are on a continuum with poems;
their articulations of career needs are certainly performative and staged,

if also evidently heartfelt. As Roman Jakobson suggests, such statements can partake of the same choices and stylizations found in art: "Every verbal act in a certain sense stylizes and transforms the event it depicts" (Jakobson 1987, 374). Thus I bring my analysis down to the detail and scrutinize word choices and turns in which ideologies and historical claims are cast.[13] Paralleling Barbara Johnson's mode of symptomatic reading, this analysis takes seriously the nuance of words in critical texts and other documents (Johnson 1987, 93). Such a strategy tends to find in texts self-differences and contradictions, unresolved materials, and debates in poetics or values. This book thus continues to propose social philology or socio-poesis as a reading practice and methodology.

It is sometimes difficult to talk about gender without tumbling into binaries, especially when these writers deployed them, often assiduously. Yet all manifestations of gender are historically variable, affirmed, selected from, reaffirmed, and deployed, even if these manifestations sometimes proceed under rubrics of "nature" or "the natural." To be gendered, to borrow Elspeth Probyn's term, is to be continuously "re-gendered" (Probyn 1993, 1). This may mean to affirm the same again and again (*re-* as repetition), but it might mean some declaration of dissent and difference, some even compromised contestation (*re-* as in redo, reconsider). Further, any poet's sense of the meanings and practices of a gendered self may shift over a lifetime and inside a poetic career. The same may be said of any critic or reader involved with these works.

If traits and inscriptions of gender can be personally and historically mobile, contradictory, and differentially deployed in persons, so, too, rhetorics are mobile in their uses and meanings in artworks. There is, for instance, a carefully constructed artless and "unthreatening poetics of sincerity" that is "feminine," as Barbara Johnson has argued about the nineteenth-century Marceline Desbordes-Valmore (Johnson 1998, 112). Yet Ezra Pound and Robert Creeley claim that their carefully constructed poetics of sincerity is masculine in implication, involving clarity beyond the baroque, decrying mushiness or obfuscatory blur. Clarity and precision, objectivity, impersonality and its apparently pure, truth-telling intentions stand up, in Pound's 1918 "A Retrospect," against subjectivity, "slither," the decadent, the ambiguous, the devious and decorative—all either "feminine" or "effeminate" in connotation (Pound 1954, 12; Easthope [1986] 1990, 79–81). Transgressive excess in Sylvia Plath performs female protest with a masculine inflection (the fine argument in Davidson 2004, 160, 170, 181–193); this is also true of the work of Anne Waldman. In Charles Olson, transgressive excess may signal a masculine imperial or appropriative imagination; in Allen Ginsberg, a male-receptive protest, including against actual women. All of this suggests that situational, mobile readings are necessary.

Why did maleness become so fraught in twentieth-century modernity? World War I and the fervent debates and social politics around it, a response to the slaughter of the male young for dubious political purposes, created male victims of male-run state power. "Old men's lies" and "a botched civilization" imagined by Pound as "an old bitch gone in the teeth" make for a rotten parentage (Pound [1926] [1950?], 190, 191). A compensatory response made maleness precious, as if to conceal that it was also cannon fodder.

Sigmund Freud and Freudianism (especially its coarser, popularized claims) opened questions of sexuality and the vulnerable, relational construction of gender; some parts of the theory ("penis envy") proposed deep (and transhistorical) structures of female inadequacy. Praise of maleness/masculinity and its appropriate power is an outcome. Sexology in general was noted for a sometimes striking frankness and an overt and tolerant discussion of sexual identities and practices, including homosexuality, despite the strain of its criminalization. Sexual liberation (well underway from romanticism on) and political struggles around sexual pleasure free of institutional doxologies and pieties were making slow and yet inexorable progress. This vitalist strand of early modernism, its pro-sex line, and the conviction that a new society would be born from erotic energies are visible in Dora Marsden, among others, linking "the struggle of feminism to the goal of liberating the life principle" (Bush 1991, 74). In 1914, spurred in part by a committee of men, Marsden changed her journal's name from the *Freewoman/ New Freewoman* to the *Egoist*, a move foregrounding individual liberation and deemphasizing social movements for change (DuPlessis [1990] 2006, 44–45). This name change also marked, symbolically, a pivot into a growing masculinist cultural hegemony, itself symbolized by Pound's increasing focus, in the 1920s, on the vitalist urgencies of male phallicism.

Suffrage struggles and struggles for full political representation (still in course now, a century later) transformed the as yet incomplete civic and political coequality of women; 1918 for women over thirty in Britain and 1920 for women in the United States are benchmark dates for achievement of the right to vote. Fears about male virility, men "unmanned" in a bureaucratic state society, losses of male entrepreneurial potential with capitalist consolidations of economic power or mass movements on the left, and male crises of control of others set off endemic alarms throughout the twentieth century and well into the twenty-first. Eugenicist and social Darwinist concerns about the need for manly men and womanly women for reproduction gave rise to gender anxieties (Tickner 1994, 48). Gail Bederman has analyzed the fears of "[white] race suicide" and male inadequacy that women's rights, immigration, and the falling birth rate seemed collectively to indicate in the 1890s and the early part of the twentieth century in the United States (Bederman 1995, 201–202).

From the very beginning of the twentieth century, Pound, Eliot, Loy, and others lived within the steady pressure of changes in female professional, intellectual, and political expectations, enactments of sexuality and pleasure removed from marital and normative claims, and changes in the civic and ideological status of homosexuals, women, and Jews, among others. As Cristanne Miller has summarized, drawing from the refocusing interventions of feminist analysis in the past decades, one may now see "modernist poetry" as "resulting from the radical changes of gender expectation and sexual definition transforming men's and women's lives during the early twentieth century." Women and men interacted in all the modernist movements in art and literature; both genders "played major roles," developed "foundational ideas," "shap[ed] literary production," and contributed to female coequality (or produced ambivalence to it) (Miller 2007, 82).

My attempt to use masculinity as an "active term" but also as a disaggregated term, simply "one coordinate of [men's] identity that exists in a constant dialectical relation with other coordinates," is sometimes challenged by the claims of the gender interactions that I have chosen (ones central to U.S. poetries), in which maleness, at least for a while, was often forcefully reiterated with an essentialist flair (Stecopoulos and Uebel 1997, 5, 4). Charles Olson, for example, held a position in which maleness was so important and humanly hegemonic that female power was viewed with ambivalence, resisted with conviction, and simultaneously exaggerated in impact and repressed. Without acceding to the melodramatic Sandra Gilbert and Susan Gubar thesis of a gender war across the century, with misogyny as its symptom and resentment about female writers' professional achievements as its driving motive, it is clear that changes in female and gay status were something about which many (often heterosexual) male writers were quite aware throughout the twentieth century, with sometimes aggressive, sometimes condescending, sometimes fascinated responses (Gilbert and Gubar 1988, 1994).

The period from before World War I through the mid-twentieth century and even into the moment of second-wave feminism was a time of uneven, gradual, but powerful retrenchment of gender equality, always in relation to sex-gender struggles, culminating in the insistent ideologies of maleness at the American mid-century (Davidson 2004). Scrutinizing and destabilizing this retrenchment became a goal of and after second-wave feminism. Finally, all writing in the long twentieth century occurs after feminism(s), after the gradual entrance of women into universities and the professions and their presence in the workforce in general, after the sexologies of early modernism, and after psychoanalysis, with its theorizing about sexuality and gender formations in the family and about modes of desire.

Given that these historical-poetical materials saturate our poetic culture, our gender debates, and ourselves, we must be both passionate and dispassionate, even simultaneously. I am neither some generalized humanist-feminist nor some above-the-fray judge of others' attitudes; nor do I evince any particularly well-turned postbinarist, postgender queer consciousness.[14] I might take some of these positions at times, but always with skeptical suspicion of each. With sex-gender materials figuring both in assumptions and in findings, in rhetorics and their various applications, in the critic and in the objects of scrutiny, in historically persuasive sedimentations and seismic shifts in genders and sexualities themselves, it is hard not to find the hermeneutic circle dizzying.

3. Pan-Gendered Feminist Criticism

Literary critical feminism necessarily involves gender studies of masculinity.[15] But why should feminist criticism treat males or masculinity at all? Because the gynocritical imperative of studying only female writers from the perspective of gender reinforces the assumption that women are the sole repositories of gender materials and the only spokespersons for everyone's gender problems. Gynocriticism suggests that women have gendered literary careers but men have purely literary careers. Such a stance (perhaps an unintended consequence) assists quondam male helplessness about these issues, as if men and male writers (and male critics) had no analytic agency where gender and sexuality issues were concerned (Brod 2002, 166). Most luridly, not treating male writers to gender analysis implies that males have no capacity for change and even suggests that males are unhistorical monoliths. Without concerted feminist critique and scrutiny of "representation of alternative masculinities" and of "regimes of masculinity," male writers will float free, seemingly ungrounded in sex-gender systems, championing ungendered universality (Gardiner 2002a, 13, 14). Because maleness is constructed and masculinity is an ideology—actually it is several sets of historically differentiated, mobile, changeable idea systems—the issues and assumptions around maleness inside literary texts and in literary careers need careful investigation.[16] And even supposing that we all wanted to be postgender now, it remains true that sex-gender materials and cultural practices are thoroughly implicated in the history of modernist writing.

Postbinarist, pan-gendered work has been done over the past decades by such cultural critics as Eve Kosofsky Sedgwick, Griselda Pollock, and Barbara Johnson—all serious general influences here.[17] This is not only necessary feminist work but also strategic cultural work for rupturing hierarchical gender systems in cultural studies, while retaining feminism's visionary investments in social transformation.[18] In any event, putting border disputes to the side (gay theory, queer theory, feminist theory?) and claiming the rubric of critical gender studies, we need to examine the saturating impact of gender within artistic careers of males as well as females, the impacts of such materials on their depictions of gender and sexuality and on their career trajectory. This involves their ideologies, their uses of maleness, their investments made via masculinity and femininity, their specific claims of powerlessness and vulnerability, and the ways they ignore, ignite, or deploy this apparently "unmarked," "universal" status. This also involves a close look at their numerous ideas about gender. It is not surprising that maleness has been one of the last social elements to be scrutinized critically: its hegemonic power is parallel—and related—to able-bodiedness as a centralizing norm.

All this may seem obvious and belated to the point of tedium. In the 2007 Modern Language Association *Introduction to Scholarship in Modern Languages and Literatures*, however, this pan- or omni-gendered position is set outside the bounds of feminist literary study. "Women's writing" in intersection with "race and colonialism as much as gender and sexuality" is proposed by Anne Donadey and Françoise Lionnet, but, despite their important "multiplicative" approach, they do not discuss studies of apparently dominant groups. "Ethnicity" does not account for whiteness studies, nor "gender" for masculinity studies, at least where Euro-American men are concerned (Donadey with Lionnet 2007, 225, 226; see 234 for black and Asian men). Donadey and Lionnet foreground only the "self-representation of marginalized groups" (225). It is possible to credit their focus *grosso modo*, but their strategy unhelpfully limits and circumscribes plausible work in sex-gender materials, although their intersections (with transnational thought, with disability studies, with the complexities of queer feminism) are crucial. Most interestingly, they do not allow that dominant groups might evince double positions (hybridity, contradictions) of serious cultural import, although oppositional groups are praised for hybridity. It is clear that the authors fervently want to resist any neglect of the study of women.

A position that feminist reception can discuss males does not automatically undervalue female writers or overvalue male writers, however; nor does it propose that discussion be uninformed by feminist intellectual premises. Hence manifesting (bad pun included) literary feminisms proposes the feminist reception of all authors, demands gender-alert reading strategies to understand the situated materiality of a writing career, a person's represented body, choices, and texts, and the social vectors in any artistic act.

At the end of an important anthology that she co-edited thirty years before the Donadey and Lionnet intervention (that is, at the beginning of this period of scrutiny of "maleness"), Alice Jardine challenged contemporary male authors to talk through their bodies (a bit as Hélène Cixous [1980] claimed women might do in her effervescent manifesto "The Laugh of the Medusa"). Jardine wants the expression of "men's relationship *after feminism*, to death, scopophilia, fetishism [. . .], the penis and balls, erection, ejaculation (not to mention the phallus), madness, paranoia, homosexuality, blood, tactile pleasure, pleasure in general, desire (but, please, not with an anonymously universal capital D), voyeurism, etc." (Jardine 1987, 61).[19] This category-rupturing list, the different kinds of apples and oranges on it, the splay of concepts, both outraged and inviting, and the bottom line that somehow invoking "the body" seemed to produce in those recent critical moments nonetheless need some qualification from literary history.

For even in 1987 these goals had already been accomplished in a number of ways by the theorizing and writing of many male writers. One instance occurs in the Laurentian essays of Charles Olson several decades earlier. His interest in "the connection between sex and the structure of the mind" and his discussion of the "dark or phallic god" who not only is—and this is mystical, if gratifying for Olson—phallic but gets to a whole set of new senses through "the FIRST SENSE, sex" create a direct conduit between the male body and thought (Olson 1997, 136, 139). Olson treated male embodiment with mythological grandeur and an uplifting binarist certitude. Because of materials like these, *Purple Passages* begins again with modernist writing by men, since modernism is already—in Jardine's words—concertedly and self-consciously "*after feminism*" (Jardine 1987, 61).

4. The Deuniversalizing Project

The production of masculinity is everywhere, and almost everywhere it is invisible.[20] Despite important social and literary studies of male subjectivity in past years, unless one is deliberately talking about gender it is still commonplace in viewing artworks by male writers to treat them as ungendered and universal in stance and not explicitly commenting on gender materials or ideologies.[21] Studying gender inscriptions in work by men is critical in its sources and implications. It undercuts the "myth of masculine sameness" (Gardiner 2002a, 12, citing Robyn Wiegman). In contrast, universalizing the male subject "den[ies] the presence of sexual difference" for males in which men (however various) remain standard and women remain lack, inadequacy, and so on (Johnson 1998, 124). Bringing poetry and poetics by men up to scrutiny as negotiating with masculinities in specific and with sex-gender in general is a move that challenges the ideological invisibility of maleness. To mark the male—the formerly unmarked gender category—mandates the end (or at least the erosion) of any universalizing category with its unspoken privileges; thus it is a version of critique.

Stating categorically that "[m]asculinity need not be simply unalterable fate," Peter Middleton framed this deuniversalizing strategy in the first contemporary book about maleness and poetry, a work literary and ethical, meditative and analytic (Middleton 1992, 222). In *The Inward Gaze: Masculinity and Subjectivity in Modern Culture* (1992) and in an ancillary article (1991), Middleton proposed, inter alia, that we should view men's poetry *as* men's poetry, not as a universal, unmarked poetry, and thus should investigate the otherwise "silent inscriptions of gender" in all their mechanisms of projection, affirmation, and resistance

(Middleton 1991, 66). His book contains several remarkable monograph-like essays whose findings point inward to a space in which unacknowledged emotion and violence both outside the law and enforcing the law are dialectically linked in male subjectivity. His personal excursus involving parenthood and comic book superheroes, his critical views of Freud's studies of key males and what is occluded and unseen by Freud, and finally his brilliant readings of postmodern theorists are all arrows pointing to that underexamined zone linking emotion and violence. *Purple Passages* works in the area that Middleton opened, certainly by the premise that criticism should analyze "the dilemmas of masculine self-reflection" and also by the finding that texts by male writers encode both "exposures of ideology" and, sometimes, "transfigurative proposals," in possibilities for self-reflection, debate, and change (Middleton 1992, 231, 11). In these particular affiliative dyads, however, perhaps by virtue of the need for mirroring and affirmation or perhaps from the arousals of textual eroticism, lie plethoras of emotionality, even exaggerated emotion, not the resistance that Middleton identifies in his materials.

Acknowledging Middleton as a key generative text for the analysis of maleness and poetry, related projects both before and after his can be loosely divided into two categories. The first category includes studies of masculinity in general, sources which tend to use personal experience, writers' biographies, novels, and films as narrative evidence; these have usually been deeply influenced by studies of homosexuality modulating to queer critical practices.[22] Indeed, the development of queer theory offered considerable leverage for deuniversalizing maleness and may even be said to be motivated by that project. The second category sees maleness and masculinity as historically specific, including recent discussions of cohorts, poetic groups, and poetic careers, with their texts and practices. Many of these analyses featuring feminist-inflected gender suspicion and sociocultural scrutiny are lively and subtle.

The general study of masculinity—social criticism, sociology, psychoanalytic theory, and historical study as well as writings from self-conscious men's movements—began in the very late 1980s but actually flourished in the 1990s in relation to feminism and to gay liberation movements. The influential literary studies about the homosocial triangle and homosexual panic by Eve Kosofsky Sedgwick (1985, 1990, 1993) dramatized the question of literary representations of male cultural patterns and addressed, variously, the queerness of the straight. Theorizing homosociality, as in the work of Wayne Koestenbaum (1989) and

Michael Davidson (1995, 2004), as well as strong readings of powerful bonds between men in Libbie Rifkin (2000) and Andrew Mossin (2010) are loosely indebted to Sedgwick's vital formulations.

Another study that queers maleness by a reading of its suffusion with the effeminate and transgressive is *Deviant Modernism* (Lamos 1998). Colleen Lamos shows how eroticisms and gender instabilities of a variety of "perverse" kinds have implications for normative ideologies of maleness—whether these errancies are effeminate, hysterical, sado-masochistic, homosexual, homoerotic, voyeuristic, or matrisexual. She unifies all these (arguably rather various) manifestations of sex-gender anormativeness under the term "errancy." This too is a reading that produces an "unsettling of masculinity," with many implications for the study of male poets who generally manifest (in Sedgwick's terms) "homosexual panic" yet a good bit of "errancy" as well (Lamos 1998, 229; Sedgwick 1990).

Over the past years Michael Davidson has considerably forwarded the project of deuniversalizing maleness in his study of misogynist homosociality in influential poetic groups—the Jack Spicer circle and the Beat poets (Davidson 1995). Davidson offers subtle historicist readings of "the intersection of cold war geopolitical issues [particularly containment] with gender" in poetry and other cultural materials (Davidson 2004, 21). In *Guys Like Us: Citing Masculinity in Cold War Poetics* (2004), he interweaves ideological discourses and poetic expression in a succinct study of the diverse but pointed materials of masculinity in the 1950s: heteronormativity, homosociality, and aggressive male bonding, sometimes within gay cohorts. Davidson frames fraternal formations bonded laterally over a particular vision of manhood—and he tracks some of the implications for female writers and for cultural representations in general: film and pulp fiction figure in his text as well as poetry. Davidson is keenly aware of the conflicts and contradictions in his materials; he sees texts "as a site or matrix of competing tendencies—some progressive, some reactionary" (Davidson 2004, 21). *Purple Passages* is also extremely interested in moments of conflict and choice, contradiction and resolution.

The general importance of these deuniversalizing critical activities is noted by Judith Kegan Gardiner in the key anthology that she edited: "Although dominant or hegemonic forms of masculinity work constantly to maintain an appearance of permanence, stability, and naturalness, the numerous masculinities in every society are contingent, fluid,

socially and historically constructed, changeable and constantly changing, variously institutionalized, and recreated through media representations and individual and collective performances" (Gardiner 2002b, 11).
The consensus, as outlined by Gardiner, is that maleness is constructed
and reconstructed in social, historical, and ideological processes. There
are numerous ideologies of masculinity and many kinds of maleness.
(This is already graphic in both Middleton and Davidson.) These vary in
historical eras and are drawn upon and recombined variously in those
eras. Gender issues are inflected with all other kinds of social location,
from sexuality and ethnicity to age and class. Power and gender inequality exist in the relations both between and among genders. *Purple Passages* foregrounds these sociocultural findings in its specific discussions
of texts and practices.

A number of studies of cohorts, coteries, and friendship groups
among modern and contemporary poets are infused with feminist
thought and assist the study of sex-gender in poetic practices. Libbie
Rifkin's pioneering study *Career Moves: Olson, Creeley, Zukofsky, Berrigan and the American Avant-Garde* (2000) is attuned to the creation
and institutionalization of several intense male communities, with their
players, interactions, staged performances, interventions, envies, emu-
lations, and differentiations. Her primary emphasis on institutions of
poetry—publishing, promotion, reception, and archive building—and
her setting of text and author in relation to these practices resist claims
of "individual genius" in favor of the analysis of activities in a dynamic
social field that she calls "career." She lucidly identifies how such cohort-
building practices as filial pieties, influence, generation, and posterity
operate in the cultural field.

Indeed, by their commitments to the avant-garde, Rifkin and Davidson's books have pertinently intervened, both in literary history and,
more loosely, in poets' self-knowledge. Their work is extremely pertinent to mine. Andrew Mossin's invested readings of male subjectivity
as a self-conscious enterprise of "ambition, assertiveness and authority"
clarify the work of Robert Duncan, Robin Blaser, and Nathaniel Mackey
as sometimes-linked lyric investigations of a feminized male subjectivity; his book also writes his poetic practice through theirs in some frank
moments concerning the growth of his poet's mind (Mossin 2010, 4).
My sense of poetic formations saturated with personal relationships
among poets is also indebted to recent work by Andrew Epstein (2006),
Maggie Nelson (2007), and Lytle Shaw (2006). These make parallel,

loosely Bourdieu-inflected analyses, often of sex-gender relationships—involving friendship, rivalry, eros, and mutual support in a cultural field; their books all treat the poets of the New York School, which, while not a totally homosexual cohort by any means, draws on and plays with contemporaneous manners and modes of gay sensibility.

Within the general framework of contemporary U.S. experimental writing (in which Davidson also participated), two other male poet-critics have made striking critical analyses of their predecessors and peers precisely from a sex-gender perspective, one in the study of maleness and the other in the study of the poetic career and its gender narratives. Charles Bernstein's assessment of Charles Olson began with the publication of the essay "Undone Business" in 1984 (Bernstein 1986), which critically notes the lack of gender coequality in that cultural zone. "Women's voices—by which I mean not a product of biological gender but of socially-mediated attitudes, circumstances, syntaxes—are completely marginal to *The Maximus Poems*. The image is of men speaking to men—and all who fall outside that discourse are simply inaudible" (Bernstein 1986, 326). He tellingly observes that "for Olson 'maleness' is patriarchally assumed to be an 'all-inclusive' term for *significant* human experience by dint of an *unacknowledged* reduction of the nonmale to insignificance" (Bernstein 1986, 328). Bernstein's essay resonates with my concerns here: to investigate masculinity as it enters poetic texts and practices and to disaffiliate from its more problematic effects. Bernstein's analyses, as well as the work of feminist thinkers on which he implicitly draws, make constant attempts to suggest that poetry (both as an individual mode of practice and as a socio-scholarly field of investigation) envisioned as if solely by male writers will just evoke more poetry and criticism as if only men were authors—an endless multiplication of sameness, culturally damaging in the long run, however temporarily affirming for those who benefit.

Part of my effort here to diversify and rearticulate individual artists into relations involving the eros of poesis is foreshadowed in "What I See in 'How I Became Hettie Jones.'" Here Barrett Watten attends to the emergence of poetry "not at the site of original genius but as a material fact in a discourse constructed between subjects": "in unrecognized literary (and domestic) labor" of those many people implicated in the poetic career of one figure (Watten 1998, 112, 104). Watten insists that to define poetry "solely in terms of the production of 'the poet' is an inadequate account of agency"—where this means both artistic production and the production of the self. Both are involved deeply with "gendered [and racial] dynamics"; both reveal the "micropolitics of literary culture" made visible via textual manifestations (Watten 1998, 103, 107). In *The Constructivist Moment* (2003), Watten outlines a remarkable analysis of five male language writers' multiauthored *Legend* for what can be discovered about masculine writing in a zone of conscious *jouissance* and scrupulous attentiveness to male bonding in their dialogues. No summary can do this analysis justice, but two male subject positions emerge that are proto-queer in their contours: penetrability and androgyny (Watten 2003, 79). The still future challenge named by this analysis is "there is no position [in this text] for woman," "(not even woman as lack)" (Watten 2003, 81).

What it means to deuniversalize male subjectivity and to emphasize its choices is established experimentally in each chapter here; this involves relations to authority, to the "fraternal social contract," to authoritarian urges, to the vital bulwark against "femininity" and against the "effeminate," to the attraction of the feminine and of passivity, to some distinct styles of maleness that are part of the gender range in the twentieth century. These styles of maleness can range from the fervently committed to the highly critical and playful. Indeed, part of the strain of analyzing modes of maleness is that these modes (and their practitioners) enter easily into self-ironizing moves that create deniability. In any event, any poet variously deploying maleness also must "place," attend to, use, reject, idealize, or otherwise deal with the cluster(s) of femaleness, femininity, effeminacy. Thus feminist reception—of women writers and/or of all writers seen from sex-gender perspectives of various sorts (textual, cultural, social, psychoanalytic, historical)—becomes a crucial critical act of reception. As Bernstein, Watten, Davidson, Middleton, Rifkin, and others show, more than being merely correctives, such studies aim to be culturally transformative. These do not seem like quixotic gestures against a monolith of the Symbolic but rather activities toward different gender regimes within "a cultural life of fantasy" (Butler 2004, 216). Representations matter—even if they operate in only an indirect, complex, and even wayward fashion.

5. Purple Passages

To open an analytic path to postpatriarchal culture (that is, to non-hierarchic uses of mastery) has been the goal of my critical work and

my work in the investigative yearning of even the scholarly study but
certainly of the essay. *Purple Passages* joins, if belatedly, my two other
books of essays to form a trilogy of feminist, oppositional work on
poetry and poetics written during three different decades. To me feminist scholarship, sometimes written "otherhow," has consistently offered
a heady mode for analytic and aesthetic pleasures and has encouraged
(even cleared) some speculative and politically urgent space between desire and knowledge. The stakes in arousal and engagement, not solely in
professionalism, are socially meaningful.

Because the practices of the poetic career and of gender are multiple,
polymorphic, changeable, and always in play and because they are proposed, drawn upon, and staged variously, my title *Purple Passages* evokes
several simultaneous premises. First, I claim my passionate suffusions
and plural positions—as a critical spectator, as an invested poetic inheritor, and as a potentially "resisting reader."[23] The word "passages" suggests
tracks to follow and to examine; it also encrypts the word "passions" and
notes the eros of all of the poetic encounters that I detail. This emphasis
on passionate dyads is necessarily indebted to the evocative, influential
work of Wayne Koestenbaum, who proposed that male-male "collaboration is always a sublimation of erotic entanglement" (Koestenbaum 1989,
4). For better or worse, however, I find too tendentious and allegorical the idea that "men who collaborate engage in a metaphorical sexual
intercourse"—an idea singularly specific in its vision if broad in its claim
(Koestenbaum 1989, 3). I view the "passions" as more diffuse if equally
erotic and committed. My title word "passages" also suggests a path away
from the "cult of masterful presence" (Watten 2000, 280) that many of
these "New American" writers encouraged. My emphasis falls on "cult"
and "presence"—"mastery" is a different concept. For them, poetry itself,
in Barrett Watten's words, was invested in "affective bonds" of love and
desire, not the least with the reader (Watten 2000, 280). It is up to the
reader whether to be thoroughly or partly seduced or not.

"Purple passages" also means, idiomatically, lush prose. If this seems
a bit counterintuitive for writers who often claimed that they decried that
rhetoric, one may still see that at least their letters and essays are indeed
lush and commanding at once.[24] Further, *Purple Passages* never under-
estimates the striking, tempted resistance of modernist poetics to the
decadent, to the perverse, and to any manifestations of the feminine or
the effete. Writing in verse is indeed perverse—given its attraction to the
hypnagogic power of the signifier: "when the word is felt as a word and

not as a mere representation of the object named or outburst of emotion" (Jakobson 1987, 378). There is the spellbinding, charm-weaving quality of verse, sometimes thematized—as in Samuel Taylor Coleridge's ecstatic, almost bigendered figure at the end of "Kubla Khan" or in Alfred Lord Tennyson's enervated Lotos-Eaters.

The transgressive, polymorphous evocation of bliss, the urge to dissolve consciousness and boundaries, the strong hedonism and "drift"— discussed outright in Pound's "Hugh Selwyn Mauberley"—are all renderings of the endless textual arousal without completion theorized by Roland Barthes (albeit for narrative) in *The Pleasure of the Text* (1975). Pound writes about this blur of temptation in exactingly ironic quatrains; that contained form and the logopoeic diction gave permission both to explore and to contain that decadent content. Although decadence, the flirtation with transgressive masculinities, and the verbal temptations of queering maleness are visible in such sonically scintillating poetries as that of Wallace Stevens, the work becomes suspect whenever sound edges out the semantic without a mode of containment. Writing in verse opens the scandalous possibility of excess, disturbance, and the (Kristevan) semiotic linked to the seduction of femininized cultural materials (Barthes 1975, 14ff.).

Thus "purple passages" evokes somewhat indirectly the traces of decadent, the aesthetic, the temptations of late and excessive romanticism that Pound and Eliot, when young, dismissed with such contempt. One case of the thoroughly perverse signifier taking over is the annihilating rhythmic/syntactic ivy of Algernon Charles Swinburne, far outpacing the semantic wall (as in "A Forsaken Garden"), not to speak of his fascination with sexually ambiguous, sometimes hermaphroditic figures. Verse as perverse proved viscerally threatening—that is, fiercely tempting—to Pound and Eliot, who, as Cassandra Laity has argued, ceaselessly evoke Swinburne as the culminating horror to be avoided (Laity 1996, 20–23). Both poets emphatically express their loathing of this cluster of perversity—female, feminine, effeminate—with the notable homage of modernist ukases. Certainly Eliot and Pound protested symptomatically both against the imitative and against the feminized.

Hence purple is motivated. It not only is the color of power and the regal, the erotic and its temptations, but is also, in our own ideological coding, a queerish color to put back into the male center of modern and contemporary poetry. I have mixed the pink of *The Pink Guitar* and the blue of *Blue Studios* to get—this.[25] This book is different from both but was created in a similar critical desire to talk of gender and poetics. Buoyed by the undecidable mix of critique and glee in Gertrude Stein's poem-essay "Patriarchal Poetry" ([1927] 1980), I make a specific (sub) definition of "patriarchal." This is a negative term only when joined with misogyny, homophobia, gender-power hierarchies, and literary exclusions. I want to claim that "patriarchal" is also a poetic tactic that exercises the capacity to maximize subject positions and stances, an imperial ranging over contradictory positions, manifested in poets' oeuvres and relationships, and emphatically characteristic of the two master poets—Pound and Olson—whose careers in U.S. radical poetries shaped the twentieth century.

It is clear, as at least Michael Davidson has proposed, that male poetic power seems to differentiate itself starkly against the feminine (and sometimes against women) and against the effeminate (and sometimes against gay men). But at other times the "patriarchal" stance is omnivorous and imperial, characterized by a contradictory interest in these zones and figures. Playful, protean, and power-seeking, patriarchal poetry is not only characterized by sexism (though it may often be) but fundamentally sustains a social subject position that is omnivorous of all others. This is, of course, a sociocultural privilege with implications of many sorts. It is not, however, impossible for females to be "patriarchal" by this definition. I intend to skirt that topic here. (And "patriarchal" might then become the "wrong" term.) A further purplish gesture is my use of epigraphs from Stein's "Patriarchal Poetry"; these speak with a sibylline grandeur throughout. Her essay-poem, with its undefined repeated title phrase going in and out of focus, is insistently suggestive. These citations refract the coloration of my analysis and offer a gloss—albeit an oblique one—on my chapters.

The phrase "patriarchal poetry" in my subtitle, out of Stein, acknowledges the omnivorous and protean claim of multiple subject positions in certain modes of poetry as well as the investigative power of critical feminism, which made the term "patriarchal" suspect in helpful ways. I both follow it (the fascination of the patriarchal is patent) and resist it (its power relations, social attitudes, and sexist exclusions must be criticized). Therefore, of course, the pun in my title on "ends"—do I have to explain it? Such practices certainly have goals (and those goals have had many impacts on poetry), but they may also be coming to an end, in a near-future poetic era: QED. This has been the era of global decolonization, and in every society the struggle of women and homosexuals for decolonization from second-class civic status has been a leading indicator of modernity.

This critical writing is committed to the real social meanings at stake, as is Joan Retallack's exemplary *The Poethical Wager*. The utopian pragmatism of writing one's way through, around, inside, and inflected by the political and social crises of the twentieth and twenty-first centuries is symbolized by her aspirated, airy "h" that adds ethics to poetics (Retallack 2003, 44). The construction of a "poethical attitude" for her too is embodied precisely in "the exploratory essay," compounded of skepticism, inquiry, hybridity, and critique (Retallack 2003, 3, 49). The overlap between Retallack's attitude and my own is considerable, in terms such as "desire," "reciprocal alterity," and the "dicey collaboration of intellect and imagination" (Retallack 2003, 5). We share the goal, to cite Patrick Durgin in a parallel mode, of producing "radical modernist literary experimentation as social ethics" (Durgin in Weiner 2007, 14).

Feminism in general could draw not only on the power of its own and the epistemological and rhetorical experiments of critical poetics but also on its challenges to cultural boundaries, its own critical negativity. It could locate itself more concertedly in Theodor Adorno's ethics of unstinting resistance to fixed formulations, his sense of intellectual mobility, and with perpetual consideration of the ways "thought's utopian vision of hitting the bullseye" must be linked "with the consciousness of its own fallibility and provisional character" ("The Essay as Form," in Adorno 1991, 16). Edward Said is another Adornoesque avatar of essays, with their "investigative, radically skeptical" and oppositional modes (Said 1983, 26).

It remains true, however, that unlike the material (particularly the work of John Cage) that Retallack discusses, only intermittently do some of the poets considered here make "art that models how we want to live" (Retallack 2003, 44). Their oeuvres, their constructions of gender, may present quite the opposite problem—modeling how we do not want to live. It was sometimes a struggle for these poets to live in a multiply gendered universe or to work with respect as well as power. Some were close to being "male separatist" in their attitudes; some were, if irregularly, misogynist or hierarchical in their functional understanding of gender relations; some were fixated on male power (Hopkins 2007, 62). These chapters, with their serious scholarly text, also enact the clashes that occur when an "experimental female" (myself) meets the claims of certain "experimental males."[26]

6. "Labor, Power, Eros"

Let me speak to you in the second person–intimate.[27] Gender/
sexuality is/are not just something that happens to you but something
that you have some leeway and leverage in. You have some sex-gender
agency. You certainly can respond to prior regimes in historical time;
you can act within the gender system that you know—say, acceding to a
masculinity that is a standard; or you can act critically or semicritically in
relation to it. You can exhibit contradictions (without thinking of them),
or you can explore and expose those contradictions. You can use gender materials as they suit you, benefit you, give you position and profit.
And you can walk out on the street and be placed in a sex-gender box
by others, whatever your changing ideas. You are not simply formed by
gender/sexuality; you deploy it and may even choose some of the terms
of the formation. I would like to treat sex-gender as a toolkit and regime
at one and the same time—a system in the simultaneous process of being
used and being built and rebuilt. This is why most of the essays in this
book emphasize specific moments of choice or articulation and indicate
specific defining moments, points where some kinds of gender relations
might have been different. This is not to enter an entirely counterfactual
universe but simply to note the specificity and intimacy of these moments of choice, some with very large results for poetic communities
and practices.

Any sex-gender regime runs by human agency, distributes and ad-
justs labor, power, and eros, and works by some kind of assent or by
human choice. This triumvirate of linked practices, named by R. W. Connell and summarized by Lynne Segal, frames male-female relations by
"three main structures," "labour, power and desire" (Segal 1990, 96; see
Connell 2005, 73–74). Connell discusses "(a) power, (b) production and
(c) cathexis (emotional attachment)" as the necessary components for
discussing a structure of gender (Connell 2005, 73–74). In this kind of
book, talking of power means cultural power with social elements, not
political power except in a cultural realm. And cultural power is often a
kind of eros, a loosely defined desire for something—fame, expression
in language, oeuvre, cultural hegemony, marks of presence. Institutional
elements, or quasi-institutional elements, have to do with putting power
into play via labor and the eros of poesis.

"Power" is the term I want to deploy in this analysis of the gender
regimes in poetic practices. Jacques Lacan's term "phallus" is not as

helpful and seems to be a way of saying power in another language, but a static, unhistorical one (Segal 1990, 90). Indeed, as Judith Halberstam argues (in an appreciative framing of the work of Paul Smith), one must "[d]islodge the phallus from its place as the primary signifier of masculinity," especially as this has become, in Lacanian theory, a transhistorical trope, blocking any understanding of historical shifts (Halberstam 2002, 354). This kind of point is also made by David Savran: "Even the phallus—and patriarchy, of which it is a prop—is a historical construction, a fiction of sorts, which retains its power only insofar as it denies its own historicity" (Savran 1998, 8).

Phallus is a Platonic universal. As with any ideal, it is static, complete, and unmoving; it is already its own tautology, partaking of the "<I AM>" of monotheistic law. Such an idea brooks no sense that gender, sexuality, or materials projected from the body have changed or will ever change in social or historical time. It proposes a fundamental, foundational form that is isolated from history or change, like a pattern book of consciousness. To make this imago a master trope of gender relations is reductive, ahistorical, and peculiarly intransigent, unaccountable to any political shifts in gender materials and relations that have actually occurred. It always situates itself before, beneath, beyond shifts that it (it is often attributed agency) will necessarily regard as epiphenomenal—or symptomatic of blocked recognitions of itself. The term "phallus" only helps to solidify and hypostasize (make rigid and unmoving) that which it discusses. This is a curiosity even if "the feminine" thereby is defined as automatically critical of master narratives from a privileged "outside." This is only a sop, however interesting.

As Jane Gallop argued first in 1981, it is virtually impossible to separate "penis" from "phallus"; the existence of the physical organ confuses and blurs the clarity of outline of the mental construct, while also proving, by use of an image, what should be proposed by argument (Gallop 1988). Gallop (1988) and Charles Bernheimer (1992) both wittily and insistently argued that you are and are not supposed to think of, cathect to, and wonder at the erect penis while thinking about the third-party law that this term "phallus" represents. Yet setting aside the penis is implausible in Lacan's theoretical matrix—patrix. The word "phallus" is too suggestive, too saturated, like a red herring dragged over the concept it is supposed to elucidate. Thus a system that claims to propose relational, interdependent genders both cathected to a law (phallus) returns functionally to designate binary, hierarchical genders where one gender possesses, if only in sometimes flagging, imperfect miniature, the sign of that law. The existing, historically founded social arrangements and visualizations of the genders have secretly underwritten the theory; at the same time, the theory evacuates the historical for the eternal. In contrast, the term "power" and discussions of a gender regime that valorizes male power allow us to see how gender is created and supported by an array of "interlink[ing]" relationships across a wider front, as both Connell and Segal propose (Segal 1990, 96).

"Labor" is O'Connell's second term: power and labor are very interinvolved in the field of poetry, poetics, and "poethics," as in many other fields. In a book about poetry, these are the labor practices of poetry as a working institution: editing, mentoring, manifesting allegiance, following, grouping, and connecting. As documentation, I use the evidence of working relationships as they are produced on the ground—reflective essays, poems, and letters between poets. These letters are documents of work that are work themselves—daily work of great seriousness for Olson and Creeley; work of cultural position-taking and the staking of claim for Zukofsky and Pound.

"Eros" is the third term of my analysis. Power, labor, and eros are intertwined in the world of art production. These are the erotic and the conceptual/analytic affiliations as they emerge in practices like mentoring, editing, and the like but also as the artists themselves investigate and thematize (and participate in) masculinity and femininity in their work. For the cultural drive that marks both the writers in this book and this book itself is, in widest measure, erotic. Power, labor, and eros in the cultural field are all three deeply erotic. This is not necessarily an eros with the sexual object of another person; nor is it procreative and heterosexual or even necessarily expressively sexual in any way. This eros is also mobile rather than gender fixed. It may be narcissistic, contradictory, and changeable. Eros is the desire to be making. That is, eros here is a work and a drive, the work of making works. Eros also means making connections of friendship and care that are generative, productive, arousing, being connected to and recognized by another. It is another kind of generalized eros from the purely sexual. This is the eros of poesis.

This erotics suffuses mentoring, editing, following, grouping, and entering into cultural power.[28] This desire for poesis is sometimes quite ruthless. None of the relationships in this book derives from or leads to pure unmitigated good—such relationships can be manipulative, deceptive, cruel, one-sided, painfully renegotiated, and thoroughly unsettling (as can my critical relationship with what I am writing about); but nonetheless the desire for making and the eros of the cultural act itself with its pulses and charges are vital to artistic affiliations and practices. Power-labor-eros is for artists a passage to the erotics of poesis—ambition, fame, connectedness, and things made.

In the realm of production and dissemination, a male poet's sense of the poetic career and the poetical is sometimes marked by heightened and intense relationships with other men (often in poetic groups or mentoring relationships)—that is, in homosocially enriching but sexually taboo relationships (Davidson 2004). Yet poetic production also may compel a man to assume conventionally "feminine" traits—empathy, sensitivity, negative capability, and the chameleon subjectivity that John Keats spoke of in two exemplary statements in his letters (22 December 1817 and 27 October 1818).

This intermingling of quasi-"feminine" sensibility and homosocial and often, but not necessarily, heterosexual ties then actually structures many artistic men (and women) as artistically bisexual—or, better, bi-erotic, polyerotic—whatever their functional sexuality may be said to be. This, in many cultural settings and political regimes, is taboo and threatening, perhaps particularly for men. The bierotic, to extend Donadey and Lionnet's argument about the bisexual, "undermines hetero-homo binary opposition," creates the possibility for "porous" sexual categories, and might even work to separate masculinity from men (cf. Halberstam 1998; Donadey with Lionnet 2007, 233). The eros of poesis is a queer erotics whatever one's sexual orientation(s) or partners. Patriarchal poetry absorbs this covertly and denies/extrudes it overtly.

Poetic masculinity takes shape in a self-perpetuating and "viscous"/vicious circle of argument resistant to flow, dependent on reaffirming against all evidence a binary sex-gender system, with sides (hetero/homo; male/female) and exact borders. In this system, cultural power and social power accrue to one side of the binary—so long as it keeps relatively untainted—neatly divided into, say, manly men and womanly women, a system in which, nonetheless, a spectrum of erotic possibilities, female cultural power, and omni-gendered materials are functioning. Because it is impossible and implausible (both theoretically and in historical and practical terms as well as in artistic representations) that any rigid binary should be sustainable or even plausible, various systems and symbolic gestures supporting and framing masculinity sometimes go into overdrive.

Two

Pound Edits Loy and Eliot

1. "Patriarchal poetry or indeed an explanation"

In the teens and twenties, male and female cultural workers were struggling with, against, and for female coequality and with resistance to homosexuality in cultural life (Miller 2007, 76).[1] Among the acts of affirmation and contestation are warding-off charms (including misogynist bluster), particularly given the fear, in T. S. Eliot's words in 1917, that writing poetry (by definition feminine or perverse activity?) would "feminize" or unman men (Eliot 1988, 204). Similarly, in 1917 Ezra Pound waltzes through a chain of genial insults to William Carlos Williams, stating: "Your sap is interrupted" (Rémy de Gourmont is an antidote for this condition) and criticizing Williams's mimicking of "the old ladies" and his lack of "robustezza" (Pound 1950, 123, 124). The "distrust [of] the Feminine in literature" (Eliot 1988, 204) mingled with chaffing allusions to the male body creates binarist, exclusionary claims of masculine cultural power.

Comments in William Wordsworth's "Preface to *The Lyrical Ballads*" prefigure this gender subtext of poetry and allow maleness to be presented as the deciding trait of general modernity, though in contestation with a parallel fascination-revulsion concerning feminine and effeminate claims in topic and style. That poetic pleasure depends on topics "metrically arranged" in such a way that "the style is manly" makes a linkage of gender and language that becomes characteristic of one strand of modernism (Wordsworth 1974, 146). The elements that Wordsworth feared and scorned are "caprices" and "a motley masquerade of tricks, quaintnesses, hieroglyphics, and enigmas"—any kind of "extravagant and absurd diction" leading to and from a "perturbed and dizzy state of mind" (Wordsworth 1974, 144, 162). These proposals, however influential on the plain style of modernism and however positive from (some of) our contemporary points of view, emphatically rest on powerfully encoded sex-gender assumptions. Wordsworth rejects poetic language evoking the feminine, the effeminate, the quirky, the "adulterated," the "perverted" (Wordsworth 1974, 161).

The imagist program of circa 1914 and the writings in poetics of both
T. S. Eliot and Ezra Pound similarly affirm a manly stylization of poetry.
Common fears, according to Gail McDonald, saw women "defil[ing]
or trivializ[ing] poetry," a field that the men were eager to see profes-
sionalized, taken back from genteel amateurism (again associated with
women and with the effete) and from nonformulated standards, including dilettantish criteria for achievement (McDonald 1993, 79). Of course,
plenty of manly men were undemanding as writers, so the gendering
of this situation was a specific choice upholding a claim of male cultural hegemony, particularly an insistence on originality as opposed to
imitation. Thus the decadent and Victorian writers (John Ruskin, Walter
Pater, Alfred Lord Tennyson, Ernest Dowson, Edward Fitzgerald, Dante
Gabriel Rossetti, Algernon Charles Swinburne) from whom both Pound
and Eliot learned so much would have to stay repressed and invisible or
publicly cast out, in order to resist both the weakness of effeminacy and
the weakness of indebtedness as accusations.[2]

The antifemale fulminations and the resentment of professional
women voiced by the young male modernists were an attempt to position themselves in an already existing cultural field that included women
with some cultural power (Gilbert and Gubar 1988, 98, 152, 231; Mc-
Donald 1993, 78–79; parallels in the art world in Tickner 1994). "Feminization" got mustered to deflect attention from the salutary shock of
female aesthetic and professional participation in modernity—women's
educational, economic, and civic gains and their presence in cultural life
as artistic producers, original contributors to foundational thought, and
editors, publishers, and supporters of literature (Tickner 1994; Miller
2007, 69). Given Pound and Eliot's own considerable economic struggles
at this time, both itched to reduce or curtail the already existing and
significantly developing cultural power of women in their milieu and seriously (though sporadically) resisted female coequality.[3] Their "feminization" worry seems to have been a hortatory and self-challenging claim.
Although influential, unpleasant, and inflammatory, this stance did not,
however, sum up their (uneven, uneasy) sex-gender activities.

Frank Lentricchia has proposed that the social world from which
early modernism emerged (in the United States) "masculinized the economic while it feminized the literary"; the solution (which he sees in the
young Wallace Stevens) was to "recover poetic self-respect, whose name
was necessarily phallic" (Lentricchia 1987, 766, 763). But why "necessarily"?[4] Male "poetic self-respect" in modernism could have taken and did

take any number of affiliative forms—for example, a fascination with and not a resistance to female professionalism and coequal participation, or cross-gender bonding over transgressive modes of gender and sexual behaviors, or even support (principled or tacit) for female access to professional venues. Modernist claims ("its rejection of sentiment, narrative, moralizing, and passivity," in Lisa Tickner's words, as well as a "*feminist* repudiation of femininity") might have much to offer all artists (Tickner 1994, 66, 67). None of these options would depend on binarist genders or on assertions based causally upon genital equipment but on a building of communities of critical practice.

That Ezra Pound did try variously, aggressively, and unevenly to assert male power and the phallic as a free-floating force is quite true; yet that this was "necessarily" the sole outcome of his dilemmas of profession and position even in the vorticist years must be questioned. Because they are shifting and often recipient-dependent, Pound's gender attitudes are hard to reconstruct. His thinking moved incrementally toward conservatism, but in a looping (opportunistic?) manner in the early years of his career, as his vitalist, pro-sex position hardened, so to speak, into phallic assertion.[5] The young male modernists could always manifest an undercurrent of misogyny and a resentment of a bigendered universe of practitioners; but, as Gail McDonald strikingly argues, Pound's and Eliot's fascination with female energy and their "ambisexual" identification with both males and females, in imagery both impregnating and pregnant, need to be foregrounded (McDonald 1993, 83–84, 85, drawing on Koestenbaum 1989, 116).

Pound's contradictions and claims about sex-gender emerge in two editorial acts: an unsolicited redaction (ca. 1920) of Mina Loy's "The Effectual Marriage" and an authorized cutting (1921–1922) of T. S. Eliot's "The Waste Land." These acts have not, to date, been discussed in tandem (not having been thought to concern the literary "process of dialogue and rivalry," in Drew Milne's phrase) or used to understand some of the conflicting sexual politics of modernism (Milne 2010, 40). Pound's editing of Eliot expressed their serious and intense relationship; even long after, Eliot always spoke as positively as possible of Pound. Eliot had asked for aid; Pound gave it fully, with his heady mix of self-assertion and entrepreneurial commitment. In contrast, Pound's editing of Loy has little known context—no ongoing dyadic interrelation, no letters exchanged (so far as we have found), no interaction or explicit critique, though Pound had already expressed admiration for her cerebral, critical poetry.

The two redactions, taken together, offer a contrasting and revealing gender narrative. In 1915, hoping for the patronage of John Quinn
for a new journal, Pound launches into manly misogyny as a strategic
way of staking a claim on Quinn.[6] Pound insists that "I have included
hardly any feminine names" and "I think active America is getting fed
up on gynocracy and that it's time for a male review," yet still he includes the two "editresses of Poetry" and several other women as participants (Pound 1991, 41). Did antifemale fulminations have real power
for him? Were they simply appealing to Quinn or pro-male bonding or
were they a blustering attempt to differentiate his potential product from
the female-edited reviews that had so far dominated modernism (Pound
1991, 42, 26 August 1915)? Was he packaging the same product but with
different slogans? His hoisted "banner" "'No woman shall be allowed to
write for this magazine'" and "give 'em the vote if you like but . . . . . . "
reveal that female suffrage, a major political change of civic status and
the topic of acrimonious public debate, is (apparently) easy for Pound to
accept but female coequality in the literary world is derided (Pound 1991,
53, 54, 13 October 1915). *The Closer to Home, the More Resisted* might be
a patriarchal proverb.

This prospective all-male review is intended to shock. Pound is a
master at stating an outrageously bold idea then modifying it with tem-
pering noises. He acknowledges some good women writers while excluding them, noting that the masculine "vigour" achieved would be worth
it (an antieffete turn), even insisting that "a few very intelligent people
(women & men) would be pleased," thereby claiming the approval of
"intelligent" persons of both genders at this exclusion (Pound 1991, 54).
Finally, he observes that the callow and sentimental are the possession of
both men and women (Pound 1991, 54). Yet at the same time "Women"
are responsible for the "rot" of failed cultures—there is the scapegoating
(Pound 1991, 54). While it is very plausible to see solely misogyny (it is
absolutely present), it is more accurate to see Pound trying incessantly
to take gender positions in both ways and all ways, but particularly in
whichever ways would give him cultural advantage (McDonald 1993,
83–84; DeKoven 1999, 178–179).

This is also visible in Pound's fulminations about Amy Lowell, a
smoke screen for his annoyance at having to share a movement (Imagism) that he is hardly sure he still wants. When Pound and Eliot propose
a *rappel à l'ordre* in 1919–1920, parallel to conservatizing postwar anti-
vanguard movements in art across Europe, and write in taut rhyming

quatrains for a few years, this interesting prosodic move toward an allusive, aphoristic impersonality occurs among other reasons to reject the
free love/free verse association (for example, in Loy) and the "Lowellian
lesbian" aura softening Imagism just as Pound was hardening it in Vor-
ticism (Burke 1985a).[7] Thus "no vers is *libre* for the man who wants to
do a good job" (Pound 1954, 12, citing Eliot; Longenbach 1999, 119). Of
course Loy's logopoeia had already achieved tight, allusive aphoristic
writing.

Far from regarding these views as a foregone conclusion, Pound
evinced much wobbling on the phallic and even on the prosodic points
throughout the twenties and particularly before 1926. For instance,
Pound claimed that he was "a male who has attained the chaotic flu-
idities" of a female, a trial balloon of androgyny, if suspect in its praise
of women's distinctiveness (Pound to Marianne Moore, 1919, in B. Scott
1990, 363). He also tries to blame cultural problems on women's participation—disparaging women for general consolidation of middlebrow
thinking and for the "obstruction" to new ideas (mainly his) and the lack
of "speed" in taking up them up that he would later blame on the press,
on the political class, and finally on the Jews. It took him some time to
find a comprehensive, multipurpose scapegoat; in this goal, women were
one transitional object. Pound would eventually settle on the "male as a
principle of form and order," reverting to the sexology of Aristotle, the
"natural"/hierarchical sexual politics of fascism, and an "anti-chaos" ma-
chismo that show how much he came to fear, not simply loathe, whatever
he could characterize as chaotic (Bush 1990, 353, 356, 354).

Yet even in 1931–1932 Pound praised the female editors of *Poetry* and
the *Little Review* and included female writers (Marianne Moore, Alice
Corbin, H.D. [Hilda Doolittle], and Loy) in his literary-history-cum-
anthology *Profile*. Pound certainly did not disdain Moore and Loy in
his earlier reviews; indeed, he was a bit in awe of them.[8] In linked 1920
discussions of Moore, Loy, Eliot, and Williams, Pound makes no critical distinction between the work of the modern men and the modern
women, treating them as one phalanx (Pound [1920] 1967, 233–246).
Pound is proud of their opposition to "glutinous imitations of Keats,
diaphanous dilutions of Shelley, woolly Wordsworthian paraphrases,
or swishful Swinburniania," phrases as sensitive to imitative pretension
as they are symptomatically dismissive of the feminine and the effete
(Pound [1920] 1967, 239).[9] Thus some women were notable exceptions to
the general rule of "women" as destroyers of cultural thrust.

Pound, as "a cultural impresario," helped to construct this phalanx in Anglo-American modernism by literary journalism and entrepreneurial activities (Rainey 2007, 87). Though about the same age as
Williams, Eliot, H.D., James Joyce, Loy, and Moore, Pound offered his
peers authoritative, incisive, sometimes colonizing advice. He accrued
much poetic capital from his production of their status as leading writers; Eliot later stated that Pound saw his poets "almost impersonally, as
art or literature machines" (Eliot in Sutton 1963, 18). In his early career,
Pound often enunciated principles in poetics well before he could follow them himself. He played catch-up to other writers while concealing
with good dollops of bluster the self-doubts raised by his own slow-
to-emerge modernist style and topics (Litz and Rainey 2000, 68; Du-
Plessis 2006a, 134–135). What Pound hated more than anything was to
be belated.

2. "Patriarchal poetry might to-morrow. / Patriarchal Poetry might be finished to-morrow"

Gertrude Stein's comments (1933) on a 1911 encounter distinguished
mischievously between Mina Loy and Loy's then-husband, Stephen Haweis.[10] The plodding Haweis thought that Stein needed to add commas
to her writing; however, the perceptive and acute Loy "was able to understand without the commas" (Stein 1933, 124; Burke 1996, 129). Only apparently innocuous marks of punctuation, commas actually personified
retrograde gender attitudes. In *Lectures in America* (1935), Stein viewed
commas as blocking characters in dramas of female agency. Commas
are "degrading," "enfeebling," and "servile" because commas channel females away from independence and self-sufficiency (Stein [1935] 1985,
220, 221, 219). "A comma by helping you along holding your coat for you
and putting on your shoes keeps you from living your life as actively as
you should lead it" (Stein [1935] 1985, 220). Commas control, cosset, and
court; they are a repugnant fusion of infantilizing mothers, manipulative servants, and sanctimonious suitors. Indeed, commas themselves
resemble dependent women: "they have no life of their own" (Stein
[1935] 1985, 219). Stein's dramatic narrative parallels Virginia Woolf's in
the overt self-sacrifice and covert agendas of ideological control in "The
Angel in the House" (Woolf [1942] 1970, 236–238). Stein's intermingling
of feminist thought and experimental syntax reveals both the political
and polemical mobility of any style (a situational point) and the links

between a feminist and a stylistic avant-garde from the earliest moments of Anglo-American modernism (a historical point).

Mina Loy's four-page poem "The Effectual Marriage or the Insipid Narrative of Gina and Miovanni" (1915) employs no commas.[11] Here a woman writer debates her own exceptionalism while depicting feminine servility.[12] Loy separates the authorial persona from the object of scrutiny ("[Mina]" and "Gina"). She also inspects avant-garde male behavior, male gender conventionality, and futurist failures to live up to modern sex-gender ideals. Loy knows of F. T. Marinetti's "disprezzo della donna" (scorn for [the cultural idea of?] woman], as a parasite, trapped in love, and "purely animal," but her satire of a futurist marriage is far from *disprezzo* (filled with scorn). It calculates the price/cost (or *prezzo*) that Gina pays (Burke 1990, 232; see also Lyon 1999, 101; DuPlessis 2006a, 135).

Gina's pleasant passivity is alternately proposed as a charming adaptation and excoriated as a servile delusion. The two characters do not communicate across the self-satisfied chasm of the gender division of labor.

> What had Miovanni made of his ego
> In his library
> What had Gina wondered   among the pots and pans
> One never asked the other
>
>   (Loy 1996, 37; Scott 1990, 248)

This is where Pound ends his redacted version, although Loy goes on for sixty-nine more lines and a prose coda. By ending her poem where he did, Pound gains in wistfulness what he loses in narrative arc, removing both the beginning of Loy's poem (one page) and the end (two pages). By his presentation of these twenty-four lines of Loy selected from her 122-line poem, Pound softened or muted the poem's feminist critique—the critique of marriage, the critique of besotted women and genius men.[13]

In contrast, the narrator's own summary judgment is palpable. Gina's womanly virtues (cooking, washing up, marketing, sexual service) and her attempts to live in "audacious happiness" for and through her man are already punctured by the penetrating analytics of the diction (Loy 1996, 39). Domesticity and marriage force the couple into the most conventional complementarity of gender roles. To exist "conjunctively" and "corporeally" (sexuality summarized with Loy's characteristic antiromantic use of abstraction) reduces them to gender polarization:

library vs. kitchen, mind vs. body, male "work" vs. female "love" (Burke 1996, 201). For

> She never opened the door
> Fearing that this might blind her
> Or even
> That she should see   Nothing at all
>
> (Loy 1996, 38)

The door leads to his library; "this" is his mind at work. With duplicitous finesse, manipulating the hemistich and the dramatic blank-space caesura, Loy leaves up in the air whether the male's whole career is a sham ("Nothing at all") or whether the female's understanding is so deficient that she would see "Nothing at all" even with plenty to contemplate. The pretensions of both genders are skewered by Loy's critical manipulation of the segmentivities of the visual text.

The motivation for this complicit relationship is revealed: "Gina was a woman / Who wanted everything / To be everything in woman / Everything everyway at once" (Loy 1996, 38). This may be Loy's least satiric moment, speaking to the relationship between her created character and her self-fashioning self—an omnivorous seeker in the realms of sexuality, gender, and art. In response to Miovanni's philosophic or just pretentious rejection of suppertime, "she learned   at any hour to offer / The dish   appropriately delectable"—a comment about what Marianne Moore, in a review of Conrad Aiken, called "woman's humiliating battery of fascinations" (Moore 1986, 284). It is clear how much, in these years, female compliance was in debate. Loy sees the relationship as a performance on the part of the female who wants perfectly to fulfill all her mandated roles, a feminine masquerade that is judged with a shock at the end of the poem.

The vacuous concepts that Miovanni elaborates—"I am / Outside time and space"—are punctured in this guidebook to male greatness (Loy 1996, 37). The syllables of "mio" suggest the Italian for "my" or "mine" (actually il mio, masculine referent) and the association of "vanni" with an adjective like vano (vain, useless) or with the noun vanità (vanity) yields a mistranslated "my vanity." This is an irresistible onomastic commentary.

Pound published his extreme condensation in quotation marks, yet under Loy's name, in *Instigations* (1920) and in *Profile* (1932); it is unknown whether Loy authorized either anthology appearance.[14] Her poem is treated differently from any other work in the 1920 anthology.[15] Pound's editing is obscurely motivated; perhaps he was fascinated by a woman critical of yet so invested in sexual passion and so drawn to objectify her own biography. His redaction was neither an account of nor a better version of her poem but a symptom of his concerns. Through the redaction, he undertook to manage her poem in the public eye. That is, the redaction cut out what Pound took from the rest of her poem to apply to "Hugh Selwyn Mauberley" (1920). Peter Nicholls has already suggested a "buried dialogue" between "The Effectual Marriage" and "Mauberley" within his general proposal of Loy's influence on Pound (Nicholls 2001); here I "unbury" and specify that dialogue.[16]

Pound's edited presentation of Loy's work would then be a covert way of removing certain original, striking features from her poem and thus of assigning himself priority for the invention of split-persona tactics, seriality, multiple points of view, double endings, and the writing into the poem of a simulacrum of the poet. In general, appropriation is an all-encompassing, necessary literary activity, in principle neither to be deplored nor to be denied. Pound's editing in this case created himself as first to do these interesting things, however, when he really was not, allowing some limited credit to Loy but not the credit of priority or originality.[17] Insofar as priority and origin as well as innovation are framed as masculine power claims, it is ideologically more "fitting" for men to be the pioneers of modernism and women to follow behind. The fact that this is not always or necessarily true is just a minor problem in the management of literary history. Pound did hate belatedness; he therefore constructed his originality by eroding Loy's.

The dual plot—the surface text of the narrator's observing Gina and Miovanni and the paratext between narrator and reader—may be seen in the work's twin titles. The term "effectual marriage" summarizes the surface text, for by the stereotyped position of Gina in the kitchen and Miovanni in his study the marriage is "effectual"—it reproduces conventional gender roles. It is also valid, legally binding—"effectual"— a meaning that produces a dry commentary upon law. The term "insipid narrative" (meaning "flavorless or unpalatable") also produces subtextual irony, given Gina's obsession with cooking saliva-provoking, mouth-watering food (or "sialogogues"). Loy's ironic term "effectual" was blissfully de-ironized by Pound, who retitled this poem "The Ineffectual Marriage."

The shift in title says a good deal. Pound missed or chose to ignore Loy's mocking point that *marriage* was working just the way it should, "effectual" as a mechanism of the sex-gender system for the solidification of gender binaries and, more precisely, for the construction of worshipful females at the shrine of male narcissists. In contrast, Pound constructed a specific case of the dysfunctional ("ineffectual") and not a barb at the whole institution. Loy's title says that all marriages (even perhaps all heterosexual relationships) are "effectual" in just the way she outlines, given the self-deceptions of the two genders, which her speaker coolly analyzes. Pound's imposed title says, temperately, temporizingly, that some marriages are good, others bad. By selecting from her poem and by placing it under a revised title, Pound puts Loy's name to a work reasserting a pleasant (if happier) commonplace and tamps down her radical New Woman critique. In Pound's version, Loy is no longer criticizing the institutions of heterosexual marriage, concubinage, and genius/muse relations but rather criticizing one particular, local compromise.[18] What Pound does achieve, by cutting the male figure Miovanni almost totally (he is mentioned only at the end), is a drastic reduction of Loy's judgment of the relationship and an empathetic portrait of a female figure mostly enervated but just a little fulfilled, like the poignant figures in his own *Lustra* (Pound [1916] 1917). His redaction of her poem tucks Loy under his own manner, makes his sex-radicalism trump hers, and positions her as the follower of his originality.

Loy's double title ("effectual marriage" or "insipid narrative") also helps to indicate that the poem has a double voice: both an observer and a participant. For when the chiastic play with Mina Loy's name and that of her quondam lover Giovanni Papini is decoded (easily, as intended), the work functions as an act of self-scrutiny. Loy has split herself dramatically: the romantic, if servile, ideal of her role is factored into participant "Gina," while the bitter, analytic, calculating observations of the situation are factored into observer "[Mina]," as narrator of the whole, as "actual" author. "Gina" has made marriage her trade and acts the part of Good Womanhood. Her narrator and double, observer "[Mina]," looks at this situation analytically, as one who sees the bargain clearly, with contempt for the calculations and for the blindness demanded by the sexual bond. Because Gina's teensy love poem (alluded to in the text) is derisory, we also find that such feminine compliance is problematic for artistic achievement. The female narrator ("I"/"We," the subjectivity of the enunciation, the observer) and the female character ("she," the subjectivity of the enounced, the participant) confront the reader with their names in reality and in fiction. This doubling seems to have been attempted, in a somewhat altered vein, by Pound with "E.P." and the title character Mauberley, who is investigated by—and perhaps identified with—his observer narrator.

To call attention to the fabricated and ideological character of this mininovel in verse, Loy has placed the word "narrative" in two exposed, paratextual places—once in her judgmental subtitle ("insipid narrative") and once in the footnote that ruptures this fable. The poem ends with a prose parenthesis: "(This narrative halted when I learned that the house which inspired it was the home of a mad woman.—Forte dei Marmi [a fashionable beach resort])" (Loy 1996, 39). The observer/narrator, speaking as "I," interrupts this "story" by a demystifying *volta* that abruptly arrests the whole work. The note changes the balance between servility and complicity by suddenly interpreting the romance we have just read as delusion and insanity.

Needless to say, by cutting this ending (along with the latter part of the poem), Pound has made it impossible to articulate this critique. Loy's ending bears public witness to the failures of unequal intimacy and of female compliance; it speaks out directly, from observer/narrator to reader, across the text of the poem. The rupturing impact of this note is made more intense by the naming of the beach resort in Italy where Loy herself wrote the poem, thus bringing a version of the actual author inside the work. Pound was to claim and use this framing structure, double personae, and odd observer/narrator as glyph of the author for his own "Hugh Selwyn Mauberley."

Pound was hardly unaware of Loy's double title, participant-observer stance, and commentary from actual author across the representation to the reader or unaware of her destabilizing ending, which he achieved with a further brilliance in the rhetorics of "Mauberley." It is Loy's doubled, interesting confusion between author and character that Pound arguably appropriates, both in the relationship between Pound and E.P. and in the one between E.P. and Mauberley. These criss-crossings have occasioned much comment and debate. Pound's witty, difficult layers of critique of the decadent and account of decadent temptations, the way in which a figure suggestively designated "E.P." chooses his tomb and writes his own eulogy at the beginning of the poem yet is present as commentator, the writing-in of a figure who must have some relationship to the actual author (but one quite hard to decipher), the rupturing ending, and the abstract words as well as the crisp stylistic remove all bespeak a use of Loy by Pound. Particularly the commentary by actual writer and observer "[Pound]" on the high-minded art of "E.P." and on the compromises and temptations of one "Hugh Selwyn Mauberley" makes a mix of biographical commentary and poetics that parallels, and arguably deepens, what Loy did with her shifting of the names in her poem.

Fundamentally, both Pound's and Loy's poems treat issues about sexuality, sexual temptation, and artistic/intellectual practice. Loy depicts far less sexual temptation, produces far more objectifying remove in her portrait of the relationship than Pound does in his poem. In contrast, as Nicholls argues, Pound's "Mauberley" experiences the temptations of sexuality, hedonism, drift, the destabilizing sense of blurred boundaries, formlessness, and the destruction of will because of a surge of sexual desire (Nicholls 1994, 71–73). Nicholls identifies a structure of feeling in Pound's modernist sexuality (shared with Joyce, Wyndham Lewis, and Eliot), in which female figures are so alluring and the dissolution of boundaries in sexuality is felt so acutely as a threat to autonomy that aesthetic objectification and avant-garde "hardness" become, for Nicholls, compensatory mechanisms (Nicholls 1994, 73). Pound's conflict between two poetic manners—a yearning decadent/sexually urgent one and a discontented, objectifying male modernist one—gives "Hugh Selwyn Mauberley" its structural intensity.

In his poem, Pound seems to treat the effeminate, the aesthete, and the sexually aroused male figure in the ways that Loy had treated the feminine and the enthralled female—by investigation and tempted resistance. For in spite of Pound's repeated announcements of phallic fervor, he also identified with this wavering figure. Despite the recent *rappel à l'ordre*, Pound praised the formalist-sentimentalist verse of Ralph Cheever Dunning, showing a flexibility about former poetic principles to remain in charge of canonizing (Pound 1932b, 127; Pound 1925, 340).[19] Ralph Cheever Dunning was a real avatar of the character "Mauberley," whose archaic, poeticizing work (sounding like A. E. Housman or Ernest Dowson) Pound championed between 1925 and 1932 for its sensibility, yearning, "marvels of precision," and "intensity, [. . .] vigor, almost violence of visual imagination" and for what Pound saw (it is quite debatable) as "rhythmic invention" (Pound 1932b, 84–85; Pound 1925, 343, 345, 343). In his 1925 review of Dunning, Pound insists that the presentational imagist criterion of composing in the arc of the musical phrase could be achieved with "freshness and precision" in a late Victorian prosodic

mode (Pound 1925, 341). *Vers libre* and logopoeia (suddenly) are not the
only paths: Dunning emphatically evinced neither.[20]

Pound often attempts to have things both ways, to come out on the
winning side by placing a number of bets, and thereby to stay as current and forward-looking as he could; Dunning is one small episode.[21]
Hence Pound both supports intelligent women and suspects their independence, is fascinated by their originality and discredits them. He takes
both *vers libre* and Imagism and then vorticist power as his banners yet
briefly attends to passéiste work of little prosodic or imagistic energy.[22]
And he tries to claim as his very own the poetic inventions of women
even when their achievements precede his interventions and inventions.
His redaction of "The Effectual Marriage" is Pound's attempt to colonize
what Loy had done, in part to take her original tactics for his "Mauberley" (1920). The result is the blurring of the achievements of a coeval
female poet and her work.[23] One thereby sees a canon being shaped
and crafted by careful exclusion of significant practitioners. Such pertinent moments indicate how we arrived at the monogendered, virtually
monoethnic, often heteronormative modernism that was canonical up
to about 1975. Modernist studies demand that the networks and cross-
hatchings among people include females and, with due cause, visualize
them as innovators. Certainly Pound constructed his male subjectivity
in a typically contradictory way: by some attempts to deny female practitioners' status as coequal, co-temporal, and original participants in literary culture as well as by some attempts to celebrate their work, when
refocused and mediated by himself.

3. "Patriarchal poetry. He might be he might he he might be he might be"

Some of the gender attitudes in two young American men, both trying for literary careers in England, seem to feed off one another, something that T. S. Eliot depicts in a stylized way.[24] "Eeldrop and Appleplex"
(1917) shows an urbane brace of males (Eliot and Pound) dismissing a
female figure (amalgamating Katherine Mansfield and perhaps H.D.).
This repositioning of the female from considerable cultural producer to
both muse figure and pretentious fake is, again, a cutting (or wishful)
response to a changing literary scene.[25] It is a key structure of maleness
in modernism, which, as we shall see, imperially claimed the feminine,
the effeminate, and its own sex-gender materials yet tried to narrow

and obliterate female claims on similar and parallel materials—this is precisely the mode of patriarchal poetry. During these interwar years, from about 1917–1918 through 1930, Pound became less sympathetic to the generalized feminist critique with which he had also evinced uneven empathy. Perhaps it was World War I that provoked a relative return to "traditional gender values" and a distrust of sex-gender risks (DuPlessis 2001, 39). Perhaps it was his growing collaboration with Eliot and his appeals to Quinn and Lewis; affiliative male relationships and their insistent rhetorics sometimes end in posturing.[26] Perhaps it was the wartime deaths of two promising friends (T. E. Hulme and Henri Gaudier-Brzeska) that enraged and altered him, indeed permanently. Perhaps it was his own marriage (1914) and the difference between Dorothy Shakespear Pound (1886–1973) and the acerbic, critical female poets whom he praised. Further, Pound's bigamous life involved a legitimate wife who maintained no professional aspirations and an almost simultaneous common-law quasi-wife, Olga Rudge (1895–1996), a concert violinist and musicologist. Pound's debate about females and professional life thus had two simultaneous and split personal outcomes. These years and Pound's specific activities make a transition in the construction of a modernism that tended to lose female practitioners and their—and the men's—feminist and critical attitudes about sexuality and gender.

The same kind of saber-rattling antiwoman line as in the Pound-Quinn letters occurs in early Eliot letters, again (symptomatically) in relation to possession of a journal. When Eliot writes his father in 1917 that he is taking over the editorship of the *Egoist*, he says the "struggle" is to "keep the writing as much as possible in Male hands, as I distrust the Feminine in literature" (Eliot 1988, 204, 31 October 1917; cf. Gilbert and Gubar 1994, 67). The Feminine could be male, of course—the confusions of social-gender with ideological/stylistic attitudes are everywhere in the two poets. Eliot (as always under heavy financial pressure) is angry that some women who do not have to work for a living in fact do, taking jobs from men, even as he admits that actual cases of this are almost null. Faced with a father whom he could not satisfy with his professional choices, a mother with noble if nonmodern literary ambitions, and vocations (poet, journalist) and a place (London) not to their taste, faced with his own resistance to finishing his doctorate (helped by the war and the dangers of crossing the Atlantic), and finally having made an abrupt, exciting, and debilitating choice of wife, Eliot had a good deal of anxiety and pain free to displace onto scribbling women, even before other sex-gender anxieties are factored in.[27]

By the time Pound comes to cut "The Waste Land," his sense of being inside various gender debates is acutely developed. Early in the twenties, these looping attitudes seem to have settled (mainly) into phallicism. Pound is concerned (as was de Gourmont, whom he echoes) at the female challenge to the "natural"/biological binary of active and passive that they postulated in sexual intercourse and reproduction. In *The Natural Philosophy of Love*, de Gourmont argued aggressively from sexual dimorphism in animal nature that any proposal undermining the direct link of females to femininity and males to masculinity was unnatural. "Feminism" and comparable political designs for female equality were therefore doomed to failure. Pound, in his turn, was prepared to be chivalrous about this failure, but he was not inconsolable about it, either. Hence when women are actually powerful, productive, and personable in their cultural claims, Pound becomes intemperate and insulting about both them and their works. As they disprove his theories of "nature," he increases both animal metaphors and sexual insults—Harriet Monroe ("that silly old she-ass"), H.D. ("narrow minded she-bard"), Moore ("spinsterly"), and Lowell ("perfumed cat-piss")—although he mentions Loy positively, perhaps because he had put his editorial hands on her work (*Pound/Williams*, 37 and 38, 11 September 1920).[28] The more tread Pound needs to feel on the cultural scene, the more manly invective he disseminates. He resented any denial of male sexual and therefore (with a notable slide of argument) cultural leadership (DuPlessis 2001, 69–77).

Yet at the same time, astonishingly, Pound did not want to be found in any "anti-feminist" position. He says this directly in his 1921 essay on de Gourmont, where his sex-radical claims about the importance of "sexual energy" for both genders still left a special place for penile leadership (DuPlessis 2001, 76). Pound identified powerfully with and as this organ, in his self-styled claim of "charging, head on, the female chaos" and particularly "driving any new idea into the great passive vulva of London" (Pound [1921], 1958, 204; Bush 1990, 357). The binary active vs. passive is notable as a structuring of sexuality and of the cultural field. While this is hardly Pound's final word on this topic, it is among his more frank and lurid ones, the more so as it virtually coincides with his temperate, antibinarist editing of Eliot.

Pound's fulminating bursts about gender before about 1925 do not match the great poem that he helped Eliot to propel and solidify. Were these formal cuts only—the work of *il miglior fabbro* with a spectacular ear—or did they, willy-nilly, create a particular sex-gender tone and atmosphere? In one genre—the complaining and aggressive letters in the teens—the male poets bitched about female practitioners, particularly about powerful editors, reframing them as conventional obstructors; yet the other genre (the 1922 poem) foregrounded—in Pound's revision—a striking empathy for the gender-doubled transgressive searcher(s) tested by the trials of waste-land sexuality. Pound's "Waste Land" intervention was made during this period of unstable debates on sex-gender ideas. His editing can be read with a gender lens to postulate some of his shifting opinions. Pound's repeated pattern of holding disparate or conflicting versions of masculinity (and of professionalism) had just occurred in one poem in his 1920 "Hugh Selwyn Mauberley." In 1921–1922, while Pound's own letters, some of his essays, and his developing attitudes tended in one direction, he helped Eliot's poem go in another. It is as if, via Pound's interventions, the two men divided the cultural field between affirmative phallic manhood and a more wounded manhood and womanhood. Pound got the phallic.

"The Waste Land" has been described often, yet it still wonderfully escapes. It is a social poem trying to penetrate the urban plethora that, in relation to both the horrors of World War I and personal grief, was saturated with a sense of doom, devastation, and despair. It is a haunted poem, filled with broken tokens of past beauties, systems, and myths, in disembodied, mysterious citations. It is a poem about abjected detritus and "osmo[tic] identities" (Ellmann 1987, 93–95, 97). It is a poem of desire, frustration, blockage, and sexual cross-purposes, with virtually no release. Fertility has been damaged; a wounded male is limned in the intermittently used Fisher-King quest myth with its Parsifal-like hero. It is a poem of unresolved contradictions—with a consistent emotional trajectory that can be "narrativized" and thereby somewhat resolved, and a suspension that hovers, perpetually unresolvable (Bedient 1986, ix–x). The seminarrative juxtapositions offer cut-off glimpses and vignettes of bumbling, burnt-out, grieving searchers, of the living dead, and of blighted hopes. All this occurs in a symphonic montage now so classic that one almost forgets its shocking brilliance. The cuts agreed to by Eliot emphasize these hovering juxtapositions and tonally veering cross-lights, rather than what Harriet Davidson reminds us are more unruly and vulgar specifics: "scenes of drunkenness, whoring, urinating, defecating, and bigotry" (Davidson 1994, 124).[29]

The shards of citation that stud the text are a reminder of our pa-
thetic cultural capital and spiritual incompleteness. Eliot uses the citations to make it seem as if there is some "secret," that an important
answer would emerge if one could just decode it. Thus the reader is
put in interpretive situations of yearning, seeking, and urgency that are
constantly frustrated, mirroring, in the zone of reception, the sexual-
spiritual frustrations of the speakers inside the poem. Part of the power
of this work lies in the evanescent sense of a final, yet always postponed
conclusion, in part because of the rhetorical juxtapositions, in part because of the dynamic contrast between poem and notes.

In late 1921 to early 1922 Eliot had asked Pound to read "The Waste
Land" in draft form and accepted his advice about what to cut. It once
had five longish narratives; only two remain.[30] Three major chunks of
narrative plus sets of other lines were removed. Pound also suggested
many individual verbal changes, often quite acute for tone and diction
(Rainey 2005, 23; Rainey 2007, 98).[31] Eliot authorized the poem as edited,
and he acknowledged Pound's help throughout his career. Comically un-
solvable is the question whether these cut sections had contained "bad"
writing. Given that Eliot became hypercanonical, if we had a longer and
authorized poem from the draft materials, critics would easily find ways
of justifying the necessity of every word. In fact, the shipwreck section
(eighty-three lines cut) contains rather "good" writing, if not always on
topic. Of course, we are quite used to "The Waste Land" as it is; the three
cut sections are disproportionately long and would unbalance the poem
as we know it, but only because we know it the way we do. Thus I ignore
"badness" to address a different speculative question: how to evaluate the
sex-gender impact of Pound's excisions.[32]

Some of the effects are quite striking. The poem achieves this with
Pound's help by his cutting out two thoroughly stereotyped depictions of
genders: a randy "man's man" and a pretentious bluestocking. Of course,
he might have cut them simply because of their being generally narrative
sections (from a dogmatic-modernist resistance to poetic narrative), but
the sex-gender impact of their removal is striking.[33] Particularly, cutting
the two (non–sailor/shipwreck) narratives makes the poem considerably
less fixed (fixated?) on two of Eliot's already existing "types"—a Sweeneyish
lout (here more genial than in the quatrain works) and a female figure
whose artistic and literary pretensions far outweigh her abilities.

After the removal of "Tom's place," almost no male heavies are left
in "The Waste Land," although there are quite a tidy number of them

in Eliot's early poems—both Irish and Jewish thugs, to give them their ethnic due. The only one left is the carbuncular clerk, and one of his more *louche* acts (public urination) has also been cut (Eliot 1971, 47). The semicomplicit semirape remains. The bar scene is gendered in a stereotyped hearty way—the madam with the heart of gold, the "fly cop" on the beat whose attempt to arrest a man for "committing a nuisance" (the urinating mark again) was nixed by a fix from one of the other gentlemen.[34] Gender banalities of these sorts are excised—despite Pound's and Eliot's earlier investment in just that type of banality. Both the inclusive cultural range with popular song citations and the smug male Babbitty voice are gone from the opening. Entering the poem now, one enters a yearning, cosmopolite mystery; there is no curtain of impervious jollity to penetrate.

The fierce problematic of sex and gender in "The Waste Land" is literally everywhere: the Woman Question and neurasthenia, incompatibility and desperation, hysteria, impotence, male wounds, homoeroticism, failures of desire and failures of nerve, commonplaces of abortion, grungy losses of virginity, perversity, degradation, rape, rancor, conflicted passion. To make a site in which a fertile heterosexuality is returned as a centerpiece is the overt (and underachieved) aim; this is wrenched and interrupted by homoerotic yearnings and propositions beyond normative heterosexuality. The heightened sensibility and arousal around desire (the hyacinth girl—perhaps Jean Verdenal transposed, whom Eliot recalled greeting him with flowers) sometimes take on a spiritualized dimension, but mostly sexuality is just sordid and sorrowful.[35] Sexual passion and spiritual yearning are here deemed incompatible, instead of being necessarily—ideally—interrelated.

Eliot's depictions of female figures in his pre–"Waste Land" work often reveal hostility, shock, distaste, and a mordant masochism at their sexual energy and emotional power. The mocking urbanity of many early poems—exacerbated sensation and irritation, arid gender relations—opens out to an uncontainable yearning mixing the sexual, the spiritual, and the existential, which is as quickly closed up or ironized. Pound's redaction of "The Waste Land" contains far less closing off or ironizing of these materials. Impotent connections, incomplete sensations, defensive resistances, frustrating sexual encounters, urban loneliness, and intense crises among the obscure and marginalized are now emphasized rather than the sardonic portraits of social types. That is, Pound tended to save Eliot from his own gendered stereotypes and rigidities and from the

powerful satiric tone that created a puppeteer's distance, not a wounded
or empathetic saturation in the materials of the poem.

The female characters now left in "The Waste Land" have shadows
and dimensionality. Even the ambiguous Mme Sosostris—inadequate
shyster or prefiguring prophet?—has a haunting part. (And past: her
"bad cold" seems to be World War I slang for syphilis.) Particularly defining are two matching female figures in "A Game of Chess," in two set
pieces with two class orientations, neither section coming to any narrative conclusion or outcome. Two kinds of stalemate about (in)fertil-
ity, hysteria (expressed/repressed), and cagy expressiveness balance
each other. In "The Fire Sermon," the powerful urgency of sexual desire
seems heightened and beautiful in the regal past but completely passive, beaten-down, and "supine" in the low-life present. In many of the
vignettes, the speaker proposes an empathetic picture of female figures
whose hopeless acquiescence or depressed resistance to sexual contact is
a symptom of the morbid lack of fertility that is mourned—and suffered.
The poem travels through loss by its séance-like calling up of half-alive
voices and half-dead, unrecognized emotions.

Despite Pound and Eliot's every emphasis on binarist extremes of
sexuality and fulminations against culturally active women, Pound did
not retain the ersatz poetess-socialite with her artistic pretension but cut
this scene from the poem. In the draft, Fresca lies abed, attends to break-
fast, defecation, and snobbery, meditates social triumphs, scribbles arch
letters—a thoroughly middlebrow female literary pretender. The aura of
distaste (particularly in references to Alexander Pope's Belinda and even
to Jonathan Swift's poem "The Lady's Dressing Room," in which a voyeur
gazes on a female's teeming chamber pot, ll. 11–12, 23) offers much sardonic revulsion both at ripe female body and at vacuous female soul. Indeed, "Women grown intellectual grow dull" (Eliot 1971, 41). And there
are other negatives still: a backwash of middlebrow and lavender high-
brow influences like "Vernon Lee, Walter Pater, Symonds" (intermixed
with some, arguably Henrik Ibsen, offering serious debates about sex-
gender). The unfresh Fresca is given a down-market cosmopolite feel
with her "hearty female stench" (Eliot 1971, 23, 41). All this self-deception
and smugness, the pretentiously cultured and sexually promiscuous, has
but one awful outcome—"she scribbles verse" (Eliot 1971, 41). The allusion to Nathaniel Hawthorne's *mot* enhances Eliot's tonal parodies
of her scribbling pretensions. In short, Fresca is a collection point for
a plethora of negatives about females: her "unreal emotions, and real

appetite" (Eliot 1971, 27, 41) construct a worst case—inauthenticity and manipulative lust.[36]

Given the fulminations about female writers that we have seen in Pound and Eliot, the excision of Fresca from the final poem is a fact of unusual richness.[37] She is, after all, the zone in which all their anxieties about female professionalism and autonomy as well as manipulation, sentimentality, and bad writing could have been broadcast, the apogee of their earlier "feminization of poetry" grumblings. Further, the satire of Fresca's "dreams of love and pleasant rapes" could have offered a sordid contrast to other characters' more pained considerations of sexuality (Eliot 1971, 23, 39). The verse is exciting, if quite nasty—and in this particular consistent with other early Eliot. Yet Pound cut Fresca, and Eliot concurred.

Why? The parts of the poem that Pound selected to retain are far less narrative in impulse and far less parodic about gender and sexuality than the full draft but more needy, yearning, upset, fragmented. By retaining these scenes of scattered vignettes and mixed-up desire, Pound emphasized the wounded side of Eliot's draft, the speaker apparently suffering with all his characters, be they male or female. In short, Pound selected one part of Eliot's existing poetic sound and resisted another part—the guarded, superior side, the Eliot of snide, powerful *vers de société*.

Pound emphasized a poem in which both male and female characters were unstrung, with no omnisciently nasty area of exemption from the sorrows that the poem outlines. Pound cuts any sense of smug fulfillment or manipulations of either sexuality or gender both in the men in the bar and in Fresca. As for coarse fulfillment, the argument that Eliot had made and that Pound emphasized posited coequal anguish. What is left of sexuality and gender is always more baffled and indeterminate, pained and grieving, than two of the cut narratives. Pound did not cut the ambiguous gender pain; what he did cut (in two of the three narratives) was sexual and gender smugness—superficial, jocular, and pretentiously fulfilled.

Both the Joycean opening and the scene with Fresca were narratives of superficial denizens of their gender, blissfully unconscious of any sexual anguish (in the enounced) and literarily imitative (in the enunciation). So resistance to sexual banalities was perhaps not the only rationale for Pound's cuts. Given that one section was provoked by Joyce's "Circe" section (in *Ulysses*) and the other by Pope, imitation was also at issue. All imitations of past work, even of much admired but recognizable work, would put these male poets in a secondary, weakened position.[38] Literary unoriginality was to be avoided (at least programmatically denounced) in the construction of modernist maleness. "Copying" and "following" were feminizing strategies; in contrast, allusion was an ironic, hermetic strategy, arguably more powerful.[39] Recall that Pound remastered Loy so that he could appear to be the originator of what turn out to be her complex formal strategies in the enunciation. Yet at the same time, in a patriarchal poetics in which male poets may take up and claim any number of subject positions in the sex and gender world, "The Waste Land" contains many sexual waverers and wanderers, rather than strong figures inhabiting one gender or another. An imperial range has been claimed by the wraith-like inhabiting of many sexual subjectivities, even if this range concerns a vulnerable, cross-gender zone.

The poem now represents bisexual maleness, male and female hysteria treated as one related phenomenon, and a compromised spiritual yearning. This is related to characters in limbo, between the living and the dead. Thus the sex-gender ambiguities do suggest a vaguely queer regime. Much of early Eliot did correlate masculinity and passivity ("The Love Song of J. Alfred Prufrock") and femininity and at least manipulative pressure, if not sexual fulfillment ("Portrait of a Lady"; "Hysteria"). Some of the cut parts of the manuscript correlated masculinity and loutishness, femaleness and sluttishness. With this removed, we are left a demoralized, unconvinced, generally infertile "femininity" plus some kind of exacerbated quester who seems to foresuffer his errant "masculinity" or his doubled gender.

Tiresias collects both the sexual and the spiritual/prophetic aspects of the poem into one efficient, non-normative figure.[40] He is, at root, a figure of sex-gender ambiguity—hermaphrodite, androgyne, bisexual? These, of course, mean different things but amalgamate both/all genders, both/all sexes, as Suzanne Churchill has argued (Churchill 2005, 23). In Ovid's version of the Greek myth, when Tiresias answers "Woman" to the gods' probing, even prurient question about which gender has more human sexual pleasure, his ambiguous punishment is physical blindness but spiritual/prophetic gifts.[41] In Eliot's poem, however, this figure does not bear witness to extremes of sexual pleasure but rather to extremes of sexual pain—indifferent, casual, cruel, and anguished. Modernity is, again, loss.

While editorial excisions and their sex-gender meanings constructed the poem, the cuts of the independent short poems that Eliot had once proposed to fill out a book-length publication have a parallel task with complicating implications. Eliot himself had perhaps cut the most Swinburnean, decadent, or "purple" of the poems that he composed between about 1914 and 1921 that were at first intended to complete the "Waste Land" volume. "The Death of St. Narcissus" involves fantasies of being raped by a male figure (the male protagonist imagines himself as a girl) and intense ambiguous sexuality in a male figure, who ends up martyring his complex desires in masochistic religious rituals (Eliot 1971, 91–97). It is plausible that they were too odd and revealing, too bizarre in their religious sexuality (or sexual religiosity), and could not be assimilated. As for the other poems ("Song. For the Opherion," "Death of the Duchess"—a shadow version of the first part of "Game of Chess," "Exequy," and "Dirge"), Pound still had notes on Eliot's manuscript about these poems, which presumably were somewhat in play for the volume. Pound opposed at least one because it was self-imitative (Eliot 1971, 107). As is already clear, imitation in any form triggered Pound's resistance. He opposed the rest because they repeated what was already in the poem and became superfluous. And, as Michael Levenson points out, Eliot had already excised many allusions to English literary works and had substituted classical and Continental texts to distance himself from his immediate local indebtedness and to claim more comprehensive cultural power (Levenson 1984, 203).

Thereupon Eliot changed the poem definitively once more. After accepting Pound's textual editing, Eliot completed his own poem by adding the notes inside it, rather than publishing a few particular lyric poems standing outside the main text. Having decided to remove all of the poems of self-immolation, tortured sexuality, riffs on the "shadowed beauty" of men, and sexual despair, Eliot chose instead, after much self-debate, to produce and insert quasi-scholarly notes to the poem to complete the volume (Eliot 1971, 101). He thereby fixes his own queer poem by framing it with rhetorics of scholastic mastery; he also extends the range of the poem by a powerful, authoritative, and influential subjectivity. In the notes, a highly literate and literary voice claims an allusively comprehensive engorgement of masterworks of European culture. These footnotes create a parallel discourse to the poem, hardly extraneous, gratuitous, or finally that accidental. In Tim Dean's elegant reading (both of Eliot's "impersonality" and of other critics), this is a work of mediumship and radical "self-dispossession"—penetrated by and powerfully violated by a plethora of voices in a striking queer, antimasculinist affirmation

(Dean 2004, 59). But the addition of the notes, in my view, alters this equation and remasculinizes and remasters this haunted, penetrated work. Such a double sex-gender negotiation is the engorging move typical of patriarchal poetry.

Eliot's inclusion of austere and impressive paratextual material (often using the "I" as a gracious, knowledgeable explainer of the origins of sources) as opposed to his quite anguished lyric poems has many implications. The notes disturb the fragmentation—and the gender pain— with a stance of mastery beyond the poetic sections of this text; the notes are invested in connecting the work to the power of high culture, to contemporary scholarship in comparative ethnography and religion, and to an array of impressive classical texts, with four languages cited in bulk—Italian, French, Latin, Sanskrit. The reception of this work was depersonalized by Eliot's creating a philological scholar-poet as one of the poem's author-functions and thus emphasizing a classicizing mastery of "the tradition" rather than leaving us with an author-function depicting modern-decadent sexual suffering, incompleteness, and anguish inside of mysterious events with no outcome. The notes thus encourage thematically extractive and universalizing high cultural readings, saving the poem and its author from grotesque splay, domestic horror, mysterious connections, and ecstatic heightening. Eliot thereby veiled some of the personal and sexual anguish with its occasional homoerotic trace; he tried, though unevenly, to masculinize the frame of the poem with scholarly authority. While it is still possible to argue that this is a very queer poem, such readings do not account for the different tonality of the notes. It is the contradiction in subjectivities between notes and poem that is so striking. The authorial voice of the notes with allusions to overarching "universal" and transhistorical culture places and controls Eliot's evident debts to *fin de siècle* motifs as well as to modernist sexual and gender debates. The paratexual notes modify and reframe the poem by surrounding its sexual and gender anguish with a distancing authority.

Pound knew this well, and it seems to have annoyed him. To underscore: Pound had not seen the notes before the poem was published; when he did, he thought they were irrelevant to the "emotional unit" of the work and to the "functioning of the poem" (Pound 1924, 97–98). He suggests that "the reader of good will should read THE WASTE LAND as I read it; i.e. *without* the notes" and states (this is important bibliographic information) that he "did not see the notes till six or eight months after [seeing the 'typescript']." He further claims that "they have not increased my enjoyment of the poem one atom" (Pound 1924, 97). He continues in the same vein, insisting that the poem is for the poetically invested "reader" but the notes "are for some other species of fauna, perhaps the Times Lit. Sup. reader" (Pound 1924, 98). That is, the division between the emotional arc of the poem and the notes identifying various citations was very clear to him; the parts seemed to call for two different kinds of "reader" with unequal aesthetic understanding. Pound comes close to saying outright that the presence of the notes modifies the "intensity and poignancy of expression" of this poem; this effect was, in my view, precisely Eliot's goal, done to muffle the indeterminate sexual anguish (Pound 1924, 98).

The critical debate on whether Tiresias is the central consciousness of "The Waste Land" also implicates Eliot's pedagogic notes, any reader's attitude (annoyance, rage, acquiescence, resistance?) toward being told what to think, as well as Eliot's ideologically motivated attempt to assert an organizing figure—stabilizing in that way what is quite porous in other ways (see Eliot 1971, note to line 218). To propose, appealing to narrative structure after all, that Tiresias is "the most important personage in the poem" and that "the two sexes meet in Tiresias" seems tendentious given the poem's non-narrative gaps, fragments, plethora and vectors, and figures emerging and withdrawing as revenants and irruptions.[42] The importance of Tiresias lies in his sex-gender proposals, not in whether he organizes (or, more assertively, unifies) anything. By these interpretive comments, Eliot insists that his central consciousness is both male and female (although an "old man"). This Tiresian gender wobbling is, in one view, quite queer, but it is also imperial and universalizing, and everything taken together constitutes a specific version of patriarchal poetry. This I have defined as the imperial ability to inhabit even a contradictory range of sexual and gender subject positions as a masculine power claim. This effect is enhanced particularly with the addition of the notes. The contrast of "The Waste Land" draft and the work we have therefore speaks to the intense contradictions about sexuality and gender at the inception of modernism.

The editing also speaks to Pound's and Eliot's somewhat different investments in the poem. For Pound, "The Waste Land"'s wavering characters involve a debate about maleness in poetry that had also taken shape in "Hugh Selwyn Mauberley." In "The Waste Land" he emphasized the androgynous, anguished, and queerish characters, thus donating one mode of gender thinking to Eliot after he had used it (and half-expelled it) for part of himself as well. The sexual dramas, lack of fertility, and blocked sexual desire are symptoms that phallicism could, arguably, cure. It is an argument that we have seen developing in Pound. While Eliot accepts the loss of his satiric treatment of stereotyped male and female types, and accepts that this is now a poem of sex-gender ambiguities, he also produces an authoritative framing subjectivity. With powerful, hermetic, and allusive notes he bolsters a sense of authority that is arguably masculine but nonphallic. Such scholarly assertion combines with the androgynous, pained, or gender-ambiguous seekers that populate the text—"I do not know whether a man or a woman" (l. 364). In short, if postwar history is pain and spiritual-sexual loss, the cure is scholarship, analytic investigation, and an affirmation of the truths embedded in classical texts. The notes restabilize the poem by couching its despair via an imperial, world historical subjectivity ranging over eras and eons. This defines Eliot's contribution to patriarchal poetics beyond the gender-ranging queerness of the poem.

"These fragments you have shelved (shored)" is Pound's mysterious aphorism commemorating their encounter, along with the gayish "slanging" "'Slut!' 'Bitch!'": one man (Pound?) as Truth, the other (Eliot?) as Calliope (Pound 1996a, Canto VIII, 28). Or perhaps Pound plays both roles, truth and epic poetry, self-divided. Or was that Eliot—his notes being Truth, the poem as Calliope? The choices that are made as these men articulate their literariness, and the contradictions and ambiguities of those choices, are propelled across the whole century (Rainey 2007, 101–102, 106–107). Pound shores up a certain aspect of Eliot and tries to deemphasize another. In fact, he shores up Eliot's interesting sex-gender "ruins" instead of emphasizing Eliot's superior satiric remove, while satiric distance and academicism are arguably how Eliot had shored himself "against" those ruins (Milne 2010, 35; Rainey 2007, 102). Eliot put back a version of that superiority and authority when he completed the work with his notes, after Pound had edited the poetic text.

With the much more ambiguous redaction of Loy, Pound tries to shelve her (in *his* library and *his* anthology) and thereby to claim her innovations for himself. Women, in Pound's irregularly affirmed truism, could not be original, complex, cynical, or critical about heterosexuality (even when they were); men (like Eliot) had to be held to originality (by cuts) and were allowed by Pound to have a complex sex-gender position including androgyny, sexual frankness, and queerish wavering.

These multiple, contradictory gender positions combined with the imperial, authoritative range of the notes are precisely patriarchal, in my argument.

So what did Pound learn for *The Cantos* from cutting "The Waste Land"? It is impossible to say quickly without another chapter, but it appears that Pound's response in his own oeuvre was an enhanced insistence on male factive heroism in art, love, and war. In the work from 1923 on (from Canto VIII with its mysterious Eliot allusion, including the Malatesta Cantos of the mid-twenties and beyond) Pound resisted making the past "poetic," wifty, and evocative but struggled to depict the past as solid, contemporary, and modern-decisive. "There are more men in this camp" becomes proleptic (Pound 1996a, Canto X, 47).

4. Coda: "Patriarchal poetry an entity"

Of course the Fresca material is not neutral.[43] Even when excised, it is a revenant itself and remains a provocative shadow text. Eliot takes up the questions of sexual license and female authorship again in 1933, eleven years after "The Waste Land," diagnosing modernism as hampered by its sexual, materialist focus. *After Strange Gods* constitutes a "moralist's" paean to racial and religious purity and to the U.S. South, praised for its resistance to modernization, modernity, heterogeneity, urbanization, immigration, and certain "undesirable" groups, notably and notoriously "free-thinking Jews" and blacks as full citizens with full civic rights (Eliot 1934, 19, 20). The modernists who encourage heterodoxy (a bad) are—no coincidence—those who focus intensively on sex and gender issues; this fastidious touchstone designates their moral limitations. Discussing Thomas Hardy and D. H. Lawrence, Eliot dismisses as reductive the driving force of passionate sexuality as motivation for their narrated characters. Eliot particularly disdains the "sexual morbidity" of Lawrence, in which the female characters might have sex with "savages" or "plebeians" (Eliot 1934, 58, 61). (Presumably a female character crucified by savages—as in *The Cocktail Party*—is a better narrative bet.) "Morbidity" is a very striking term for these matters: it is a crossing point for general mental states (gloomy, unwholesome, extreme, unreasonable) and, as a technical medical term, for diseased parts or structures, corrupted, vitiated, and infected.

Sheer femaleness in a writer presents the lowest, most easily dismissed case in Eliot's hierarchy of effects. Femaleness and females (tautologically) produce only the "feminine," defined through Katherine Mansfield's story "Bliss," described as a "perfect" handling of the most "limited" and "*minimum* material" (Eliot 1934, 36). This polemically forces the minor and the female to overlap, given that no other female modernist is mentioned: not Stein, Moore, H.D., Loy, with whom he had varied but seriously literary dealings, or even Woolf, whom he knew well.[44] One thereby sees in 1930s Eliot a desire, reaffirmed, to segregate female authors to a "feminine" mode already disparaged as hopelessly miniature and therefore as culturally and morally inadequate. Male authors will certainly struggle toward cultural, social, and spiritual adequacy, but they may be consoled in those struggles by their carefully constructed assumptions of gender superiority.

Three

Succession and Supersession, from Z to "A"

Patriarchal Poetry connectedly.

GERTRUDE STEIN, "PATRIARCHAL POETRY"

1. Men of Letters

Certain cautions apply to literary-critical uses of letters, including the sets of letters crucial to this book. The letters in any selected edition appear by an editor's best judgment at the time; in addition, untold texts may be lost.[1] Letters are an emotionally invested practice in which contestation, raillery, intimacy, revelation, and exposure are staged. Because poets with a preternatural sense of their historical career may write for the archive, not, or not only, for the recipient, sincerity may be particularly performative. Reference problems can be startling: letters are allusive, deploying initials for poems and persons, nicknames, typographical play or suggestive error, glancing, unclear allusions, unfilled-in pronouns, and shorthands of all kinds. In letters, one sees graphic inscriptions sometimes almost minute to minute within the time of writing, the little adjustments and articulations involved in creating a serious working bond; misunderstandings and quarrels, jokes and teasing, self-interest and manipulation get frozen, exaggerated, and magnified. Letters among poets mix narratives of desire, success, and the frustrations of never having enough recognition. Indeed, the arrival of letters may stand symbolically for recognition and fame, which explains their uncanny affective power.

Letters are driven both by the writer's response to another and by a self-mirroring process that the epistolary genre encourages. Hence letters show figures making and remaking themselves in "correspondence," speaking to the self by speaking to someone else. In letters emotion is visible before it hardens, literary hopes are exaggerated or confessed, and particular, even random or thoughtless turns of phrase become talismanic. Hence through letters a critic constructs—as Andrew Epstein proposes—not "biographies of these friendships" but rather "defining dialogic encounters and their effect on literary production" (Epstein 2006,

10). So epistolary intimacy is both welcome and fraught, and letters are rhetorically tricky, dense, layered, and full of guarded nuance. Thus they are susceptible to close reading.

Becoming a literary leader (the switchboard, the go-to man) was one of Pound's achievements, and his construction of networks of correspondents was key. Even if he made parallel statements to many people, even if some letters became repetitiously formulaic, the power of his epistolary intimacy was defining. Pound energetically affirmed in galvanizing bulletins that "the fate of culture" depended upon instantaneous and full-scale action on fronts he defined (Timothy Materer in Pound 1985, xi). As early as 1915 T. S. Eliot felt that "an attitude of discipleship" was what Pound demanded (Gordon 1999, 102). An antic, intense emotional charge emerges in the "dialogic encounter" between Ezra Pound and Louis Zukofsky (Epstein 2006, 10). Many of Pound's letters, but a number of Zukofsky's too, are written in a distinctive cant (James Laughlin calls it an "Ezratic lingo")—allusive, orthographically creative, imperially multidialectal, sardonically seriocomic, almost as if the poets were morphing among rapidly changing social positions (Laughlin 1987, 50). Pound assumed this voice habitually in his correspondence; it was catchy and catching, probably because, as Michael North has argued, assumption of racial or ethnic dialect is a masquerade encapsulating a sense of vulnerability and a desire for power (North 1994, 77–83).

2. Maleness, Mentorship, Mastery

As Christian Bök suggests, "Your mentors become your tormentors."[2] In mentorship, two conflicting pedagogic models structure different social metaphors of maleness (Brown 1988). In Wendy Brown's discussion of political theory and manhood, the fraternal model depends on mutual, lateral self-fashioning and interactive learning, the aggressive friendship that Andrew Epstein titles *Beautiful Enemies* and that Peter Quartermain calls "instructive kin" (Epstein 2006; Quartermain 1992, 68).[3] The paternal model postulates a fountain of wisdom and male power from which, as suppliant, one imbibes—as from the oedipal father or the pre-oedipal father. Harold Bloom has dramatized this as one high-stakes oedipal struggle, ignoring the possibility that in the poetry world (not the monotheistic critical world of canon formation) alternative figures might desire to assume this patriarchal role and that the "applicant" actively chooses and may even shift among different pedagogic figures, as both Christopher Beach and Zukofsky suggest (Bloom 1973; Beach 1992; Zukofsky [1967] 2000, 135).

The relationship of Pound and Zukofsky is an episode in mentorship within patriarchal poetics, in the ambitions both men articulate and in the particulars of negotiating both scope and autonomy for Zukofsky. But their models were at odds in this relationship. Pound had a father-son or apprentice-master model, while Zukofsky, though cast by Pound as performative "son," attempted to enact a fraternal dyad. These models both exist within the "filiative," in Edward Said's terms, with the fraternal choice trying to pull toward the "affiliative" or nonfamily model of lateral bonds of compatriots (Said 1983). The filiative is a relationship like father to tribe or offspring; it is hierarchic and framing. The affiliative is a chosen, comradely, contestatory, nonhierarchic social relationship (Said 1983, 23–24).[4] The tendency of modernity (says Said) is toward the affiliative; yet fraught and much-debated passages back and forth between these positions are more typical of these poets.

If these male-oriented family metaphors are thoroughly problematic, they are nonetheless also authorized by the participants. Pound and Zukofsky express their ambivalent fondness for each other by stylized uses of father-son terms. This topos was instigated (1928) by Pound's claiming to the young Zukofsky "the fak that farver is SOMETIMES RIGHT" before Zukofsky began playing with this metaphor in the early 1930s (*Pound/Zukofsky*, 20).[5] The many teasing and serious father-son allusions in the correspondence indicate that Zukofsky was given and assumed the role of "Joonyr," "Boy," "sonny," "your infant chile," and "deerly beloved son" in relation to Pound's "favver," "yr. aged parent," and, by 1931, "granpap" (*Pound/Zukofsky*, 34, 39, 62, 78, 101, 56, 123). The terms were clearly appealing enough to both, assimilable, perhaps, to Freud's acknowledgment of regression to the infantile in their mutual transference. At the same time, the family words are very stagy, a mask for Zukofsky's pride at his competence and abilities.[6] The struggle between the fraternal, lateral model and the paternal, age-hierarchic model of mentorship marks their relationship.

In his early twenties, Zukofsky evinced the attributes of all fine candidates for mentoring or sponsorship—ambition, boldness, confidence, deference, and intelligence. As Williams observed to Pound, Zukofsky's "mind is really silky," and he "enjoy[s] excellence" (*Pound/Williams*, 87, 12 July [1928]). Zukofsky constantly defined himself as a collaborator or co-conspirator, Pound's coequal and not his epigone or apprentice.[7] Both the dynamics and the contradictions of that claim are vivid; at the same time, he insistently seeks instruction, approval, advantage, criticism, praise.[8] The pleasures of homosociality and patriarchal power made it quite difficult for the younger partner to define the relationship with as much success as the older one. This sounds simple, but it had some complex, long-term consequences.

The Pound/Zukofsky letters show mentoring bonds from the moment of Zukofsky's first mature work, emerging strikingly in 1926 but particularly around his guest editorship of the February 1931 issue of *Poetry: A Magazine of Verse*, brokered by Pound. Zukofsky is simultaneously granted (lip-service) independence and given so much advice and instruction as to position him as Pound's instrument.[9] The overall impression of lists of names, obiter dicta, suggestions, interventions, and encouraging comments is overwhelming, particularly when Zukofsky is told that this editorial "opportunity is larger than you had grasped" (*Pound/Zukofsky*, 52, 25 October 1930). Pound generously and challengingly proposed that Zukofsky's intervention could even be something that "will stand against Des Imagistes," a confrontation, however, that Pound already had won long ago with vorticist declarations (*Pound/Zukofsky*, 45, 24 October 1930; see also 46). This is a proposal of replacement and belatedness at once: Zukofsky is told he could be in his generation what Pound was in his, a new patriarch of a new group or movement—but in a decade-old formation. Despite this, Zukofsky is thereby placed as an insider within Pound's poetry universe, particularly to answer again, with Poundian tools, what Pound now viewed as flaccid poetics.

Pressured both by Pound and by Harriet Monroe, *Poetry*'s editor, the young Zukofsky seemed to satisfy both—and himself—by his prose essays framing, sometimes with surgical scare quotes, "Program: 'Objectivists' 1931," "Sincerity and Objectification," and "An Objective" (Zukofsky [1967] 2000). By its suffix -*ist* the rubric "Objectivists" suggested an -*ism*, thus seeming to name a movement, although it did not. These essays were thus taken as a "manifesto" of "Objectivism" (a term consistently rejected by Zukofsky)—not, as they were intended, as a general literary ethos.[10] Yet the poetics of "sincerity" and "objectification" proved to be fungible. However reluctantly formulated or even opportunistically invented, Zukofsky's rubric "'Objectivist'" became talismanic for a number of poets over the next decades.

Zukofsky discusses these terms in poetics while protesting loudly about designating a group with the rubric "'Objectivists' 1931" rather than so designating the work of a congeries of talented individuals (*Pound/ Zukofsky*, 65, 6 November 1930). A crucial consequence was that Zukofsky was fiercely unwilling to separate the generations of practitioners by age-group (with overtones of a new group forming to replace the old). Instead, Zukofsky attempted to construct his editorship on a fraternal model—Pound, Williams, e. e. cummings, and Eliot were all invited to the issue among his examples of good writing.[11] Zukofsky so completely resists the idea of division by generations that he asks Pound repeatedly for a contribution (*Pound/Zukofsky*, 67, 6 November 1930).

Zukofsky's reaching for desired fraternal companionship notably uses imagery based on the male body and its vagaries. His cross-generational model proposes a fraternity of spermatic poets and claims the same general status for youthful masturbators (his term) and older men, husbands with wives and children (see *Pound/Zukofsky*, 67, 6 November 1930). There is no age hierarchy, no group; seminal metaphors are potent enough. "We" stand only for literary excellence. In the event, the only one of the earlier modernists who agreed to be published in Zukofsky's issue of *Poetry* was Williams; he was also the only one of the older men with whom Zukofsky had a fraternal relationship of coequal mutual mentoring.

Indeed, Williams speaks directly (7 April 1928) to their relationship in their correspondence.[12] He appreciatively notes their bond, a balanced reassurance to Zukofsky on the fraught topic of generational or age difference (*Williams/Zukofsky*, 544–555). "I did not wish to be twenty years younger and surely I did not wish you to be twenty years older. I was happy to find a link between myself and another wave of it [literary ambition, poetry] [. . .] it [our friendship] proves to me [. . .] that the thing [literariness] moves by a direct relationship between men from generation to generation" (*Williams/Zukofsky*, 5–6). The unself-conscious gendering of the poetic project is notable. But so too is the metaphor of the "'chain'" of writers related by poetics (*Williams/Zukofsky*, 32). At the same moment when Zukofsky was the play-along "chile" to Pound's "favver," a fraternal model of mutual mentoring characterized his relationship with Williams, with cross-generational homosocial bonding in the brotherhood of poetry.[13]

For Zukofsky, the tensions between influence and originality were prime. In this context, age is something that Zukofsky will come to mark a good deal throughout his career—as several times in *Prepositions+* when he will turn the generational gap (of twenty-five years) to a mutual confluence of interests transcending age. In the contexts of both the Wallace Stevens and the Henry Adams essays, Zukofsky notes the relationship between literary men born about twenty-five years apart (Zukofsky [1967] 2000, 28, 51). In several of his essays beginning in the 1930s and extending to his discussion of Stevens (originally delivered as a lecture in 1971), Zukofsky has drawn a subtle, condensed portrait of influence, including at least the general *Zeitgeist* as well as a confluence of interests between two totally autonomous persons, one of whom simply *appears* (with ironic emphasis) to be affected by the other. Zukofsky proposes—indeed, insists—that any such similarity may well be coincidental, not direct and definitely not subordinating for either member of the exchange. In addition, through the agency of the affected party, there are choices and negotiations to make with literary traditions in general and in specific (see Zukofsky [1967] 2000, 135). This deemphasis of direct literary influence, intelligent and suggestive, is at the same time a studied processing of that moment early in his career at which Zukofsky, faced with Pound, had to take up some attitude—resistant filiation, cultural coequality—to Pound's mentoring of himself as younger writer and, with a preternatural quickness, to the implications of their relationship for literary history.

3. "Poem Beginning 'The,'" Eliot, the Wimpus, and the Poetic Projects of Young Manhood

Zukofsky staked himself on the literary life, on his joining the line of practitioners in a tradition defined for modernism by Pound. Such ambitions often contain buried struggles around maleness. Perhaps as early as 1922, when "The Waste Land" was published, but certainly beginning in 1925 and completed by 1927, Zukofsky wrote "Poem Beginning 'The'" as a satiric farrago and elegy, tonally extreme and surpassingly literary and virtuosic. Zukofsky's first mature work, constructed with an antic resistance to "The Waste Land" and commenting on Eliot's further evolution to "The Hollow Men" (1925), is inflected with imitation, defiance, and subtle twists on Eliot, as Maeera Shreiber notes (Shreiber 2007, 105–127). The issues and problems of belatedness that this work creates are real, as his ambition expresses emotions around descent, genealogy, tradition, and originality and as he faces and absorbs the work of contemporaries. "The" insistently and even arrogantly (citing from Shylock out of William Shakespeare, yet) proposes with a contemptuous: "The villainy you / teach me, I will execute, and it shall go hard but I / will better the instruction" (Shakespeare, *Merchant of Venice*, III.1).[14]

"The" was Zukofsky's calling card to Pound, who published it in the third issue of *Exile* in 1927 as well as in *Profile*, his literary historical anthology of 1932. In December 1930 Zukofsky gave Pound an account of contemporary literary history, insistently proposing himself as part of that company, not belated to it (Stanley 1994, 47; Perelman 1994, 175). In the poem, too, Zukofsky alludes to, plays with, and amalgamates modernist work. Making one streaming "dream" of all those modernists' names and works in the First Movement acts to contain, organize, and control them. The poem's lines are comically, aggressively numbered, as if each is something ticked off on a list of accomplishments. To write as a person who, even as he arrives, is at that moment late/belated is the bizarre (and painful) situation of young Zukofsky. He dramatizes this by playing catch-up by allusive citations, with the implicit claim that his belatedness has thereupon ended.

Given the themes of male impotence, female casualness and casuistry about pregnancy, general infertility, and gender wavering in "The Waste Land," the randy scandal of Zukofsky's "Peter Out" section in "The" takes on eye-rolling meaning. Nowhere is Charles Bernstein's point about "the founding significance of difference for American poetry" more graphically demonstrated (Zukofsky 2006, xvi–xvii). Zukofsky presents the companionable (and arguably circumcised) penis as a supplement to the faded blocked sexuality anatomized in both "Prufrock" and "The Waste Land," and to any number of obsessive canards about circumcision in both general culture and Pound. Sandra Kumamoto Stanley makes the witty point that this sexual organ parallels the unseen Prufrockian addressee in the poem beginning "Let us go then, you and I" (Stanley 1994, 64). Zukofsky is also making a pun on Eliot's depictions of impotence; to peter out is an idiom about sexual failure, but bringing this particular "Peter Out" for an airing activates him by exposure to exciting cultural influences. Thereupon Zukofsky presents a raunchy urban American culture—the culture of music halls, vaudeville, and revues with showgirls, along with black and white popular song—as worth a cultural visit, along with great artists and great comic strips (Zukofsky 1927, 8). Zukofsky's proposal of this aggressive modernist high-low cultural mélange plays with stereotypes about Jews, lechery, frankness, and the lower body.

Zukofsky's comments about Eliot's "Waste Land" in his December 1930 letter to Pound are placed inside a paragraph on "A," along with a complex denial that he is belated to Pound's *Cantos* in his own just-begun long poem. These materials about rival long poems contain aggressive core statements concerning maleness. Barely two years into his public career as a poet, Zukofsky situates himself and (according to him) is already critically situated as a follower of both Eliot and Pound. He is not sure what his attitude is—immediate glee at the quickly achieved power of that position and wariness about its costs seem about equally divided. He uses the letter as a lawyer might, to outline the charge of imitation, following, and "indebtedness" and to respond in his own defense. The gist is: I am not slavishly following; I was accepting the "challenge" you had set (*Pound/Zukofsky*, 79). Again two models of literary relationship are in collision—the fraternal (challenge to challenge) and the paternal (he comes after, is imitating, is epigone).

The strange word "wimpus" is a collection point for these conflicts around manhood and cultural claim. Zukofsky says that he was answering "The Waste Land" in his poem in order "to tell [Eliot] why, spiritually speaking, a wimpus was still possible and might even bear fruit of another generation" (*Pound/Zukofsky*, 78–79, 12 December 1930). Because Eliot and his work are the topics, critics have long assumed that the word "wimpus" is punningly cognate with "whimper," in "*not with a bang but a whimper*," the poignant, much-parodied end of Eliot's "Hollow Men" (1925).[15] This identification is quite plausible, if not irresistible: Zukofsky's reply to Eliot could not thereby be clearer, and "Hollow Men" had been published recently (Eliot 1963a, 92; Scroggins 1998, 132; Shreiber 2007, 106). In "The Hollow Men," male figures reveal spiritual hopelessness, reduced to the physical level of dried bits and the rhetorical level of riddling paradox. In Zukofsky, the anticlimactic feeling and the questions of "spasm" and "potency" from "Hollow Men" are indeed in play, but differently than in Eliot's depiction of the hapless and impotent within a hopeless modernity (Eliot 1963a, 92).

For the "wimpus" to which Zukofsky alluded is an actual object, touted by U.S. tinkerer, health/"sexual vitality" advocate, and bodybuilder Bernarr Macfadden, who, among activities as a self-promoter, huckster, and journalist, found time to "invent" the wimpus, a prosthetic device for sustaining erections (Hunt 1989, 160).[16] "Invent" is Macfadden's claim, yet the device appears in other contemporaneous advertisements as "the Erector" and the "Robut Man"; the same item had different names with different manufacturers (McCoy 2000, 214, 216).[17] It is an invention "that would remove the embarrassment of men inflicted with temporary impotence" (Hunt 1989, 160). For Macfadden, "manliness" was not only a physical norm that could be improved upon by diet, bodybuilding fervor, and the use of his products: "manliness was the product of a properly exercised sex organ" (Fabian 1993, 56). Hence the wimpus. It apparently did not work all that well. But it certainly works to penetrate this mordant comment by Zukofsky.

What is the wimpus doing here? Who or what is impotent? To whose organ is the wimpus attached? What is playing the role of the wimpus? Using this word, Zukofsky reads Eliot's male characters as impotent, evoking the diffident, neurasthenic figures often found in early Eliot ("Prufrock," the speaker of "Portrait of a Lady," and these "Hollow Men").[18] Or perhaps it is this recent poem by Eliot that demands a wimpus; its yearning repetitions are boring and weak. Or more boldly— possibly the poet Eliot himself needs this device. This would be a time-honored, if nasty, way of bonding with another man (Pound) by offering a joking depiction of the (postulated) male troubles of another. And even stranger is this proud claim: Zukofsky's poem provides the wimpus for a prior poet, for a prior poem, and for modernism itself.[19]

In Zukofsky's opinion, with the wimpus offered by his "The," that drooping sense of spiritual impotence in Eliot's poem not only could be cured but could thereupon be made to "bear fruit"—result in issue. Eliot's career to date then becomes the impregnated female ground for a newer career. Zukofsky's own long poem "A" is explicitly charged with being the fulfillment of "The," out of Eliot's "Waste Land" (*Pound/Zukofsky*, 79). Zukofsky stands ready to complete modernism: to prop it up, as needed; to revive it; to make it fecund. And he is ready with arrogant and witty metaphors concerning potency. Now the wimpus, or its enveloped organ, is not going to bear fruit—that does require another entity. But claiming all places, zones, and genders in sexuality as solely the male's is, as we have seen, part of the imperial ethos of patriarchal poetry.

In Zukofsky's self-characterization of his poem, all the citations, the lively, if obscure narrative, the satiric Popean energy, and the ringing radical conclusion together create a wimpus for Eliot's poem and its ideas (*Pound/Zukofsky*, 79, 12 December 1930). To offer one's own poem—its manner and its matter—as a prosthetic supplement to stiffen the spiritual impotence that Eliot depicts in his poems, even to "impregnate" the "Waste Land," is teasingly aggressive. Aggressive? It is downright vulgar, a low blow. Citing his own poem, saturated in an allusive Jewishness and

Yiddishkeit, as a spiritual wimpus for the rapidly Christianizing Eliot is a devilish, fearless, and cocky remark.

4. Zukofsky in the Pound Aura

Zukofsky continued to struggle over what to do with Pound and his enviable cultural power, his refusal to enact the mentoring relationship using the model of fraternal cooperation and lateral bonding that Zukofsky desired. On 18 November 1930, after the multiple letters of advice to Zukofsky about the "Objectivist" issue of *Poetry*, Pound finishes his interventions and thereafter turns to a slightly offhand critique of *"A."*[20] This turn has a stinging impact. Zukofsky gets told in rapid succession that the seven sections of *"A"* have not adequately "digested meat of his forebears" (really meaning Pound himself; *Pound/Zukofsky*, 75); that the work is a bit "perfessorial"; that it shows some "progress" but still has a distance to go (*Pound/Zukofsky*, 76); that it should not continue after the seventh movement (is not cut out to be a "life work")—something Pound repeats more emphatically a year later (*Pound/Zukofsky*, 105). Further, that it has the potential for a "succes [*sic*] d'estime" but that it should not yet be published (*Pound/Zukofsky*, 76–77). As a last blow, that the work could be "remedied more or less by procedures" that Pound could reveal—but does not. This gets said in the abruptly nonfamilial guise of "yr /   vnbl /   frien'" (*Pound/Zukofsky*, 77). Given that Pound had performed paternal personae and fatherly posturing in letters just preceding, the change of speaking subject is striking. So too is Pound's teasing disengagement: "Wot you want me to tell you about it that you can't find out for yourself??" (*Pound/ Zukofsky*, 75, 27 November 1930) and "I strongly suggest that *YOU* send me a crit. of it before *I* say anything more about it" (ibid., 76; see also 77).[21]

Pound ends this letter: "Have you see J[oseph] G[ordon] Macleod's Ecliptic? I mention only to show the 'need' being felt for longer poems built on a plan" (*Pound/Zukofsky*, 77). The need? Perhaps Pound was noting a market for such work, as Macleod's poem had just been published by Faber and Faber, with Eliot's implicit approval. Is this to say that *"A"* needed a plan? This is a relatively benign, hardly discouraging remark about *"A"*; but by the time it occurred, it is probable that Zukofsky was in no mood to credit any amiability.

Zukofsky's long poem project had been put on notice. The bilateral ambivalence of Pound's withdrawing and Zukofsky's desiring recognition constructs a fraught dialogue perpetually in process between them.

At the very end of Zukofsky's letter back (12 December 1930), the Macleod reference emerges again (*Pound/Zukofsky*, 82–83). Rather than reading the whole of Macleod's poem, just published in a 77-page pamphlet, Zukofsky has read (standing in a bookstore because he could not afford to buy it) the one section "Leo, or, The Lion" published in the July 1930 *Criterion*. This section stages a conflict between a proud lion and a thunderstorm, with impressive descriptions of aggression and struggle. The metaphoric section ends without any sort of male triumph, but a moment when "all purpose and desire / Vanish like matchflame in a broader fire, / And all the want that fills his aching head / Is to return, to drink, to go to bed" (Macleod 1930a, 39; Macleod 1930b, 674). Thereupon Zukofsky makes not only a remark about form but an evaluation of content and even author. In his discussion of the poetic tactics of Macleod, Zukofsky was quite approving but took the occasion to doubt that poem's "virility" (*Pound/Zukofsky*, 83).

"Virility"? This comment about the long poem of another young writer evokes the charged realm of manhood and potency. After the near-sexual excitement of this storm/machine and the rain, the lion simply walks away in an anticlimactic turn. Hence Zukofsky can wonder aloud at the poem's "virility" (apparently the nonconsummation of a narrated encounter) and also implicate the author of that poem in his remark.

The Ecliptic is a *Bildungs*-poem, fragmented but yearning for wholeness and reintegration; its major preoccupations are sexuality and subjectivity.[22] The bits of the self are elaborated through the signs of the zodiac. "Each sign thus contributes to a single consciousness" along an ecliptic, that imaginary line among the constellations (Macleod 1930a, 9). This is the plan to which Pound alludes, a scaffolding like the Odyssean one Eliot said that Joyce had provided for *Ulysses* and one that in 1930 Pound might have felt he still had for *The Cantos* in allusions to Dante Alighieri's *Commedia*. This kind of scaffolding was suggested to Zukofsky as a "plan" for "A." Macleod's poem is somewhat obscure in its private allusions, very learned in its classicizing materials. It shows an artful, baroque modernism, reminiscent of 1930s W. H. Auden, Edith Sitwell, or Hart Crane—a high-toned playing among diction levels, hermetic allusions, syntactic complexity, and metrical skill.[23]

Even from the few pages he scanned, Zukofsky surmised the tension around maleness and sexuality central to the text. This remark about "virility" resembles the question of "wimpus"; it indicates some interlinked investment in one's own poem and one's career in manhood for the young poet. Doubting the "virility" of a representation by a contemporaneous male poet is also a way of slapping back at Pound's praise for Macleod's poem when presumably Pound had an even more striking example of a long work by a young man to consider: "A"'s first sections. Whenever Zukofsky feels belated before he had even started—and Pound's praise of another young man would certainly provoke this—he marks the spot with a male-inflected image.

What is the "pisscology," in Zukofsky's pun, of his need to write his long poem (*Pound/Zukofsky*, 78)? Answer: his grappling with a highly articulated generational belatedness while having the intense conviction of literary equality with Pound. Zukofsky will be, he wants and hopes to be, part of the modernist Chosen. At the age of twenty-four, when he states that he has lost and will not recover an ability to write short poems, he says that his long poem is somehow thereupon a default position, replacing inadequacy with ambition (*Pound/Zukofsky*, 78). This throwaway remark on failing to write short poems is a smoke screen: he is now necessarily involved with, marked by, and in a relationship of challenge and belatedness to the *Cantos*. For even if one begins a long poem by default or by offhanded accident, one has (in fact pretty soon) to notice that one is doing this in and for itself, not simply, say, out of the incapacity to be short. Further, Zukofsky's stagy anguish is hardly true. He wrote short poems throughout his career. Avoiding saying (exactly to Pound) that he is directly challenging Pound in beginning a serious long poem seems to be the purpose of his comment.

But Zukofsky wanted to be credited for carrying out the challenge effectively, not sidetracked by praise of another young male poet, Macleod (b. 1903). All this is intimately related to a question of old versus young men and generativeness mixed in with generations. Thus he aggressively queries a Poundian dictum. In a citation from Pound of Constantin Brancusi's claim that the making of sculpture was not for young men ("jeunes hommes"), Zukofsky belligerently challenges the implicit doubt that a young man was capable of a big work: "what's jeune got to do with it—if Abram could have a chile at 110 & at 16 what's the difference. La Sculture etc—is that why 'A' shouldn't have been written?" (*Pound/Zukofsky*, 82, 12 December 1930).[24] Just because Zukofsky is young, does Pound actually think that the poem "A" will be *ipso facto* inadequate?

This angry, proud, and overstated question—rejecting age hierarchy and asserting capacities for generativity at all ages—was not assuaged by Pound's kindly smoothing of the feathers in his next letter, telling

Zukofsky not to worry about belatedness, even though he is up against more challenging elders (Pound, Eliot, Williams) than Pound and his peers were (early Yeats, Bliss Carman) (*Pound/Zukofsky*, 85). This remark did not help.

However good Pound's advice is, that letter is provoking. Zukofsky is about seventeen years younger than Pound. For him not to continue to worry about belatedness and mentorship would take more than Pound's generous and possibly self-preening permission. Zukofsky had set himself the poetic program of equaling three of the most distinguished moderns—by accepting their challenge, as he says. He is unlikely to turn back, but he does sometimes also humbly seek instruction, perhaps as a way of keeping his long poem in Pound's purview (see *Pound/Zukofsky*, 81, 12 December 1930). Zukofsky wanted to be able to work through belatedness without feeling that it implied a hierarchy. Dealing aggressively with a temporal/generational but not poetic belatedness cuts a track for Zukofsky's ambition for the next years.

A year later, in December 1931, Zukofsky makes an even bolder assessment of his work. He has had a year and a half to revise "A" but has found nothing to change—nothing. The various critiques (often concerning the poem's obscurity) made by René Taupin, Williams, and Pound himself have not undermined Zukofsky's sense of the importance and value of the work.[25] This is certainly both a proud claim and a claim of parity. Indeed, Zukofsky's analogies deserve notice. He affirms that he has read and reconsidered his poem multiple times, and yet he will change nothing. In one of his frankest—and most amusing—evocations of interwoven metaphors of physical masculinity, Zukofsky puns on the "rocks" of John D. Rockefeller—linking poetic riches with potency to characterize the "stirring" success of his poem to date. He says that "A" is physically arousing to him as well as intellectually pleasurable, claiming this by making a witty and sly application of one sentence from Leo Frobenius. My translation of the German that he cites into direct—and vulgar—English would simply read: he has a cock but no balls. Zukofsky is contrasting this sad situation (of maleness but no masculinity, no guts) with himself and with his arousing poem (*Pound/Zukofsky*, 111, 7 December 1931).

My poem, says Zukofsky, is arousing in a specific, charged way. It is potent. Poetent. With slangy allusions to rich men and to the "fellers" of Rockefeller, he unleashes a joshing but powerful message, producing class affirmation as well as poetic affirmation via the explicit topos of physical manhood. Zukofsky is again aggressively testifying about his own and his poem's male power. His long poem and some metaphors of manhood are, at key moments, tied into each other; they form a distinct node of material inflecting the ongoing propulsion of this work. They are also claims designed to resist any ascription of career weakness and second-class status.

Yet the composition of "A" after 1930 (after the first seven sections have been completed and have served as the topic of this exchange) falls off until 1935. The relationship with Pound is hardly the only barometer of this shift; nonetheless, the project has gotten all mixed up with Pound because of Zukofsky's anguished and possibly staged disclaimer of similarity, following, and belatedness and his interested claim of dissimilarity, parallel projects, and originality. This strongly suggests that Pound's epistolary resistance, offhandedness, and coolness toward the project had a chilling effect on Zukofsky for a number of years.[26] Zukofsky does not want to replace Pound or to view him as a patriarch but to parallel him as another "makir" or "fabbro." However, what might be called a patriarchal structure of poetic practice—an age hierarchy as well as a sociocultural difference that became more and more divisive—proved difficult to alter. Indeed, it appears that Zukofsky began to entertain a particularly inflected replacement fantasy in a very *sub rosa* way, a career fantasy saturated with assumptions from Jewish hermeneutics and non-hegemonic theology. The crossing point in this exchange is Pound's anti-Semitism.

5. Pound and/or Zukofsky: Copying

Zukofsky's 1935 accusation that Pound copied a motif from him marks the next stage in their relationship. Zukofsky notes that Pound's allusion in Canto XXXV to the St. Matthew Passion and the audience wearing black copies the opening of "A"-1 (*Pound/Zukofsky*, 167, 8 April 1935). Canto XXXV begins "So this is (may we take it) Mitteleuropa"; the reference is to the story in free indirect discourse of a Jewish maestro "conducting / [. . .] the Mattias Passion, after requesting that / the audience come in black clothes" to mourn the crucifixion (Pound 1996a, Canto XXXV, 172). The local allusion seems beyond harmless—perhaps copying, perhaps accidental, perhaps indeed intended by Pound as a nice reminder of Zukofsky's poem. This canto—and Zukofsky's hypersensitivity to it—does not simply concern this tiny allusion to Zukofsky's

"property" (if it even could be so construed): this is the canto in which
Pound (on the same page) points out "the intramural, the almost intravaginal warmth of / hebrew affections, in the family, and nearly everything else," charging all Jews, and certain male Jews, with both the
regressive and the female/feminine (Pound 1996a, 172–173). That is,
Pound's depiction of the young artistic Jew affirmed that figure's unmanliness at the same time as he "alluded" to Zukofsky's words.

The topos of the Jew as male-feminine had a long history in
nineteenth-century discourse, crystallizing in the early twentieth century with the broad-brush claims of Otto Weininger's *Sex and Character*
([1903] 2005), to which Pound alludes (in another context) and whose
lurid arguments he absorbed (DuPlessis 2001, 69–71). Bryan Cheyette
and Laura Marcus place Weininger's writings at the "heart" of modern
European culture, the place where a feminized male Jew, a masculinized/
eroticized female Jew, and the lecherous Jewish male help solidify a
countertopos: heroic and virile nationalist and anti-Semitic thinking
(particularly in Germany). "Remasculinization" would certainly be
Pound's position, in his typically secondhand refractions of such thinking (Cheyette and Marcus 1998, 3–4). Weininger argues that modern
culture is both Judaicized and feminized, degrading to the virile male
and to the racially pure or Aryan (Robertson 1998, 23). Ritchie Robertson surveys the stereotyped "equation of Jewishness and femininity"
and its various sources in the "nineteenth century imaginary" among
playwrights, novelists, journalists, philosophers, even a rabbi, and early
psychoanalysts (Robertson 1998, 28–29, 25). There is a transferring of
views about women in general to male Jews in general as dependent,
weak (not masculine), chameleon-like copyists, "receptive" and therefore unoriginal, irrational (not objective), and prevaricating as well as
sensual (Robertson 1998, 27). In this explanatory stereotype, Jewish men
were effeminate, unmanly, intuitive, damagingly nonaggressive—in a
word, feminine.

This passage about the "intravaginal" is one of the indicators of
Pound's often vile and here somewhat satiric fascination and disgust
with Jews. He sometimes played these mixed attitudes in Jewface (in
Yiddish-inflected dialect), as in the poem that Zukofsky published in
An "Objectivists" Anthology (1932)—the notorious/ridiculous "Yid-
discher Charleston Band" (DuPlessis 2001, 172–173).[27] This manic identification with (appropriation of) the "extravagantly racialized" dialect
with the warding, superior gesture of mockery is characteristic of some

Anglo-American moderns who satirize in order "to keep the boundaries absolutely clear between the self and its all too familiar Semitic other" (Cheyette and Marcus 1998, 9; see also 19). As others have argued, Pound reveals a "repressed identification with 'the Jew'" that emphatically plays out in his relationship with, and abjection of, Zukofsky (Ellmann 1987, 189; Cheyette and Marcus 1998, 8).

In Canto XXXV the Yiddisher sound is somewhat more benign and superior, in "the tale of the perfect schnorrer: a peautiful chewisch poy / wit a vo-ice dot woult / meldt dh heart offa schtone / and wit a likeing for to make arht-voiks" (Pound 1996a, 174). This is only benign, however, if it does not seem to be about yourself. A schnorrer is a beggar, a para-site, a sponger, someone who habitually takes advantage of the generos-ity of others, always trying to get something for nothing. If this Yiddish word characterizes Zukofsky in a tale *about* him, the remark is a striking rejection. Or was this a tale told *by* the schnorrer, who frames (with a colon) this condescending portrait of the artist as a young Jew? In either case, Pound was emphatically stating that such male beauty in face and voice made a Jewish artist and his artwork always feminized, perhaps parasitic—by definition, by ethnicity. Actual maleness was therefore not enough; maleness and "chewishness" did not combine properly, if at all. The combination came out feminized, too pretty, too effeminate, too soft, too unoriginal. In calling attention to Canto XXXV, Zukofsky was certainly saying "message received" about Pound's sly portrait of the art-ist as a young (feminized male derivative) Jew. And what he says back to Pound is not I reject the aspersion of the feminized or I am shocked at your depiction but, in a complex turn: You are the unoriginal one; you are the follower; you have copied me.

Pound's anti-Semitism had become increasingly fierce in the let-ters of 1934 and 1935 before the comment in which Zukofsky discusses Pound's "borrowing." Zukofsky's almost derisory attribution of two epi-phenomenal lines of Pound to an "origin" in his own work constituted a way of defending against or containing the sting of Pound's prejudice. To say that Zukofsky was first with this image of the St. Matthew Passion in "A"-1 is to claim priority, precedence, and—importantly—originality, to try to puncture Pound's fondly teasing (and meanly superior) slurs. So much for the canard that Jews "copy," "mimic," and are unoriginal. It is Pound the borrower who is actually imitative, a repeater of the culture of others, Pound who is the (imaginary) Jew, the chameleon, Pound who is belated.

"Intravaginal" is a particularly astonishing body-evoking word in the Pound canon. It is not, however, unique. A similar word gets used in one of Pound's 1934 letters, in a mocking threat to Zukofsky about economics. "Cease the interuterine mode of life," says Pound, and learn economics "if you don't want to be confused with yr / ancestral race and pogromd" (*Pound/Zukofsky*, 158, 6–7 May 1934). Such allusions to ethnic hatred and terror-killings include the shock of throwing Zukofsky's self-professed "anti-Semitism" back at him. Pound's letter is filled with slashing anti-Semitic remarks of one sort or another in the guise of self-righteous political teasing. In these two similar words (intravaginal/ interuterine), the male Jew is depicted inside and between the walls of the female body—in uneuphemistic sexualized spaces—the vagina, the uterus.[28] He is thereby protected, cozy, unmanned and unmanly, if also (another stereotype current in the early twentieth century) a bit lecherous: "intravaginal" suggests an act of intromission.

Zukofsky's earlier male-and-penile based imagery in the letters of the late 1920s and early 1930s might have been motivated to preempt any such stereotyped thinking about the femininity of male Jews. Given all the images of maleness and potency that Zukofsky had proposed in his correspondence with Pound, the evocation of this "feminized Jewish male" material was designed to cut Zukofsky deeply. Constructing a feminized Zukofsky was a Poundian way of never having this co-conspirator of modernism be considered his equal, for a female/effeminate, derivative Jewish poet was never the equal of a self-styled virile male innovator. Thus Zukofsky's career becomes one "site" where Pound's debates about women authors in the 1910s and 1920s are repositioned. The Jewification of the secular Zukofsky by Pound, caging him by anti-Semitic barriers to discourse, and Zukofsky's own strategic, unpleasant, and awkward claims that he is an anti-Semite too all had a sex-gender narrative as well as a Semiticized one. Zukofsky had repeatedly claimed in frank and even vulgar allusions that his maleness and his literary ambition were one; his maleness stands as a guarantor of his cultural claims as a critic, as an editor, as a poet. All this effort ends in "interuterine," a precise insult of unmanliness, along with some later insults about Zukofsky's intelligence and his falling "back into racial characteristics, and ceas[ing] to be L/Z at all" (*Pound/Zukofsky*, 163, 6 March 1935). But in particular Pound insists that Zukofsky is now belated (again), unoriginal, behind the times: "Most americans miss the boat / but it is more irritatin' to see 'em catch it; and then step off"; "I can't hold the boat FOR you" (*Pound/Zukofsky*, 163).

6. Implications for "A"

It is very hard to treat "A," a notably impervious poem. "A" is almost impenetrable in its motives, its control, its privacy, its outcomes. It is a poem of textual invulnerability. Any or all of its sections will undoubtedly always be best-in-category given that the categories are so singular, so unique a measuring and trumping of cultural material. We find a homophonic translation of parts of the Book of Job ("A"-15) and the Psalms (intermittently, including "A"-23), a thousand-line epos in which every line is a citation, sections "employ[ing] a word-count prosody," a retelling of a Plautus play, a Joycean "history of the world," a double canzone on Karl Marx and Baruch Spinoza, using the same form and parallel lexicons (Scroggins 2007b, 188).[29] The work is a sampler of aggressive mastery in language and design. Its verbal acuity is unsurpassed and yet also hermetic, sealed.

The reading offered here views "A" only in the context of one relationship (with Pound) among the several that Zukofsky had in his life and poetic career. The first parts of "A" (precisely through "A"-9 and perhaps further) seem to be loosely Poundian, done under the rubric of the fugue, which, as Burton Hatlen reminds us, was then the central mechanism—at least Pound claimed it was—of the *Cantos* (Hatlen 1997). The oft-cited question in "A"-6 about testing the plausibility of the fugue in its uses for the structure of a poem suggests that Zukofsky uses the fugue exactly and exactingly as a test of Pound (Zukofsky 1978a, 38). Zukofsky proposes this organizing strategy throughout the early part of "A," and especially with the *stretto* construction of the galloping sonnets of "A"-7. Hatlen's argument (which he takes through "A"-12) supports a sense that Zukofsky tracks Pound deliberately, going him one better, actually carrying out and completing what Pound said, rather loosely, that he was doing.[30] This is also clear in observations by Bob Perelman and others: there are uncanny parallels between Pound's and Zukofsky's choice of projects, whether these be translations of Guido Cavalcanti or the construction of a literary textbook (Perelman 1994, 24–25, 177). Pound may well have thought so too. In a benign remark that retains some proprietary rights over Zukofsky, Pound stated in April 1937 to a correspondent who asked about *The Cantos*: "Take a fugue: theme, response, contrasujet. *Not* that I mean to make an exact analogy of structure. Vide, incidentally, Zukofsky's experiment, possibly suggested by my having stated the Cantos are in a way fugal" (Pound 1950, 294).

After or at the first half of "A"-9, that is, around 1940, Zukofsky takes a very important turn in control of his fear of being under the influence of any master or forbearer. How will he escape belatedness? In a 1930 letter he had proposed to escape through an impenetrable hardness of diction that draws on his second-generation immigrant propensity for torquing and distorting English (*Pound/Zukofsky*, 79, 12 December 1930).[31] So, with this diction of opacity, he will write the long poem as a lyric, by which I mean not a short poem but a long poem built rhetorically as if it were short: an intense, sonically thick, metaphysically dense, layered, closural, and sometimes even private work. This also has the effect of answering the strictures against the long poem enunciated by Edgar Allan Poe.

Thus "A" is hard because as a through-composed long poem it is made like a metaphysical lyric or epigraph. "A" has very little slack; it is a poem that does not relax. The intensity of the lyric, the jeweler's sense of every word as faceted, precious, and multiply determined, has given Zukofsky's long poem a diamond-like hardness. Every single word stakes the claims of the whole project, the whole poetic career (see Zukofsky [1967] 2000, 228). The importance of verbal intensity to Zukofsky is shown in his response to L. S. Dembo's serious question: "Do you conceive of ['A'] as having an overall structure?" (Zukofsky 1969, 218).[32] Zukofsky turns the answer from large to small and from structure (scope, design, plan) to intricacy of diction, condensation of syntax, verbal focus: "It's the detail that should interest you all the time" (Zukofsky 1969, 218). Dembo is observing the sheer overall scale of the thing, its obviously daunting scope and largeness. Zukofsky answers by insisting on smallness and the local detail as sustaining interest (Zukofsky 1969, 218).

Zukofsky is an inheritor of Judaism's own interior historical debates between the Enlightenment and the Orthodox observant Jew: modern vs. marked manifestations, a universalizing ethos vs. particularist signs of one's religious affiliation. His secular claims are his way of distancing himself from a group with which he does not want to affiliate directly, stating that, unlike his own Orthodox father, he is a nonobservant, critical Jew (*Pound/Zukofsky*, xx). Thus he claims a disinterested or objective ability to examine evidence and judge Jews without identifying with them. Zukofsky insists that he makes as compelling a critique of Jews as Pound insists that he himself does. Zukofsky even calls himself an anti-Semite (*Pound/Zukofsky*, 28, 19 December 1929). As a way of stating nonaffiliation, this is extreme, and in the historical context it becomes at once poignant, risky, and chilling.

Thereupon Zukofsky is startled to realize that by the mid-thirties Pound was deadly serious. Pound's prejudices were not susceptible to reason, economic analysis, any functional critique of his demagogic bedfellows, or political debate. These explicit arguments are presented by Zukofsky in letters of the later 1930s to both Pound and Williams, who also showed a loose, general anti-Semitism. Zukofsky played the part of token exception in Pound's eyes, something that Zukofsky could tolerate all too well given his own sense of "singularity." Finally, in 1940, he directly criticizes Pound on his ethnic fulminations, naming anti-Semitism explicitly and telling him to stop (*Pound/Zukofsky*, 204, 15 April 1940). This is the last letter between the two in the Ahearn edition (*Pound/Zukofsky*) until 1951. Of course, the war and the Holocaust intervened.

The main implication of this relationship for "A" lies in Zukofsky's Hebraic-inflected appropriation of the Christian doctrine of supersession. Jews in general do not accept theological supersession—the trumping of Judaism by Christianity's "fulfillment." Nonetheless a cultural, secular, "Pauline" Jew might have both some knowledge of and some uses for this material.[33] We know that Zukofsky was indeed interested in Christian thinking and certainly in J. S. Bach's St. Matthew Passion— a masterwork of Christian redemptive universalism within the cultural heritage of the West. We know from Mark Scroggins's discussion that Zukofsky was interested in the question of redemption, which he solves for himself by evoking the flower "liveforever" and the triumphs of art in lieu of salvationist doctrine (Scroggins 2007a, 98–101). Zukofsky transposes these materials and ideas into his relationship with Pound and more precisely in the relationship of the two long poems, one by the self-styled "father" and the other by the reluctant "son." "A" is not simply a brilliant culmination of Zukofsky's own younger poem "The" but also a supersession of Pound's *Cantos*. That is, the Zukofsky poem is a fulfillment, not a replacement.

When Zukofsky transposes supersessionist thinking from the theological to the cultural realm, he implicitly proposes that his work becomes the trumping fulfillment of Pound's. "A" "fulfills" the *Cantos* in the same way that Christianity fulfills Judaism—by minoritizing the prior structure, by reducing its texts and doctrines to stages on the way to something greater, more redemptive, differentially articulated, and absolute. Replacement is static, occurring within the same system. Supersession transforms the system. Of course, Zukofsky secularizes supersession and distorts it to serve his poetic purposes. He secularizes it by applying this concept to the cultural texts of the long poem rather than to biblical texts, as in the "New" Testament allegorically "fulfilling" or "completing" the "Old." He distorts this concept it by casting Pound's *Cantos* in the role of the superseded text and by casting his own long poem in the role of the text of fulfillment—but a text of fulfillment at once Judaic, Pauline, and secular. He has denied or contained direct influence from Pound by repeatedly rearranging what he knew about the *Cantos*; but finally the best way to trump the situation is to surpass the model by fulfillment of the prophecy.[34] In this case the writer inflected with Judaism constructs that Jewishness as the temporal end—the end and culmination—using the Christian/hegemonic cultural terms against themselves. This also turns the cultural model of Jewish-Christian temporality backward. The fact that Pound was contemptuous of Christianity except in its pagan/syncretic and "mystery cult" versions is not relevant to this argument; *The Cantos* stand for a rival formation.[35]

But in what sense is "A" a Judaic poem? "A" has twenty-four movements; Zukofsky noted that to write a long poem is always to flirt with one's own mortality, making a wager with life, death, and/or God, a wager with and against time (Zukofsky 1969, 218).[36] This suggestive twenty-four-ness clocks in to completion, yet this work is not tied in any other way (metaphoric, thematic, allusive) to the twenty-four-hour cycle or to the chronometrical. So this number is more than a wager with the clock of mortality, more than an allusion to the age at which Zukofsky began the poem. It is emphatically an allusion to Bach's *Well-Tempered Clavier* (in two books, each twenty-four pieces).[37] Finally, twenty-four is the number of books in Hebrew scripture. While there are thirty-six named books, Jewish tradition counts the twelve minor prophets like Joel as "one" book—thus twenty-four.[38] Zukofsky's poem becomes arguably more Judaic as the project goes on—taking this term to mean not religious adhesion but a secular cultural project: hermeneutic, materialist, lettristic, stubborn, and self-commenting.

Did we not suspect all along that Zukofsky acts as if writing a secular, personal, and modernist version of the multigeneric Hebrew scriptures? As the scriptures take on a number of generic tasks (prophecy, law, genealogy, lyric, prayer, family narrative, historical interpretation, chronicle) and have different political-social motivations and rationales, so does the Judaic "A." "A" is also "like" the Bible in that the "author" is often simply a redactor or editor of a lot of texts, compiling them and correlating them. So Zukofsky behaves at one and the same time as if he is the God-like origin of the word and the rabbinical committee of editors of the word. He is not only the prophetic "son" fulfilling that Pounding "father" (as in the relational games of the late 1920s) but the maker of a text first fraternally equal to Pound's text but then triumphantly surpassing that work. Zukofsky becomes the poetic *fabbro* who will supersede (complete and transform) the terms set for him.

At the end of Zukofsky's career, this debate about mentors between the fraternal coequal and the hierarchic paternal reemerges dramatically. One section of *"A"* (*"A"*-17, "A Coronal") is devoted to William Carlos Williams (after his death in 1963) and dedicated to Floss Williams, his widow. It is a documentary elegy, presenting multiple, intimate connections between the poets. *"A"*-17 eulogizes Williams indexically and chronologically, cataloguing some of the times in Zukofsky's career when Williams had been at issue, with citations from letters exchanged between them that illustrate the varied bond.

Despite an arguably similar (if not parallel) connection, Zukofsky writes absolutely no such section of *"A"* for Pound, although the whole work contains a few brief, perhaps even deliberately minor allusions to him. One allusion notes (with a mordant wit about obscurity) that Ezra's first name is the answer to one line of a crossword puzzle; this mention is indexed (*"A"*-14, 352, 820; one of four indexed allusions to Pound). Indeed, the critical and evaluative shorter poem "Nor did the prophet" is importantly analyzed by Mark Scroggins as a meditation on Pound in St. Elizabeths and on Pound's allusions to the Hebrew scriptures in *The Pisan Cantos*. Scroggins incisively argues that "Nor did the prophet" originally had been conceptualized as a section of *"A"*-13 but that Zukofsky apparently decided not to use it. It is thus that Zukofsky deliberately excluded any extended section on Pound in *"A"* (Zukofsky 1991, 146–147; Scroggins 2007a, 270–272). To underscore: this is in stark contrast to his elegiac homage to Williams.[39]

7. A Conclusion or Two

The fact that Zukofsky's long poem ends certainly differentiates it from Pound's *Cantos*; Pound's apologia for his nonending had just been published in several striking fragments in 1968. Zukofsky might have been spurred thereby to focus on completion even though neither *"A"*-23 nor "A"-24 had yet been begun. Literal completion does distinguish his long work from Pound's.[40] Yet the double ending of "A" (text and paratext) has to be—and will undoubtedly remain—one of the most unusual endings in the history of the long poem.

The poem's first textual conclusion, "A"-24, is a *Gesamtkunstwerk* collage, dated 1968 and called "L.Z. Masque." It was assembled by Celia Thaew Zukofsky as a gift, but the poet declared it to be the poem's ending (Scroggins 2007a, 412). "A"-24 is a holograph of the complexity and density both of the whole poem and of the whole literary career. This ending has a lot of critical suggestiveness and emotional finesse. It is family constructed: Paul Zukofsky also had some serious input in suggesting the use of G. F. Handel, as registered in an "official" formal acknowledgment of him at the end of the poem (Zukofsky 1978a, 806; see Rifkin 2000, 91–92). As creative compiler, Celia Zukofsky chose meaningful citations from Zukofsky's prior works and placed them as four layered voices with the Handel performed at the same time. This redaction of his work constructs an allusive network or miniature library in which Zukofsky has become intertextual with himself as well as with certain other cultural artifacts. "A"-24 is a bolus presenting the multiple, contradictory positions that he has taken in his oeuvre, with self-citations, self-quarreling, and palimpsests.

"A"-24 might also well be unperformable, *pace* the attempts by the West Coast Language poets in June and November 1978 (http://www.writing.upenn.edu/pennsound/x/Zukofsky.php) and the January 2009 performance in Sussex, England. We cannot take it in with our current "listening" devices; it is like a *Singspiel* (musical drama) built of cluster chords of layered speaking voices. It is meant to present five simultaneous montage lines, intertwining at times but clashing sonically during most of the work. The Handel is familiar, catchy, rhythmically exact and offers a continuous classicizing resolution for the four sets of loose ends that simultaneously unroll in the voices. The voices do not sing but work with degrees of unnoted *Sprechstimme* (a cross between speaking and singing); they also overlap considerably in their time and pace of speaking. While the librettist-editor programmatically demanded that the voices be clear and distinct, this might actually be impossible, particularly since dynamics (marked in the text by relative size of the words) always make one voice (besides the harpsichord/piano) dominant (see Celia Zukofsky in Zukofsky 1978a, 564). I speak as a listener to a recording; as a quondam performer (he was the pianist in 1978), Bob Perelman remarks with even more authority on the mutual clusters of interference of the various lines, unrolling in parallel play, with "*isolated*" moments of clear statement "vividly foregrounded" in contrast to the clots of the rest (Perelman 1994, 186, 253).[41] Given all this, we might see the work of "A"-24 as engineered to explore a crashing conflict between music and words, an example of self-canceling reception among the parts that brings the whole house of art to a cacophonous conclusion. Forget heavenly harmony—this is a totalized secular struggle, perhaps even a struggle between the medium of the father and the medium of the son as mediated by the mother.

The interface of making and unmaking in "A"-24 is thoroughly appropriate to the level of intensity and negativity to which this text finally aspires. What could actually conclude a poem like this? Who could construct an adequate realization or summary statement capacious enough? After all, "epiphany" and any revelation aside from continuous text and continuous interpretation are outside of this poetics as being a Christian structure of feeling. A summary statement referencing Zukofsky's whole career is the choice; the poem becomes a matted palimpsest of citation and allusion paralleling a musical suite spoken as if from within a long-ongoing conversation among his works. This striking extension of single authorship into doubled authorship in "A"-24 and the index drastically multiplies the author-function into commentary and into a fractal remaking of text.

"A"-24 might be unperformable or might indicate a Platonic ideal of a performance—silent, unrealizable, or tacit on the page, but an idea of literariness and musicality together in a literary career. The final section is emphatically proposed as a modernist *Gesamtkunstwerk*—words, music, and performance at once. This differentiates it from *The Cantos*. Even though Pound had a small musical career and did compose music, he never thought to put this in *The Cantos*, except for some notes (birds on the wire) in Canto 75, transcribing a medieval manuscript. In contrast, the co-operative Celia and Louis Zukofsky piece puts a score inside the Book. Thus it settles—one might say—a score with Pound, who did not construct achieved closure, in some measure because of the political debacle of fascism. And it settles a score with Stéphane Mallarmé, too, or in any event scores on him as well as on Pound, pointing to Mallarmé's (unachieved and unachievable) ambition to put the world in a Book. An extreme (hence also perhaps Mallarméan) aesthetics demands an unreadable speech and an unplayable opus. Yet, however qualified, "A"-24 does exist, and by its multifarious citations of Zukofsky's oeuvre it is deliberately positioned to complete, or close, the poem, using that plethora of genre allusions characteristic of endings of such lifelong works. The whole 24-section work also, of course, closes with a musical-textual performance of secular art, just as the poem had opened with allusions to a musical-textual performance of religious art.

Compared with "A"-24, the other ending of "A" has not yet been particularly noted in the criticism. This is the paratextual index—the actual final section in the book. It is not a summary or a part of the poem as such, or even an official numbered section, but an important gesture to and in words. Indeed, Zukofsky had originally proposed an index even more quixotic than this, apparently including only the words "a," "the," and "an." Celia Zukofsky intervened, adding a number of other words; Zukofsky then worked on her proposals to develop the twenty pages of index now published.[42] Zukofsky's index to the poem constructs a second "conclusion," the purely verbal asyntactic conclusion or an antic (anti?)conclusion. The index draws on the ateleological structure of alphabet, proposes paratext as text, and mocks the pedantic and plodding with its own jaunty resistance to any functional reference or scholarly use. Incidentally, very, very few poetic texts have indexes written by their authors; those two genres are conventionally viewed as oil and water—impossible to mix.[43]

From the beginning of his career, Zukofsky had been concerned with paratexts. His poem "The" puts the Eliot-like notes in the front rather than in the back—another piece of snide, possibly Jewish contrarian humor. In "A," ending with an index indicates Zukofsky's verbalist emphasis on individual words, not to speak of the "lettristic" and very Hebraic notion that the alphabet is a prime mode—an allegory—for writing, because all words are implicit in it. This alphabetic intention conforms to the last words that Zukofsky himself composed for this book in "A"-23—his alphabetic "summary" (Zukofsky 1978a, 562–563); it also recalls the famous B-A-C-H notes, using the name of another master as an organizing motif for a key autobiographical section at the midpoint of the poem ("A"-12).[44] From A to Z is the motif, giving the gift of this poem from the alphabet to its maker and then back to the alphabet: Thanks to the Alphabet.

The index still contains those indexical definite and indefinite articles with which Zukofsky began this part of the work, along with the four elements (earth, air, fire, water), and any number of paired opposites

(sun/moon, being/nonbeing, day/night, death/life, father/mother, space/
time). "Man" is indexed along with "son" and "child" but not "woman" or
"wife." That lacuna, given everything, is a curiosity; Celia Zukofsky certainly appears repeatedly as a figure in the poem, not to speak of being a
facilitator of its concluding. The index contains a great number of body
parts, including body itself, arm, blood, brain, breast, breath, eye, face,
hand, head, heart, mind, mouth, neck, palm, and skin. This has serious meaning in the Christianizing context of elevating "spirit" and the
mind-body split to hegemonic status; the (Jewish/human) body answers
in all its enumerated physicality. There are clusters (family, home, love)
and also singularities (Jew, not Jewish; Christ but not Christian; horse;
poet; music).

This index is a fantastic phantasm of language. Is it indexical? It does
point toward the poem that it caps but that it cannot, of course, cap-
ture. Yet in many ways the index is anti-indexical, simply because all that
pointing is fundamentally inadequate—to what is the writer pointing?
The only way to "index" this work would be to type it out again. The
whole is equal only to itself. Of course, this is theoretically true of any
poem, but with some poems (including Zukofsky's work) one sees that
fact more intensely. Obviously, with such a decided gesture, Zukofsky
undercuts the conventional expectation that this or any index could possibly denominate all the important categories in the poem (although it
does touch on some), could present all the important proper names (such
as Goethe, Mallarmé, Mickey Mouse), or could even give any "scholarly"
account of anything. Though part of "A"-15 is devoted to the funeral after
the assassination of John F. Kennedy in November 1963, there is no index
entry for Kennedy (cf. Zukofsky 1978a, 361–365). In short, this index is
an unassimilable outrage (outrigger?): comic, incomplete, mocking of
any mode of summary and fulfillment.[45] This poem may supersede *The
Cantos*, but it cannot "fulfill" itself—it can only be a perpetual midrash
on its own ambition.

Did I just use the word "unassimilable"? Did I just say "incomplete"?
How Jewish it is. And nothing is more "Jewish" than that in this poem the
spirit killeth but the letter giveth life, as St. Paul did not say (2 Corinthians
3: 1–6). At least the letter giveth inordinate complexity. With the letter and
the alphabet, textuality is never over. In this index, as Peter Quartermain
has proposed about the homophonic translations of Catullus, we have the
spectacle of texts at "an end of language"—language disappearing into its
own materiality—and bizarreness (Quartermain 1992, 120).

These different endings are two summae, arguably engaging the (much cited) "integral function" of poetics offered in "A-12." "A"-24 presents an ending in music, and the index is an ending in key words as building blocks of the dictionary, thus making an integral, not a sublime transcendence (see Zukofsky 1978a, 138). Despite being a long poem, "A" is the opposite of odic. There is little or no ecstatic loft anywhere (this is, in fact, remarkable); instead it proposes interior impaction, noise, and incomplete lists. Language—the letter—is not a transport to somewhere else; it is the constitutive material grit of the word/the world inside which we live and on which we comment.

"A" is a text of a secular Judaism invested with a Judaic hermeneutics and a Pauline attitude to fulfillment as supersession of a rival long-poem text. "Jewish hostility to the idea of fulfillment" suggests, in poetry, a resistance to epiphany or "the instantaneous unveiling of presence" in favor of a midrashic return and return again to the layers of meaning and allusion built into a text within a work so intricate that it is inexhaustible (Handelman 1982, 187, 120). And thereby Zukofsky does supersede Pound's totalitarian categories. The Cantos, as Bob Perelman argues, concern the light shining beyond the word, the image as a ball of light that does not even have to be read, scryed, or interpreted but is simply known (an epiphanic structure of feeling, a revelation) in "transverbal seeing" (Perelman 1994, 70). Zukofsky's work supersedes this poetic ideology with one of permanent interpretability and verbal-textual plethora. "A" is many things, but among them it is an exacting, lifelong response to Pound's poetics, including his sex-gender attitudes and his politics.

Part Two

Four

Poetic Projects of Countercultural Manhood

Patriarchal poetry an entity.
What is the difference between their charm and to charm.

GERTRUDE STEIN, "PATRIARCHAL POETRY"

The men are in a sense brand names themselves, a minor dream team
representing jocular freedom and masculine America.[1]

JULIANA SPAHR, *Power Sonnets*

1. The Countercultural

The works of Beat and "New American" poets of the 1950s in the Pound tradition were overtly countercultural and countercanonical. The poets stood on the periphery of American culture in chosen and flaunted marginality at the moment of the fixing of the Cold War and United States post–World War II hegemony. The most dramatic instance of cultural marginality was Charles Olson; he renounced two relatively centrist career paths (in the Democratic Party and its political appointments and in the normative university) to propose an alternative vision of the United States and an energetic geocultural vision.[2] Olson emphatically did not accept "the Americanization of the world, now, 1950: soda pop & arms for France to fight, not in Europe, but in Indo China, the lie of it," a prescient statement about the economic penetration of U.S. products, globalization, and the forthcoming American war in Vietnam (Olson 1987a, 44, 21 October 1950). He did, however, postulate a posthumanist American "ENERGY" (Olson 1987a, 34–46).

Allen Ginsberg, who brought the Popular Front politics of the 1930s forward into the 1950s, articulated a visceral, principled identification with deviant Others—people in minority cultures, internal exiles for political reasons (Communists, anarchists, antibomb radicals), exiles for psychological reasons (the dissident/odd, psychotic, crazy, or driven mad), as well as sexual exiles and outcasts, mainly male homosexuals, the sexually promiscuous, and others who did not enter the family economy.

Robert Creeley, uninterested (then) in these overt realms of socio-politics, nonetheless ironically engaged normative gender tokens of the 1950s (home, family, breadwinner, wife, and husband, female and male), exploring the fissures and quirks within their putative ideological seam-lessness. All three poets investigated United States culture; they resisted literary aestheticism, wanting to integrate research, social critique, and future-looking energies with artistic expression "as the wedge of the WHOLE FRONT" (Olson 1987a, 46; see also 11). Their poetry and poet-ics were proudly peripheral, stylistically nonconforming, and intellectu-ally outspoken.

These poets' ideological, cultural, and political critique of the "Amer-ican century" also implicated gender and revealed considerable opin-ions on manhood. They championed strong-minded, pushy, outspoken, feisty, shrill, self-consciously posing and even hysterical masculinities in contradistinction to the more buttoned-down, centrist manhood normalized in the 1950s. They voiced dissident and analytic critiques of masculinity yet simultaneously claimed the powers and privileges of conventional manhood. This combining of countercultural critique with the benefits accruing to normative gender roles is a central contradic-tion. To echo an observation of Australian sociologist R. W. Connell: they were "fighting against hegemonic masculinity while deploying its techniques" (Connell 2002b, 197).

Creeley, Olson, and Ginsberg, like other countercultural U.S. male poets of the 1950s, brought normative male expectations into question. They aggressively displaced kinds of hegemonic masculinity by using mobile gender materials, fascination with male display and emotional minutiae and (in Ginsberg's case) with a critical, though not necessarily self-critical, homosexuality. Indeed, Creeley, Olson, and Ginsberg even participated in the "male revolt" identified by Barbara Ehrenreich as a muted sociological motif throughout the 1950s, a critique of the "bread-winner ethic" and its economic arrangements (like family wage) (Ehren-reich 1983, 12–13). And the poets did so with very self-conscious tropes around maleness, sometimes assuming the exaggerated subjectivity and political position of hypermasculinity.

Michael Davidson has proposed that among the Beats and the Spicer group emerged a new homosocial male subject, mainly among gay or bisexual men, who generally enacted this position in textual (not sexually expressive) ways. That is, the men's links with each other were "homo-textual"; gender bonding apparently overrode sexual preferences

(Davidson 1995, 198; Davidson 2004, 14). To generalize from his finding, affective relations among men—friendships, cohorts, affiliative dyads— often reinforced male gender power in particularly compelling ways. One outcome of this generalized homosocial ethos was that in the 1950s these poets implicitly or explicitly rejected the possibility of making a bilateral critique of gender norms for women, thereby excluding females from the benefit that males got from destabilizing gender arrangements. Their resistance to a critique of women's roles did not necessarily apply to some women's attack on the *sexual* norms of the 1950s, where there were benefits (as well as problems) for both genders in sexual liberation.

Hence, in their negotiations with orthodox, hegemonic masculinity, these poets attempted to alter male roles without making "femininity" and female roles budge much, if at all. This exclusion was unconscious, though sometimes conscious; it was unthinking or half-thought; it was uncritical, and perhaps sometimes deliberate; it was innocent, and yet sometimes maliciously motivated. In this desire to alter male possibility but not to question female social positions, this peripheral cohort participates in centrist thinking. This is particularly dramatic because the members of the cohort did not take whiteness or Americanness "as unmarked, neutral positions of superior reason," in Suzanne Clark's words, but they did assume male gender and its privileges as such an unmarked entity (Clark 2000, 3).[3] Hence maleness and its projects were exempt from any critique that called for coequal and coeval genders, although many ideas about sex-gender were set forth, studied, and troped upon throughout their oeuvres. Some even included the feminine—for themselves. Thus again, one sees the imperial mode of patriarchal poetry in the countercultural zone, claiming a rich variety of sex-gender positions available for men to deploy.

To gender Edward Said's work on culture and imperialism and to construct a mechanism for feminist reception, we could say that these male poets "deconstructed and demystified" the male "center" but neglected to continue the critique by inventing "a new system of mobile relationships" to change power relationships between center and periphery that might make those binarist terms entirely moot (Said 1993, 274– 275). Allegorically speaking, the center claims the goods of the periphery but ignores the periphery's coequality and right to power. This geopolitical language should also remind us that the decolonization of women, across cultures and nations, was one of the (as yet unfinished) struggles recommended in this postwar period and that Simone de Beauvoir's *The*

Second Sex (1953; French original 1949) was a major salvo in that decolonization of women.

The poems of these particular male poets often "othered" men—that
is, depicted males as marginals, often critical marginals. This is accomplished powerfully and compellingly in key texts. But often enough in
their work female figures were recast as insistently normative, centrist,
controlling, a place that females occupied not so much in power relations as in ideological fantasy, despite a few exceptionalist female companions in the countercultural realm.

2. "One Patriarchal Poetry / Two Patriarchal Poetry / Three Patriarchal Poetry / One two three / One two three"

Allen Ginsberg's "Howl" was written in 1955, the same year that
Disneyland opened in California.[4] "Howl" is seriously anarchic in ideology: no law, norm, rule, or sense of decorum goes unassaulted; it is
principled in its negation of postwar normalcy through apocalyptic pessi-
mism and utopian arousal. If Disneyland is centrist, "Howl" speaks from
peripheries.[5] Disneyland offers nice sanitized rides, beneficent controls,
and unthreatening sideshows, a carnival purged of the perverted, deviant, and criminal carny. In contrast, "Howl" speaks of endless rides across
a landscape, intense drug, spiritual, and sex-induced highs and crashes.
One contains and commodifies pleasure; the other is outside behavioral
constraints or control, seeking a permanent infinity of ecstasy. Ginsberg's
"Howl" offered a radical critique of the conformism and denials of the
1950s; the Beats (who had formed around Jack Kerouac and consolidated
with this poem) were depicted as declassed men, sultry and intellectual at
once. When the poem was performed, the poet himself embodied ecstatic
heightening and countercultural negativity. The rip-out of repression in
this poem and its auratic surround was both shattering and liberating.

The first section of "Howl," now often anthologized, is a symptomatic catalogue of individual incidents unrolling narratively as if depicting
the sequential activities of an existing cohort of young men. "Howl" produces its effect by inspiring various disjointed marginals to view themselves as one "group," using the techniques of catalogue, anaphora, and
repetition rhetorically to unify isolated incidents. It deploys the Whit-
manic list as a mode of community formation and consolidation. The
expansiveness of the list and its insistences have the effect of hailing the
reader as part of the cohort.

Ginsberg also sporadically employs particular grammar-shifting tactics in imagery, so that social displacement is signaled by small bits of syntax that are "misused" in almost every line, parallel to the "misfits" enumerated and thus accumulated. Drawing on such generic traces from religious culture as sermon, prophecy, jeremiad, and exorcism, Ginsberg offers rhetorical cues for joining up on the right side and excoriating the wrong side. These poetic-formal cues propel both the sociopolitical critique and the dynamic reception that the poem excited.

Section two is an insistent ritual diagnosing and exorcising of the sociopolitical disease—Moloch—or a Goyaesque capitalist-militarist monster. Section three eulogizes one exemplary man, a patient in a mental hospital, and verbally explodes asylum walls in a way that appropriates bomb anxiety and makes a cataclysm of the world that produced this and other forms of politically sanctioned madness. Indeed, in the poem's 1957 obscenity trial, Judge Clayton Horn decided that "Howl" was protected speech of "redeeming social importance," because the poem indicts "materialism, conformity, and mechanization leading to war" (Ginsberg [1956] 2006, 174).

"Howl" is a postwar poem shadowed by the trauma of the United States' use of the atomic bomb on civilian populations along with the totally unspoken fissure of the Nazi-fascist Holocaust for Ginsberg as a self-consciously, if secular, Jewish poet.[6] In perpetual extremis, the wandering characters listen "to the Terror through the wall," and their orgasmic highs plus the aura of "kind king light of mind" descend vertiginously, becoming the "crack of doom on the hydrogen jukebox" (Ginsberg 1984, 126). Both the bomb and the war are explicitly present at the end of the third part, in which electric shock treatments and allusive citations of the U.S. national anthem become fused with an apocalyptic after-time destroying institutions of containment: "I'm with you in Rockland [a mental institution] / where we wake up electrified out of the coma by our own souls' airplanes roaring over the roof they've come to drop angelic bombs the hospital illuminates itself   imaginary walls collapse [. . .] O starry-spangled shock of mercy the eternal war is here" (Ginsberg 1984, 133). Note, however, that the solution is spiritual transfiguration, not political transformation.

The work is a postapocalyptic act, assuming that we are living beyond end time—a moral, political, sexual afterward that is not simply aftermath but defines a totally "new time," as James Berger sets forth in *After the End* (1999). The poem invites all the excluded peripheries to stream into the new-time center: antiwar pacifists, homeless wanderers left over from the 1930s, addicts using just about every drug imaginable, gays (closeted or not), visionaries without institutional religion, people experiencing psychotic breaks, the suicidal, the radical, the Communist, those turning the tables and "investigating the FBI," hystero-comic dada energizers, all who are "madman bum and angel beat in Time" (Ginsberg 1984, 131). The "best minds" have become crazed and "hysterical"— a feminizing word to apply to men—having to confront "the scholars of war" and what passes for normalcy (Ginsberg 1984, 126).

Ginsberg views insanity either as a higher form of sanity or as a hermetic key that opens a true analysis of sociopolitical reality. "Beat" has a variety of meanings from exhausted to exalted, from aggressed upon to pulsating, from defeated to struck and transformed, all of which make a rich cultural amalgam of intense authority from the fusion of low and high. Ginsberg united these sexual and political outcasts on the page of his poem as an act of challenge to the status quo. His syntax supported this goal by some phrases that transcended syntactic containment and thus created new fusions by stylistic fiat. Sometimes these fusions revealed little local bits of irony, humor, and self-judgment that made the poetic surface emotionally lively and intellectually compelling. "Howl" is not simply a relentless jeremiad but one scintillating with the delicate intimacies of its linguistic combinations and with amused self-regard amid the ecstasy.

Through "Howl," Ginsberg (and his peers) became the antitype of the American 1950s. In the Cold War context, according to J. Edgar Hoover (director of the FBI), Senator Joseph McCarthy, and other right-wing polemicists, Americans needed to fear an "enemy within." "Howl" is a poem that accepts that callow designation and twists it to its own polemical advantage: you want an internal enemy—Communist, homosexual, radical, feckless, irresponsible, "sick"—we are it. The poem rejects political and psychic norms, identifies with the mad, with the Cold War "other," and with criminal culture, discusses drugs, and idolizes men rejecting both sexual and economic "normalcy."[7] In Ginsberg's legendary poem, a triumphalist U.S. culture is confronted with amoral, rebellious, and marginal others, the enraged, ecstatic, and mourning.

The gender anxiety of (at least) white men was central to the culture of the 1950s, and poets like Ginsberg, with his hysterical rant, seemed its worst nightmare. Questions about what constituted manhood, how it could be upheld and maintained, and what forces (homosexuality, effeminacy, passivity, sexual receptiveness) undermined its border were serious themes in middlebrow social thinking throughout this period, along with geopolitical scare words like "weakness," "subversion," "undermining," and "deviousness" that could as easily apply to stereotypes of homosexuals as to "reds."

"Howl" eulogizes both hypermasculine and feminine men. It praises the declassed intelligentsia and the crazed obsessive; it affirms the impulsive lumpen and delinquent; and it turns repeatedly to sexuality for its evidence, promiscuously depicting bi-, homo-, and hyperheterosexual acts. So one of the scandals of the Beats, for David Savran, "was their production of an unprecedented kind of masculinity," one incorporating a queered "male homosociality" as well as a feminized attraction to narcissism and erotic allure (Savran 1998, 65). Beat power was their enactment of "an obsessive oscillation between feminized and masculinized positionalities, between victim and street tough, martyr and tyrant, aesthete and proletarian," which, for Savran, evokes Freud's concept of "feminine [passive] masochism" (Savran 1998, 67, 68). In that last respect, incidentally, "Howl" used a sense of a sexual continuum parallel to Alfred Kinsey's six categories of sexual behavior, notable for not dividing the world into heterosexual on one side and homosexual on the other. One triumph of "Howl," ideologically, is its attempted dissolution of hegemonic sexual norms and its queering of gender boundaries—for men.

The textual villains in "Howl" are not the socially or sexually deviant, but powerful institutions of centrist control and containment: "the narcotic tobacco haze of Capitalism," "the sirens of Los Alamos," "Madison Avenue," the "foetid halls" of asylums, and the antiecstatic "Moloch"—the Canaanite God of Fire to whom children were sacrificed, according to Hebrew scriptures. The whole second section is devoted to excoriating—even exorcising—this figure. "Moloch the vast stone of war! [. . .] Moloch whose soul is electricity and banks! [. . .] Robot apartments! invisible suburbs! skeleton treasuries! blind capitals! demonic industries! spectral nations! invincible madhouses! granite cocks! monstrous bombs!" (Ginsberg 1984, 131–132). Moloch is a negative force, patriarchy, the war machine, institutions of confinement (factories, jails), the government, totalitarian conformism.

Indeed, the repression of ecstasy and male (often gay) sexuality expressed symptomatically by Moloch's "granite cocks" leads to "monstrous bombs," because this hyperhardness without orgasm can only be relieved by explosions of atomic proportions. This is emphatically a critique (indeed, a somewhat comedic critique) of the repressive features of patriarchal authority. Certainly normative masculinity is finished in "Howl"; the poem is entirely in the peripheral subject position of the male outcast ecstatic. The depiction of metamorphic maleness evinces an uncontainable, unfixable sexuality—promiscuous, vulgar, sometimes polymorphous, aggressively homosexual, and rather tepidly hetero-sexual. The subversion of Ginsberg's poem was enormous, because it represented a hypersexuality that took shape in the poem as frank, specific, affirmative, and excited depictions of homosexual sodomy and oral sex, with a strong bent toward sexual receptivity. The male figure is graphically receptive—the open language of ecstasy mimicking both sexual passivity and orgasmic ecstasy in the spondaic thrust of exclama-tion marks.

However, the subversion of normative 1950s values in Ginsberg's po-etic text was gender-coded for men only. Its alternative value system of revelation and spiritual nakedness does not specifically include female agency and desire in what it represents or depicts.[8] While lavishly eulo-gizing critical and acting-out male figures, "Howl" has very terse, tense allusions to female figures. They appear briefly as three shrews of fate, two of whom condense sites of 1950s normativity in "the heterosexual dollar" and in sexual reproduction, while the third "does nothing but sit on her ass" and repress real intellectual creativity (Ginsberg 1984, 128). A female figure briefly appears as the oedipal mother in a taboo but decod-able allusion ("with mother finally ******") (Ginsberg 1984, 130). And fe-males occur as some random waitresses and "innumerable lays of girls" (this does not mean songs) on the road (Ginsberg 1984, 128). While male figures in "Howl" have many activities and outlets (from sexual to men-tal, from critical to ecstatic), the female figures are far less particularized and essentially have no heads. The heterosexual acts are often as grim as those female "snatches," and never as textually vivid as homosexual sodomy.

"Howl" disparages and marginalizes its female figures and is there-fore indifferently uninterested in whether women are part of the critique of American society it offers. But the poem actively suggests that females are part of the forces of conformity and containment. "Howl" is a world of comradeship, homosocial bonding, homosexual lovers, and male-male ejaculatory happiness and flare. Female figures in "Howl" receive sperm, misogyny, and contempt, without being offered a capacity for transformation.

One key geopolitical theory and practice of the 1950s was "containment," which operated internationally in a struggle against the Soviet Union and against both freely chosen and imposed Communist or socialist political systems. The correlative anxiety was invasion, infiltration, undermining, sapping; contemporaneous science fiction dramatized this by fantasizing about "alien invasions." The postwar international policy of containment has been viewed in some sociocultural analyses as homologous with internal gender politics. Although "containing Soviet aggression" often meant containing autonomous liberation movements and civil wars, the "domestic version of containment," in Elaine Tyler May's phrase, proposed a strict, idealized, and ideologically normative set of sex-gender roles (complementarity, sexual repression of women combined with mild encouragement for sexual expressiveness within marriage, legal inequality, workplace exclusion, economic inferiority) (May cited in Savran 1992, 7). Containment can frame both the lived relations of males and females and the "problem" of any non-normative sexuality—homosexuality, for instance. These are still powerful texts in the twenty-first century, the subject of political struggle for female and gay recontainment and of nostalgia, parody, and disgust.

If the United States in the 1950s was a culture of containment as Michael Davidson argues in *Guys Like Us* (Davidson 2004, 5, 54–56), this also implied protection of the white and male core against deviant forces: strong women, male feminization, blacks as icons of difference, and homosexuality imagined as weakness and perversion. While "Howl" proposed the uncontained, expressive male, deployed manipulative tropes of race ("leaped on negroes [*sic*]"), and made icons of nonconforming male figures, it posited women as incidents along the way or as witches of containment. To have nonhegemonic maleness shift to absorb feminization, sexual "deviance," and political otherness (of class and race) is a very large social gain in ranges of subjectivity—for men. For the unconventional masculinities emerging on the peripheries of U.S. culture of the 1950s, the feminine and a certain flamboyant male display become interesting and attractive, but not interesting when attached to women. Nor were female gender border-crossing, lesbian identifications, and "masculinity" in women viewed as engaging; indeed, this kind of female challenge to gender norms was reviled and taboo. The net gain in mobility is for men; in this worldview, the female has far more limited gender options.[9]

Despite this ideological contradiction, some nonconformist women were inspired by "Howl"'s countercultural presentation of visionary

resistance. Some young women of the time concocted an amalgam
of liberatory possibilities from an "on the road" mix of Ginsberg and
Kerouac. Indeed, Wini Breines argues that the young women, although
they were "girlfriends and fans" of Beat men, more deeply "wanted to
be them" (Breines 1992, 147). Cross-gender identifications in (at least)
female reading strategies have been a very common and important tactic for the consumption/reception of artworks. (And why limit this to
female interests? Reading itself may be fundamentally a queer practice.)
Breines has argued that dissident (white) girls in the 1950s "utilize[d] and
adapt[ed] male versions of rebellion and disaffection," identified with
"outsiders, hoods and greasers" and the "oddball" rebels in Beat subcultures as well as with the increasingly mainstream disobediences of rock
and roll (Breines 1992, 130). She notes the way in which "males were the
inspiration" for this muted female revolt and sees some of this inchoate dissidence emerge as feminism about ten years later (Breines 1992,
137–148). In her account, Beat sensibility made a notable contribution
to the liberation of women despite the misogyny of some Beat denizens
and many Beat texts.

Another optimistic refraction of Beat importance despite gender attitudes is chronicled in a 1994 letter by Anne Waldman included in her
long poem *Iovis* (Book II). Responding to a woman who had asked about
the "'boys' club mentality'" of the Beats, Waldman acknowledges the
general misogyny in their early writings but goes on to remind her inter-
locutor that "the Beats are popular because they represent an alternative
[. . .] to the status quo. An antithesis to bald commercialism, selfishness,
spiritual vacuity, political advantage, double-dealing, lying, dishonesty,
racism, general all-around uptightness" (Waldman 1993/1997, II: 145,
143). This moving reaffirmation of the argument of "Howl" also suggests
that a text can open the possibility for gender critiques that it does not
itself make—indeed, that it resists making.

3. "Patriarchal Poetry or made a way patriarchal Poetry tenderly"

Robert Creeley tells a richly ambiguous story of manhood in his
poetry of the 1950s.[10] The landmark Creeley collection *For Love, Poems
1950–1960* (1962) is distinguished by an antic, unbowed, playful, appropriative attitude to gender anxiety in the formation of the male subject.[11]
Speaking retrospectively, Creeley said that he first "married (mistakenly)

in the hope of securing myself emotionally" (Creeley 1989, 368). Baldly, he followed the postwar experts who prescribed early marriage "as the prerequisite for a healthy family and sexual life" (E. May 1989, 158). Any number of his poems allude thematically to domestic situations and abrasions—the surface of this "mistake" arrives in comic disarray, both literal and allegorical. Marriage appears in *For Love* as an ironized and fondly criticized institution. Normative relations, as celebrated in these twisty lyrics, are ineffectual in achieving conformist goals, as we see in tonally duplicitous stanzas: "She walks in beauty like a lake / and eats her steak / with fork and knife / and proves a proper wife" ("The Bed," Creeley 1962, 66; Creeley 1982, 162). The doggerel-laden Lord Byron allusions, harrying a famous romantic line, and the cheap offhand rhymes, not to speak of the *sub rosa* phallicism of the female (steak/stake; fork/ knife), destroy much solemnity here. Many of these poems simultaneously mock and sentimentalize the marriages—but not always the genders—in which the poet participated. The poet/speaker is courtly and critical, angry and urbane.

"The Crisis" notes: "Let me say (in anger) that since the day we were married / we have never had a towel / where anyone could find it"; this bohemian disorder becomes a point of pride (Creeley 1962, 19; Creeley 1982, 113) At other times the allegory presents idealized woman, castle, stronghold along with the rueful, delighted mock courtly "My love's manners in bed / are not to be discussed by me" ("The Way," Creeley 1962, 72; Creeley 1982, 168) or the "My lady / fair with / soft / arms," which modulates into existential query very fast, showing that those "fair lady" sentiments are simultaneously crucial and inadequate ("A Token," Creeley 1962, 123; Creeley 1982, 221). Creeley's poems in *For Love* undercut the whole narrative of the unattainable "white goddess" female via the accessible, possessable (or at least discussable) term "wife" and further undercut all, while using such rich literary sites as the Petrarchan "fair lady" imagery and romantic longing. Certainly, as Barrett Watten notes, Creeley is well within a conventional "lover's discourse of tradition" with all its studied and staged contradictions: "alternately aggressive, ameliorative, Christian, sadistic, Petrarchan or anti-Petrarchan, either praising or degrading its object" (Watten 2000, 286). He also is flippant about all of it.

In "Going to Bed," as in other marital poems meditating on sex, adultery, desire, potency, or suspicion, the lines "think to understand if / the last time you looked / you were still a man" bespeak the desperate, self-regarding, or ironized question with a cool frankness (Creeley 1962, 95; Creeley 1982, 193). "Being a man" is not simply maleness but an ideological manhood and sexual potency that are constituted again and again as the central ground of the poems, claimed, lost again, investigated in an endless cycle. "Soon everything will be sold / and I can go back home // by myself again / and try to be a man" is a poignant, proud statement about trying and trying to be that difficult thing (Creeley 1962, 117; Creeley 1982, 215).[12] In his 1989 "Autobiography," Creeley is explicit, if also self-mythologizing, about this concern in his early period: "Clearly what I needed, and probably still do, was a sense of what constitutes manhood" (Creeley 1989, 43).

Many poems in *For Love* approach the problem of choosing appropriate gender roles (husband, father, head of household) and falling aslant, never definitively solving the problem. Various tones then ensue: pride, bitterness, irony, rage, poignancy, drollery, bafflement, offhand surviving despite it all. Manhood, in early Creeley, is a site at which the figure does conform to the Petrarchan "experience of fragmentation, wounding, or loss of psychic intactness and control" (Johnson 1998, 124). Each wound is recuperated by investigative scrutiny, however; Creeleyesque manhood is constituted in the powerful investigation of the wounds of manhood.

Creeley, like other countercultural male poets of the 1950s, tried to make "masculinity" and male expectations change or be subjected to scrutiny. In this task he was understandably invested. But he was interested in investigating and even changing masculinity without making "femininity" and female roles change much, if at all.[13] The poem "Wait for Me," told in alternating voices, exemplifies this ragged half-critique (Creeley 1962, 43; Creeley 1982, 137). One voice, italicized, is like an advice book or normative article about marriage, crudely stating an answer to Freud's oft-cited, exasperated question "What do women want?" In Creeley, a woman wants to have a man whose "*manliness*" is not in doubt, and a home, so she will not be alone. The second voice is the male's, agreeing that he wants the same "only / [. . .] more so." But that same voice denies what he has just affirmed in affirming her position: "You / [. . .] think marriage is / [. . .] everything?" Thus in the more mobile male voice, attitude and tone slide across several conflicting positions; that voice ends by saying "Oh well, / [. . .] I said," an unreadable resignation, a throwing off of the issues, or a temporizing. The two genders are actually quite out of sync.

The title "Wait for Me" seems to mount an appeal. The poem's odd word—and of course it is key—is "*hypocrisies*," suggesting that both are playing roles, each manipulating the other. Both gender inauthenticity and severe normativeness seem particularly located in woman; to claim manhood in these poems, one "throws" off any such "hypocrisy," resists what the female figure represents. The poem looks like a dialogue; voices visually alternate on the page, in italic and roman type. The content privileges the more mobile and critical male figure, however, because he is able to enunciate a variety of opinions. This whole poem shows a characteristic approach to and backing off from final statement. We can see a male position constructed for the speaker, the shadow of "hegemonic manhood," but we also see the speaker sidling up to this position, putting a foot in, removing that foot, backing off, engaging it, resisting it. The male speaker moves in and out of several positions about manhood, and this shifting motion mimics the energy of critique without making any actual critical statement about gender arrangements.[14] This energy is particularly located in the poem's hesitant, nonphrasal enjambments.

The poem "The Invoice" (an itemized bill of money owed) is a self-parody about roles. It consists of three stanzas, two heavily invested in norms: the speaker's letter to a man asking for money and a letter presumably to a woman asking for love or a relationship: "dearest M/ / please come. / There is no one / here at all" (Creeley 1962, 86; Creeley 1982, 183). He is depicted as wanting the most banal gender goods: manly money and womanly presence.

> I got word today,
> viz: hey
> sport, how are you making it?
> And, why don't you get with it.
>
> (Creeley 1962, 86; Creeley 1982, 183)

This final stanza isolates the speaker as not man enough in two ways, financial and sexual. This stanza shows his lack of success in both homosocial bonds (borrowing money) and heterosexual bonds (seduction). Both voices respond that they owe the speaker nothing; his "invoice" fails.

By constructing a speaker as an outcast from these gender norms or stereotypes, Creeley illustrates the position of critique (outcast), but he has not challenged the norms. The stanza contains two rejections, both playing on hip colloquialisms (suggesting that the letter respondents are more "with it" in hipness than the speaker) and both using the open deictic "it." The line break after the word "hey," making the word that follows be read ironically, is particularly pointed in the judgment of manhood: he is a "sport" or deviant, not a sporty guy. Using "viz" (the abbreviation for *videlicet*, meaning "namely" or "it is permitted to see"), however, has the effect of proving the poet's competence—in language (in the enunciation, the poem as artifact)—and at the same time reiterating his speaker's incompetence in relationships (in the plot inside the poem, in the enounced).

This outcast figure, mocked by both interlocutors, is one type of male hero within lyric poetry, for telling the story of male inadequacy (yearning, displacement, hurt, pleasure in another's cruelty to oneself or in rejection) is part of male poetic power. In Barbara Johnson's intense question: "Why is male masochism the secret that it is lyric poetry's job to keep?" (Johnson 1998, 123). Yet poetic competence, linguistic cunning, and wit compensate for this self-confessed set of patterned rejections.

The structure of manhood in early Creeley can also be explored by Lee Edelman's analysis of the plot or the moves around maleness. (Edelman is making a critique of this plot, but the bold outline is helpful.) A man is self-divided into a dominant-masculinized male and a submissive-feminized male—a kind of binarist cohabitation inside one subjectivity. The masculine half compels conformity from the other half, demands that the other half "submit." Actual women are occluded here; they are secondary players in a male story of self-fashioning, again involving abasement—but of the feminine in oneself. Thus to be normatively male is to police oneself for this passive feminine; a sense of power is the reward (Edelman 1994, 27–28). In this explanatory narrative, men must police themselves, so one result is that men can be seen and can see themselves as victims of patriarchal power, not as agents of such power (Edelman 1994, 27–28). However, there is a counternarrative too: one might sometimes negotiate with that feminine vulnerability inside oneself and also emerge with a sense of power. This seems to be the goal—and the wit—of Creeley's early poetry.

Vulnerability *as* power in Creeley emerges in "The Lover," a poem unusually frank about gender markers. For Creeley was certainly one of the first people of any gender to mention Modess (sanitary napkins) in literature, indeed, to talk of their purchase. In the 1950s, shame and hyperdiscretion around menstruation made the large and bulky brown- or blue-wrapped packages of that necessity "invisible." The advertising in the 1950s was also euphemistic to a startling extreme, showing beautiful, bejeweled women in gorgeous evening gowns, with the ad copy saying only "Modess . . . because." Because *what* was unclear until menarche; the ad bifurcated the female body ideologically into an unspoken, sometimes messy underside and a brilliant, showy, fetishized surface.

In contrast to the ideology of containment and invisibility in the popular vision of menstruation, Creeley's poem "The Lover" is invested in expressive messiness, here the stain of a possible blush—but of the *male* body.[15] The poem debates what honest stance to take up in relation to a male's helpful but embarrassed purchase of this "feminine" product. "What should the young / man say, because he is buying / Modess? Should he // blush or not. Or / turn coyly, his head, to / one side, as if in // the exactitude of his emotion he / were not offended? Were / proud? Of what? To buy // a thing like that" (Creeley 1962, 41; Creeley 1982, 135; entire poem cited). If a man is sent to the drugstore on that mission it means that he is trusted, convenient, sexually active, and mobile, that the woman is not pregnant and has the power to ask for the favor but is also needy (menstruating and cannot go out without a Modess!—thus slightly immobile) or lazy or forgetful (didn't she know that she might need a Modess?). In other words, the situation preceding the poem, quite non-normatively evoked in the word "Modess," is already an efficient nexus of gender dynamics.

This poem shows a male figure, self-consciously debating what attitude to take up, what relationship he has to his own manhood, how he embodies it, given a woman's physical womanhood. The speaker first debates taking on a feminine coyness in a male body (blushing and drooping) and then thinks of assuming half-offended annoyance. Finally, he takes another position—exploring all these moves, discovering the "exactitude of his emotion"—which nonetheless remains deliberately opaque to the reader. Manhood is often expressed in early Creeley as a vulnerability (to nuance of emotion) that becomes a form of power. Creeley consolidates male pride in his ability to debate which attitudes to take up (what "should" he do with the amused embarrassment of this purchase?). Among those attitudes, a blushing girlishness is all the more appealing in the body of a helpful male. The phrase "buy // a thing like that" is unreadable in tone—it seems to combine an abashed sense of exposure and a gruff pleasure to be that intimate with a woman and still not lose male power. The speaker first takes up the feminine position and then ends with an obfuscated male pride. He is at all points of a gender compact: the title "The Lover"—on one level a straightforward title alluding to his place in a heterosexual couple—becomes a pun on his narcissistic investigation of various positions, a self-wooing of himself as blushing, coy man by himself as self-debating man.

This poem might well illustrate Barbara Johnson's stark finding in her discussion of Charles Baudelaire that "masculine privilege is enforced precisely by male femininity" (Johnson 1998, 127). Why? Possibly because both genders can be effectively positioned without accounting for the divergent and potentially destabilizing impact of historical women who have their own complex and conflicting relations to femaleness, femininity, and womanhood. More? The assumption of femininity is a way for men to claim vulnerability, weakness, sweetness, even powerlessness. The male feminine is a friendly way of denying, obfuscating, or cushioning the impact of male power, both inside the speaker and to the observer/reader.

Creeley and the men about whom Michael Kimmel speaks "seem to be looking for power rather than reveling in their experience of it" (Kimmel 1994, viii).[16] For many men do not feel that they have any particular power. Indeed, men can feel a disjunction between their "aggregate social power" and their "individual experience of powerlessness," a disjunction that they manage in various ways (Kimmel 1994, viii). To the observer, such a stance seems genial, while to the user it is a way of disowning what happens elsewhere (not in his subjectivity, not in his poem) in the affirmation of male power. Indeed *all* men in the real world are not responsible for what some men do in the name of manhood. To men, patriarchal power and its assertions are often felt as always elsewhere.

The male-feminine is emphatically a critique of rigid patriarchal ideology; it also imperially increases male gender range. In *Out of Bounds*, Laura Claridge and Elizabeth Langland similarly propose that a male writer "experiences the patriarchal construction of his masculinity as a constriction. He may, that is, appropriate the feminine to enlarge himself, a process not incompatible with contempt for actual women," although, one might also add, these features are not necessarily linked (Claridge and Langland 1990, 4).[17] The force of Creeley's work comes from this contradictory tension between vulnerability and power, his interest in establishing the hegemonic rules of manhood, which he at other times debates.

Debate across a border expresses itself continuously in Creeley in his sharp, syntactically unusual line breaks, fissuring statement across phrasal syntax. Creeley sometimes uses his stanzas serially as well, so that different stanzas take up different ideological positions; thus one is never sure whether any conclusion, as in "The Way," apparently ringing with normative advice about marrying, is unstable or ironic. In the many shifts in his lines and stanzas, Creeley can express and exemplify tension, wariness, a simultaneous resistance to normalcy and evocation of normalcy in love relations and gender expectations. His jagged line breaks and the lines' extreme shortness (so one jumps quickly to another) and the shifts in ideological position among the stanzas (so that a poem manifests several opinions) suggest, for Sianne Ngai, spatial displacement in relation to anxiety.

Speaking about anxiety and male subjectivity, Ngai offers the generative observation that anxiety, with accompanying disorientation, dizziness, and "an experience of suspension or delay," is the price paid by the male subject in his quest for adequate knowledge or understanding (Ngai 2001, 17–19 [quotation on 15]). This anxiety is projected or relocated onto others from the self—the throwing of anxiety outward—an effective strategy to "reinforce the boundary between center and periphery, and thus the distinction between 'here' and 'yonder' on which the experience of threat depends" (Ngai 2001, 18). Creeley works with deferral and delay in the formal mechanisms of poetry, a "thrownness" in syntax, line, and stanza; sometimes, as Ngai observes, the thrown material stays attached to the other. But more interesting is the self-reflexive way in which the cast-off material boomerangs back in Creeley. Sometimes the speaker takes up confrontative positions as "the other." He then throws those positions far from him, ejecting them, and yet moves the speaking subject over to inhabit those positions. His mobility is notable. This contradictory displacement and embrace explains how Creeley can be simultaneously critical of the materials of manhood and invested in them.

Creeley's essay "On the Road: Notes on Artists & Poets, 1950–1965" (1974), a summary of investigative manhood in the fifties, ascribes male gender to experiment and innovation. Women, Creeley argues, cannot understand the process-oriented mode of new art. Even when actual women—Ann McKinnon Creeley and Robert Rauschenberg's unnamed wife (Susan Weil)—are reasonably intelligent and ask appropriate questions, they are not swift to comprehend the possibility of praxis; they are, like all women depicted in this essay, aesthetically conservative. A woman wants the expression of prior, already-formulated intentions; a man wants curiosity, attentiveness, energy. Further, the women do not assimilate and practice the inquiry that generated the work of the new arts of the 1940s and 1950s: abstract painting (Franz Kline) and free poetry (William Carlos Williams) (Creeley 1989, 374–375).[18] Creeley uses gender difference to distinguish striking differences in poetics. However true or untrue this grim binary might have been in any individual case, it is hard to credit as fact (and not sexist projection) that differences of poetics (old/new; conservative/experimental) are so unequivocally mapped on gender difference (woman/man)—as if no woman was ever aesthetically radical and no man ever poetically conservative. It is a "straw woman" argument.

Hence this essay ends with an unmotivated throw-away line, self-mocking and yet intransigent in its gender narrative: "You'll have to tell mother we're still on the road" (Creeley 1989, 376). These female figures are construed as maternal, confining, anchored, and immobile, the site of all manner of psychic baggage that one must cast off. The male practitioners escape by evoking the famous "on the road" gender narrative of free men, practicing a homosocial wildness (with occasional sexy females present). Some women in this universe are indeed intense and capable (in Creeley's general narrative there are always a rewarded few, like Diane di Prima)—but the men of whom Creeley speaks are unfailingly intellectually mobile and more intense, having greater capacity for poesis. Creeley never explicitly excludes women from his sense of "company," a recurrent and evocative word about grouping and one firmly in his lexicon. In his later career, Creeley's "company" became markedly more gender-expansive, if never completely so. But in this 1974 assessment looking back on his early career, he depicts most women as disqualifying themselves. For in this world something simply happens inside women (though apparently not ever as an outcome of their interactions with men . . .) that results in men having to constitute themselves as artists by leaving women behind.

Being on the road is the implicit narrative of one of Creeley's signature poems, a defining poem of masculinity in the 1950s. "I Know a Man" depicts two men (or perhaps just one, self-divided, talking to himself) in a car. This is certainly a poem of masculine self-instruction toward forming a new company of men in motion. One of these men is wishing for a bigger car, maybe one with the aggressive and baroque tail fins of the 1950s, display and consumerism to brighten a sense of pain and anguish. Night driving takes on symbolic resonance as a marker of inchoate anxiety: "the darkness sur- / rounds us, what // can we do against /

it" (Creeley 1962, 38; Creeley 1982, 132). The poem resembles Olson's "In Cold Hell, in Thicket" in that the solution is to continue to do what one is doing but in a more mindful way than before, with greater alertness and intensity, as seen in the elegant confrontative "drive, he sd, for / christ's sake, look / out where yr going" (Creeley 1962, 38; Creeley 1982, 132).

The two male figures are fraternal equals. Yet the friend is underknown; the speaker is said to call him by the wrong name, a common name: John. John has advice, and it is the advice of "outward": to drive in the here and now (even if you want a bigger car), and to "look / out"—a double idiom, meaning not only caution but attentiveness, a gaze at what is. The poem is an allegory of poetic style, a poem of poetic self-instruction, saying not to hunger for bigger, more bombastic rhetorics.

Instead, subtle investigation of one's own emotional articulation is achieved through line breaks. Three lines over four stanzas offer the opportunity for eleven line breaks, and in this poem the line breaks constitute meaning as thoroughly as overt statement does. The line breaks are made by the rupture of very closely knit elements: subject and verb ("I // sd"), possessive pronoun and noun ("my / friend"; "his / name"), parts of a verb ("sur- / rounds"; "look / out"); preposition from object ("for / christ's"), an interrogative phrase ("what // can"). These construct, through a specific poetic mechanism, the splits in subjectivity, the self-questioning, that constitute the poem's meaning.

One phrasal line break (from more banal free verse prosodies) is offered as a solution: "why not, buy a goddamn big car." That's one form of manhood; the other is, of course, "where yr going." This valued manhood is simultaneously a jagged, situational attentiveness and a claim of power in motion signaled by the shifts along the line. Line break as well as statement propose an ideologically freighted contrast of noun—as affirmed possession, stasis, suburbia, and consumerism ("big car")—versus the verbal as dynamic and admonitory process ("yr going"). Opposing visions of manhood are poised in this poem. Line breaks invite the reader to value fraternal responsibility, critical negativity, and modesty and to resist affirmative hegemonic maleness.

Yet tough-guy manhoods are present in the diction of the poem, for "goddamn" enhances and admires that big car even as the car is rejected. Tough talk also occurs in the swift colloquialisms of "sd" and "yr" that come, in part, from Ezra Pound's example in his swift, instructive letters—the orthography is clipped, focused, no blabbing, no bellyaching: a manly shorthand—get on with it (so to speak). All this has been dubbed the manly "hard-boiled style": "a carefully controlled blend of colloquialisms, terse understatement, objective description, all narrated in a detached tone" (Pfeil 1995, 109). But it is not only that; it is also an indication of quick emotional shifts. And it comes from the epistolary mirroring in the emotionally mercurial letters between Creeley and Olson, through which intense changes of mood perpetually pulsed.

The "yr" fuses the possessive ("your") and the positional ("you are") as a double way of manifesting and affirming one's mobility ("going"). It is Creeley's tact to combine the objective terseness with enthusiastic, volatile meditation, a lot of male affect, an intense and freighted feeling. Many of these poems emerge from the legendary male-male energy of the epistolary encounter between Olson and Creeley. These were two vulnerable and voracious men engaged in self-fashioning not only by inhabiting a broad-band aggressive verbal maleness but also by constructing a psycho-political world of gender-exclusive manhood for their sustenance.

4. "Patriarchal Poetry did he leave his son"

As Michael Davidson has argued, there was a compact of heterosexual and homosexual men in the formation of 1950s poetic manhood, despite the possible homophobia of the straight men or the exclusionary campiness of the gay men (Davidson 1995).[19] Masculinity in 1950s poetry was produced in this intense homosocial compact, across lines of sexual preference. This homosociality was not necessarily interested in triangles of romantic love, using an "exchange of women" to get to male bonding, in the foundational terms that Eve Kosofsky Sedgwick set forth. Indeed, in the case of the poetry and letters circulating between Creeley and Olson, it was not the naming of homosexual desire (or a homosocial rivalry over a woman) but the homosociality of admitting male emotion, vulnerability, blockage, passionate cultural desire. Their homosocial pattern was the accelerated exchange of the eros of poesis with each other: outspoken excess, hysterical intensities of hopes for poetry and for their own achievement.[20]

Homosexuality was a seriously stigmatized identity/choice/set of desires in the 1950s; at any moment, straight poets could evince homophobia or homosexual panic at the rich homosocial terrain that they inhabited (Sedgwick 1985, 89). And yet in these countercultural poetries, despite ambivalence to homosexuals even unto homophobia and despite fear of the effeminate, the construction of masculinity for heterosexual poets was also seriously affected by the sexual frankness and body consciousness of gay male poets and the confrontative flamboyance of non-hegemonic cultural figures who manifested transgressive forms of male display.[21] In artistic communities, there was a forceful pressure from homosexuality on straight male self-fashioning, on the male imaginary, on the splits and debates about what masculinity was in the 1950s, given the sensual attention to male embodiment, sexuality, and physicality in overtly gay works.

The New American and Beat poets/writers resisted, negated, and berated the Organization Men, conformist and centrist types, whether from a position of localist particularity (Creeley) or global entrepreneurial mythopoesis (Olson and Ginsberg).[22] The areas to be avoided in conformist manhood included effeminacy, of course, but also virile display and swashbuckling hypermasculinity as forms of male masquerade. Yet in the 1950s certain semitaboo but attractive cultural icons combined these deviant traits—the James Dean/Elvis Presley phenomena (of the early and mid-1950s) proposed a value in petulant, ephebic bodily display and flaunting of style and tough hypermasculine stances that were more than slightly scandalous for their overt sexual display. Alternative poetry was positioned and staged as cultural protest against "conformity"; thus it made a discursive identification with virile display and/or hypermasculinity in class terms and sexual terms.

Yet, as art historian Abigail Solomon-Godeau points out in another context, "an eroticized and androgynous representation of masculinity does not necessarily transgress—and, indeed, may affirm—the patriarchal privileges of masculinity, however inflected" (Solomon-Godeau 1995, 74). Writing about three motifs in French painting of the eighteenth century, all involving a soft, voluptuous, sensual male nude, Solomon-Godeau remarks that here the masculine has been "repositioned so as to occupy the conventional place of the feminine," yet in none of these "nonphallic masculinities" is there "any particular quarrel with patriarchal law and order" or any subversion of it (Solomon-Godeau 1995, 73). This finding holds true for this poetic moment.

Charles Olson spoke with some conflict and despair about the eros of poesis and a rich array of exemplary male figures, because his attraction to powerful men who already were doing the artistic work he wanted to be doing led to a self-debate. He was heterosexual, yet he had profound feelings of desire in relation to specific men, and he was not sure how to read his needs. Ralph Maud cites a passage dated 8 March 1948 from the "Faust Buch" #41 held at the Olson Archive at the University of Connecticut, Storrs. This passage is discussed by Tom Clark, who is tenderly fascinated by its homosexual implication, and by Ralph Maud, who sternly denies it. In it Olson lists a number of men (including Edward Dahlberg and Ezra Pound) and says these "relations [are] sexual at base" but goes on to analyze the pattern as curiously, fascinatingly "mighty homosexual to me," although "the sexual root in me is male enough"—by which he means heterosexual (Maud 2008, 95). Certainly one can be masculine (even masculinist) and homosexual—though Olson might not have thought so. The terms that Olson used are quite suggestive: "unresolved 'amours,'" in this case with the visual artist Corrado Cagli and Pound (Olson 1975, xxiv). His honesty on this point is fortifying: this is precisely the eros of poesis; it neither bespeaks nor insists on decisions about sexual object choice but frames the erotic force of the poetic career.

Sexual preference, wobbling identity, and homosexual desire treated as a scandalous revelation are all set to the side here (Clark 1991, 106–118; Maud 2008, 95–96). Without shrugging off any self-debate or any agony and personal pain in poets, I want positively to recognize the eros of poesis, its enthralling and productive qualities. This powerful bond and cathexis with another creative person is formative and formidable. Clark seems to make this cathexis suspect: "a pattern of excessive dependence, a conveying of powerful affect beyond the bounds of mere casual camaraderie" (Clark 1991, 113). What is wrong with this, one wonders? The affect is powerful, the dependence perhaps less positive ("excessive"), but so what? Neither sexual preference nor biographical relationships are key, but rather the erotics and desires of the literary bond: the eros of poesis.

Olson's poem "The Lordly and Isolate Satyrs" (1956) is a major poem, four pages long, self-consciously examining masculinity and facing its erotic charge with an exemplary vulnerability and determination (Olson 1987b, 384–387). It is one of Olson's "Homeric hymns" with very long lines of six or seven lavish beats each, a poem of grandeur and breadth, reaching behind the façade of civilization for some active, animating principle of power. Using materials from a dream, and in a plural voice ("we" is the pronoun of choice), Olson writes of hypermasculine "satyrs," a motorcycle club aggressively invading a beach, exhibiting a terrific male power and self-possession that might, if allowed to, complete the speaker as it "completed the beach" by which the poem is set.[23] Their ceremonial emergence and virile display challenge the viewer. Normalcy and the normative have been totally changed. This shift in vision is provoked by their hypermasculinity, whose climactic image is "their huge third leg like carborundum," a simile assimilating a penis, a motorcycle, and the trade name of an industrial abrasive (Olson 1987b, 387). The movement of the poem occurs through the meditative elaboration of the facets or angles of this vision, a recording of the stages of realization in a diction combining the vatic, the discursive, and the colloquial.

"One of the most powerful archetypes of manhood," says Peter Schwenger, "is the idea that the real man is the one who acts, rather than the one who contemplates" (Schwenger 110). These binaries of action and contemplation, however, are interestingly modified in this poem. The action of the "we" who speak the poem is contemplating these avatars, meditating on their significance, actively "talking" the poem. The contemplation of the poem is a kind of action, responsive, twisting and braiding a complex reaction to the dream vision. The action of the poem is simply that the motorcyclists show themselves in epiphanic splendor, sitting on their very male equipment; then they start to leave ("now stirring / to advance, to go on wherever they do go restlessly never completing / their tour") (Olson 1987b, 387). Olson carefully interprets contemplation as action to allow the force of "real manhood" to be distributed to the speaker of the poem.

The speaker evinces identification and wariness: "Hail the ambiguous Fathers [. . .] Hail them, and watch out" (Olson 1987b, 385).[24] The word "hail," now theoretically marked by its status in an Althusserian understanding of subjectivity, is precisely germane: as the speaker pays ritualized homage to the figures of the motorcycle gang that he has conjured from his own dream, these figures from his own subconscious are "hailing" him—calling him into an enriched maleness. The poem offers a narrative in which this onlooker, at first awestruck and fearful of the "monumental solidity" and phallic totality of these invaders, ends by an identification with them. "These are our counterparts" and "they're here, the Con- / temporaries. They have come in" are lines indicating this transformative connection with what, after all, is a "temporary" vision projected from himself but seems to have been awarded historical status. It brings the self into the absolute present and into an affirmation of phallic completeness that functioned as a fundamental principle in Olson (Olson 1987b, 386). The poem provides an account of the bliss of

identifying with these Outlaw/Fathers, drenched in pleasure and satisfaction. It is as if Olson has seen a vision of patriarchy itself and found it
good, so good that one must "watch out."[25] That watchfulness may concern the constant fascination with a taboo and suspect homosexuality
that might cast a shadow on the power of this eroticized vision.

The poem is a fantasy of patriarchy confronting itself and completing itself in several ways: with its own mysterious androgyny, its own
male/male gaze, its own introjection of the size and outlaw status of
some males. The power and the types of maleness evoked are varied, but
all are on the periphery of orthodox masculinity. The poem seems to be
a way of recuperating masculinity despite Olson's macrocultural analysis
of the end of the humanist phase of history. That is, for Olson, the end of
the humanist era of history is not—repeat, *not*—the end of patriarchy or
of the patriarchal era of history.

The hegemonic center is exactly marginalized, while the marginal
men enter into their patriarchal endowment and heritage. The poem
gathers these marginals together into one gigantic male presence, even if
the components are uneven, conflicting, and vulnerable. The mentions
of the Yiddish vegetarian poet, of bodhisattvas, and of "on the road" activities make at least part of this work a response to the Beat poets, alluding to Ginsberg, whose poem "Howl" was one step ahead of Olson
in gathering the despised (male) others into a social compact of outsiders.[26] The motorcycle figures have probably come from Marlon Brando
in *The Wild One* (1954), playing "the tough but sensitive motorcycle
gang leader" in one of the breakthrough films about mid-fifties male
outlaw figures (Miller and Nowak 1977, 333). Other male figures manifest wounded maleness: "fifteen year old boys," "red-neck farmers" (like
many figures in part I of "Howl," they could undoubtedly be identified
with actual men). All male figures in the poem can be completed by the
solidity and challenge of the "lordly and isolate" figures, "the Fathers behind the father" and "the Androgynes," who are compared to the hieratic
Easter Island statues and to gods (Olson 1987b, 384). So this motorcycle
gang is an amalgam of hypermasculinity, homosociality, male display,
and outright phallicism as knowledge.

These figures are "Fathers" but "ambiguous Fathers" and "the Androgynes / the Fathers behind the father, the Great Halves" (Olson 1987b,
384). The speaker sees these male figures in a vision of another side, "the
ambiguous Fathers" who open out a whole terrain of manhood that involves the feminine or a nurturing paternal. In this poem, Olson seems

to draw on a striking pre-oedipal connection with the maternal father; this poem is illuminated by Freud's "Wolf-Man" analysis of a "narcissistic masculinity predating the oedipal crisis" that "implies a powerful cathexis of male genitals" and a desire for the father (Connell 1994, 14; Connell 2005, 9).

Despite some negative remarks, both the "androgyne" and the "hermaphrodite" are positive and powerful figures, though sometimes "hermaphrodite" means homosexual and is resisted (*Olson/Creeley*, V: 76–77). These terms show Olson's general indebtedness to Carl Jung; at best, both terms indicate the capacity to mend a split in a lamentably divided consciousness by fusing male and female into an archetype of power. The androgyne is a powerful and appropriate figure for men, fully creative and forceful because of an imperial sex-gender doubleness (*Olson/Creeley*, VIII: 91, 24 October 1951; see also Olson 1989a, 35). A male works both by will and "by way of woman" because both genders are mixed together: "he she-male as well as she as male"—the "androgyne" is "prime" (*Olson/Creeley*, V: 76, 15 March 1951). By some kind of sex-gender mix and crossover, one may inwardly appropriate the force of another gender, whatever one's personal sexual organs (which in any case say nothing about their specific uses). Androgyne offers, in theory, a subject place for a powerful female as well as male. It is a figure that will avoid spiritualizing and idealizing females (see *Olson/Creeley*, V: 77). It appears that even the gender division into two unequal genders is, for Olson, a form of "generalization"—which he claims to resist in favor of the particulars of any case.

But there is another line of thinking in Olson about the power of the androgyne. By the time the female and male elements meet up in his gendered poetics, female ownership of femaleness and maleness—in all imagined powers and its contradictions—is less interesting than male ownership of all elements along the gender spectrum. The modulation from somewhat earlier Olson to later Olson precisely concerns the place of the female in active cultural life. Again, as in Pound, one sees a person who began his career trying out a variety of contradictory sex-gender materials that sometimes had a place for powerful women. As his own cultural power and desire to manifest that power increased, he became considerably less curious about sex-gender coequality and more interested in an imperial imagination and enactment of patriarchal power.

The terrain of "The Lordly and Isolate Satyrs" with its androgyne/hermaphrodite may be glossed by Olson's 1953 poem concerning

Herman Melville's poetry ("The Collected Poems Of," Olson 1987b, 278–282). Here he proposes a theory of gender that involves idealizing male hardness, along with an alchemical tincture of the feminine, so that the base of imagination is "hermaphrodite"—a male who can assimilate the feminine but always be potent.[27] In the "Lordly and Isolate Satyrs," the mythological figures have totality and presence because they contain both genders while remaining uncompromisingly male. This is signaled by a metaphor of size. The satyrs are larger than us because they contain the feminine, too; but they are particularly large because they are unremittingly masculine.

My proposition that these countercultural poets sought to transform maleness without transforming femaleness or considering that transformation or allowing for it is once more illustrated here. This poem contains one female figure among the male avatars. She is the partner of the (male) Leader in the convertible and is described as a "dazzling" figure who uses hair dye (something both tacky and glamorous in the 1950s). At first, this female figure is not singled out: "She was as distant as the others. She sat in her flesh too" (Olson 1987b, 386). Yet the poem's speaker cannot sustain this similarity between the dream males and the dream female. At the moment of male transformation, the mystery and self-possession of the female figure is neutralized: she is cut down to size, brought back to the regime of binary and unequal sexual difference. This narrated dream of an enriched manhood still works according to normative ideological rules about male and female that keep females on the periphery. Of the dreamed males Olson says: "These are our counterparts, the unknown ones. / They are here. We do not look upon them as invaders. Dimensionally / they are larger than we—all but the woman. But we are not suddenly / small. We are as we are" (Olson 1987b, 386). "All but the woman." There is no imagining of female transformation; further, the female figure apparently cannot be larger than the human men in the way the dreamed Fathers are. One cannot "be familiar" with the males, but one could want to "be familiar with" the imagined female (Olson 1987b, 387).

The male speakers accept themselves "as we are" by both introjecting the gigantism of "Fathers behind the father" and at the same time describing the female figure not as gigantic but of a manageable size and of heterosexual access. Her presence helps contain the tremendous male-male eroticism of the dream. Within the dream, love, adoration, touching, and caring from man to man are part of this picture, but so is an awestruck distance: "We have no feeling except love. They are not / ours. They are of another name. These are what the gods are" (Olson 1987b, 387). Olson keeps these materials in play, evoking male-male love and eroticism without homosexuality. This is bliss indeed; enacted in Olson's relationships, it may well explain his electric power for men. Indeed, the only function of this one female figure in the poem is as a token guarantor of normative sexual desire. She provides the right outlet for all the almost taboo eros of the poem and has only one other function—to be inferior.

This poem is a collection point for any number of key materials of 1950s countercultural maleness: pure phallic imagery, carefully affirmed and carefully managed claims of androgyny, the supplement of femininity without its inferiorizing taint, affirmative heterosexuality, homosocial cohorts without homosexuality, male display and hypermasculinity, marked gender asymmetry or the enforcement of male-female difference, conflicts between actual social power and a sense of powerlessness, even an offhanded, mainly casual misogyny.[28] But many of these traits are as centrist as they are countercultural. Where does this leave us?

From such analyses of particular poems by three key countercultural poets in the U.S. context, one element stands out. Whatever the particular style, mode, sexual choices, or careers of these men, all three tacitly agreed that the benefits and fascination of investigative manhood stopped at the gender "border," to return to that geopolitical metaphor. The benefits and growth points that their investigations offered these poets, the rich and exciting ways in which manhood was used in their poems in image, theme, and ideology, were central and defining to their poetic careers. But, at the same time, in these works and in the ideologies (and sometimes institutional practices) that sustained the works, "women" were generally immobile, disenfranchised, possibly reviled—fascinating, sometimes tempting and dangerous—and so forth. That is, in their view of the world in the 1950s, "the female" had little or no countercultural or critical possibility.

In the 1950s and into the 1960s three vital U.S. poets offer three kinds of peripheral maleness, all examining taboo or countercultural forms of masculinity in their poems. One is overt about intense, orgasmic homosexuality as part of transformative vision; another is interested in hyperscrupulous male self-consciousness and contemplation; and the third draws on the male display of heroes of hypermasculinity, on the historical heroism of the local and particular and the workaday intelligence of men in a key economic/historic place (in Olson 1983, *The Maximus Poems*). In specific individualized ways, all three poets make a critique of hegemonic maleness as it functions socially. At the same time, all draw on ideologies of the center in order actively to resist the sense that textual females (or, indeed, real women) could themselves have a large stake in the gender shifts in male subjectivity occurring on the countercultural periphery. Their sense of manhood was mobile and even grand; their sense of the potential for and in women was static and suspicious. To see men investigate and even change some gender ideas without their appreciating that women could want, in parallel ways, to investigate and even change gender ideas is to feel a lost opportunity, on which we might still be able to make good. For these critical poetries of sixty years ago understood only part of what needs to be known, knew only part of what needs to be done.

5. Coda: Kitchen Debate

In the "Kitchen Debate" of Richard Nixon and Nikita Khrushchev in Moscow in 1959, the two world leaders hectored and heckled each other over the model American kitchen, trying to best each other and toast each other at the same time. It was a nasty, staged moment, in a "get tough on communism/capitalism" mode. They could not even agree to disagree, except when Khrushchev said, "Let's drink to the ladies." Nixon responded affirmatively: "We can all drink to the ladies." It is here that two pugnacious representatives of two rival world systems could agree. They toasted the waitress, a working woman who happened to be available (Savran 1992, 31). So—to the ladies, that icon whose deployment solves or covers over all contradictions between whatever center one represents and whatever periphery one wishes to excommunicate. Because the "ladies" are considered subordinate figures in all systems, one may drink to them safely and disturb absolutely nothing at all.

Five

Sex/Gender Contradictions in Olson and Boldereff

> *All of a woman's troubles proceed from the fact that she never admits to herself her fundamental inequality.*
>
> FRANCES BOLDEREFF TO CHARLES OLSON, CA. 16 APRIL 1949

> *[B]ut somewhere I must say how strongly I protest the accepted version of woman's character [. . .] I only desire to drop a hint as to how the life was lived, the life wherein God set one woman free.*
>
> FRANCES BOLDEREFF TO CHARLES OLSON, CA. APRIL 16, 1949

1. Bigmans

Consolidating, analyzing, and deploying maleness in writing are self-conscious, visceral activities for Charles Olson, a "gender project" central to his poetic career (Connell 2005, 72; see also Mossin 2007). Olson's self creation from about 1949 to 1956 (focusing here on 1949–1952) produced a mythically invested protean masculinity, to become influential within the ideologies, affiliations, and practices of contemporary poetry. His efflorescence was achieved in relationships (tracked in matching chapters) with Frances Motz Boldereff (1905–2003), a typographical designer and self-taught scholar; and with Robert Creeley (1926–2005), a fellow poet.[1] Olson struggled with his responsibilities to Boldereff, whose intellectual, sexual, and emotional enthusiasms were vital to his vocation, and to Constance Wilcock, his common-law spouse and support (Clark 1991, 157). However magnetic the biography is, I am treating this relationship as an event in the cultural structuring of gender in poetic communities. It is a working relationship in which the passages back and forth between the filiative (familial/sexual bonds) and affiliative (social/professional bonds) were volatile and metamorphic.

At clearly identifiable moments, Olson approaches a critique of contemporary gender, particularly of male-female relations, but he resolves the contradictions that he faces by choosing and rechoosing the normative, genius-oriented, relatively privileged masculinities of the time. This solution was not unique to him. The immediate postwar period saw a retreat from the modernist debates and activities that had started toward gender-equality, civic and professional status for women, increasing tolerance of sexual minorities, and the inquiry into difference without hierarchic outcomes. By "establishing an extreme return to bourgeois notions of a totally segregated masculinity and femininity," the late 1940s and early 1950s "interrupted the historical struggle for a modernization" of sex-gender regimes, a struggle that was, as my Pound, Eliot, Loy materials illustrate, serious and fraught in earlier modernism (Pollock in Orton and Pollock 1996, 223–224, 223). This conservatism is of a piece with contemporaneous psychology—the move, as traced by R. W. Connell, from the complexities of Freud to the simplicities of Theodor Reik. What Freud had seen as a "complex and fragile construction"—sexuality and gender—was codified by Reik into "gender orthodoxy" and "conventional heterosexuality" (Connell 2005, 11). Consequently, even Jung looked radical in the 1950s, although his key argument that creative men were infused with a female aspect depended on an ahistorical, binarist worldview (Connell 2005, 12–13).

Olson's specific choices and ideas made him—as Robert Duncan later said—"patristic" in his actions but richly multiple in his imaginary (Duncan 1995, 26). That is, he became both a patriarch in power terms and (in my use of the term) patriarchal, deploying multiple, imperially ranging subject positions as part of that power and its charms. Olson selected his gender modes and regimes, which included an intense mysticism about women propelled and supported by Frances Boldereff.[2] Although Boldereff (see the epigraphs at the beginning of the chapter) insists on her "fundamental inequality" as a woman, she also protests loudly and clearly, torn about the self-abnegation and self-effacement that historically have been strategies of muting female ambition. Her protest is full of a strange pride, as if she were the one woman chosen by the universe to suffer the political contradictions of sexuality and gender in the most acute and painful way. At the same time, she wants to compel the world to acknowledge that women do have a soul—it is a measure of her despair that she felt this was in question—and that female achievement is possible. Her sexual freedom, intellectual panache, inabilities to reconcile herself to secondary status, and manic emotional-intellectual force belie that "inequality" to which she has constantly to re-reconcile herself. When she claims and reclaims that "essential inequality," Charles Olson's response is a terse "((SHIT))," but his conflicts on this very matter are also powerful and formative (*Olson/Boldereff*, 28). They are formative not only for a private relationship but for modeling some limiting yet charismatic sex-gender modes for poetic institutions and practices.

Olson's early poems of incipience, "Bigmans I" (written ca. 19 May 1950) and "Bigmans II" (written ca. 8 August 1950), curiously foreshadow the narratives involving both Boldereff and Creeley (Olson 1987b, 147–154, 651). Indeed, the works mark Olson's passage from one to another. "Bigmans I" (sent to Boldereff) shows that a male figure must move from his mother's house to a "sib," aka "the whore." These are tropes about a muse "who is ground, who is fountain, who is night"; "sib" flirts with incest or a *Doppelgänger* motif; "whore," used positively, seems to mean sexually liberated female (*Olson/Boldereff*, 342). In "Bigmans II," a giant male figure, sage, seer, and builder on a mythic scale tries to civilize and teach; but because he is himself riven and torn, he "made bull trouble among his folk, / he was so rampant, wild, and unacknowledged to himself" (Olson 1987b, 151). Those around him say "he crowds us on"; "His wildness now has gone beyond our present needs. / His muscularity offends our other lives" (Olson 1987b, 152). But far from giving up on this masculine figure, they pray for the appearance of a heroic counterforce—"a man of such impetuous heart"—so that the two figures can struggle with each other and leave society in peace (Olson 1987b, 154). This counterforce might well have been a glyph of Creeley—at this moment the correspondence between the two men had become scintillating.[3] The two fictional males might also be different stages or phases of the same male figure, however: impetuous physically and emotionally. The poem shows that Olson claimed high stakes for male gender materials as simultaneously blocking and enabling.

In his analysis of the 1940s and postwar period, art historian Michael Leja presents what he calls "Modern Man discourse," which "enlisted the notions of the primitive and the unconscious in the cause of rescuing a dominant ideology, whose notion of subject was crumbling, from threats posed by its own historical effects" (Leja 1995, 16). Leja shows that the "gendered nature of the new subjectivity" helps us understand both "the marginalization of women artists" and "the representation of women" as earth mother/primitive and as the embodiment of unconscious forces or the anima (Leja 1995, 16). Certainly Olson accepted with glee the loss of any "centered" subjectivity. He also participated in "a heroic struggle" affirming primitive and unconscious materials as against rationalism, control, and "overdependence on [mind]." Females viewed as powerful Great Mother goddesses and in Gaia roles are part of his mythography;

thus he can both honor females and be crudely dismissive of historical women seekers-after-knowledge. To reject rationalist consolidations,
professional banalities, and trite ideas about progress, to draw deeply on
"the primitive and irrational," was the path of liberation (Leja 1995, 16,
199, 204). Olson championed that path.

2. Writing from the Body

After an era whose genocidal ferocities had burned millions (re-
gardless of gender) to ash and after a war whose conduct bombed people
into smudges, it is hard to believe that binarist gender ideology in general (as in postwar normative social psychology) was so luridly affirmed.
It seems a desperate attempt to reestablish masculine/feminine stereotypes after a historical experience that may have had specific gendered
occasions and disparities but hardly gave males any superiority to their
bodies. The stunned realization that an era had shifted with this recent
destruction of bodies, particularly by Nazi-fascist instrumentalization, is
of course an Olson trope; it comes from his essay "The Resistance" (1953)
and from such early poems as "La Préface" (Olson 1987b, 46–47; written
in May 1946). Indeed, Olson's response was to reaffirm the body and to
critique body-mind splits.[4]

Writing ten years earlier (in 1936) about her desperate sense of femaleness and influenced by such a turn-of-the-century apocalyptic
thinker about sex and gender as Otto Weininger, Frances Boldereff, in
contrast, concludes that woman is reduced to her body but that man can
transcend his. Further, "it is because man *can* be free from his body, can
possess his own soul in strength, that a woman so passionately believes in
him. It is also why she hates him" (*Olson/Boldereff*, 30). One might argue,
contra Boldereff, that man may possess his own soul so fully because his
material body and soul-making needs were often met within conventional culture by female helper figures. In any event, Boldereff argues
that man transcends the physical and can be mind, but woman is mired
in her body (especially because of childbirth and maternal commitments thereafter) and therefore is lodged in immanence, to use Simone
de Beauvoir's terms. Boldereff also concluded that the female is moon to
a male sun, that "the direct [cultural] tasks belong to a man," while the
tasks of a woman are "indirect," a very useful formulation for Olson if
also quite commonplace at the time (*Olson/Boldereff*, 15, 4 March 1949).
Her stark binarist thinking and its painful impact on women contrasted

with his attempts to resist body-mind splits, especially for men. Thus gender became fraught intellectual and emotional territory for both.

In the late 1940s and early 1950s Boldereff wavered between assertions of exceptionalist superiority and outrage at gender inferiority. Her tensions concerning normative female roles were electrifying. Olson wrote side-comments on some of her thoughts from a letter of 16 April 1949; their scintillating dialogue about gender reveals Boldereff's passionate commitment to ideas that led directly to her frustration and rage and shows Olson's occasional questioning of well-entrenched ideas about the subordinate roles of women.[5] Boldereff's opinions on second-sexdom are why I have argued that, by desiring indirect influence on a Great Man plus self-effacement, she offered Olson a script for her own erased status (DuPlessis 2006a, 88). Olson enthusiastically, if somewhat guiltily, took her muse function and her many research inspirations as a triumphal validation of his self-fashioning, and he strove energetically to become the Great Man that her theories evoked.

Olson did not believe in being free of his male body, however—precisely the opposite. In the post-Holocaust, postwar era: "It is his body that is his answer [to fascist murder, to fragmentations and to 'spirit in the old sense,' or 'the cross'], his body intact and fought for, the absolute of his organism in its simplest terms" (Olson 1966, 13; Olson 1997, 174; written in 1953). An embodied "Man" is "resistance" (Olson 1966, 14; Olson 1997, 174), creating a "human universe" (Olson 1966, 53; Olson 1997, 155; written in 1951). "The meeting edge of man and the world is also his cutting edge" is Olson at his most suggestive for poetics (Olson 1966, 62; Olson 1997, 162). This, too, is the Olson for whom a newly asserted phallic fascination (potency as poetency) was an almost mystical force, quite similar to and given impetus by the thinking of D. H. Lawrence.

Drawing from Lawrence's literary and theoretical work, Olson speaks eloquently "of what happens to the best of men when they lose touch with the primordial & phallic energy from which man [. . .] takes up nature's force" (*Olson/Creeley*, II: 95).[6] Sexual materials are palpable in these letters, which speak about male potency frankly and with a kind of wonder. "The phallic & art" and the "primordial & phallic energies & methodologies" are crucial; Pound and Lawrence are such central "creative men" because they exemplify this power (first and third quotations from *Olson/Creeley*, VII: 241, 3 October 1951; this essay-letter is titled "The Law"; second quotation from Olson 1997, 173). Olson is significantly invested in thinking from and in the male body, and Lawrence offers a model as well as a rhetoric. The "dark, or phallic god, who is not phallic as penissimus alone but the dark, as night" is a passage to the "well-spring" (*Olson/Creeley*, III: 63, 1 October 1950; similar observation in Olson 1997, 139).

Olson deeply admired Lawrence's novella *The Escaped Cock*, in which Jesus, after his (apparent or actual) death, renounces the tedious demands of resurrection, simply to be reborn into life itself and specifically into sexuality. Jesus is transfigured by this salvation (male potency) that is truer than doxological salvation.[7] After his brilliantly depicted physiological revulsion and reluctance to be in this life, the undead Jesus and the priestess of Isis stage a ritualized sexual encounter. What interests Lawrence is the moment when the Jesus/Osiris figure can declare of his sexual desire and emergent potency, "I am risen!"—precisely about "the blaze of manhood" (Lawrence [1929] 1973, 57). This very Laurentian narrative climax of phallic resurrection appropriates biblical narrative and diction (even with a striking vulgarity) to accomplish a critique of Christian-Platonic ideological claims about the lowness of the body. A humane pantheism manifested in male potency meets 3,000 years of bodily repression, dismissing the theological obfuscation of disembodied transcendence. Lawrence reliteralizes resurrection as erection.

In his essay "The Escaped Cock," however, Olson also claimed that Lawrence failed in this story because "Lawrence was not yet able to take woman down that next step towards his Etruria" (Olson 1997, 139; similar observation in *Olson/Creeley*, III: 64). "Etruria"—actually the land of the historical Etruscans—is here propulsion to "change." For Olson, the "climax" of this story "is not what happens to the characters or things" but what causes change, particularly intersubjectivity—"what happens BETWEEN things" (Olson 1997, 138). One might also gloss this as idealized sexual redness or passionate suffusion, the "red thread" of "sex" and "orgasm" (Olson 1997, 139). Olson continues his critique: "[Lawrence's] 'woman' here loses by goddessissing the actuality of Constance (Frieda), an actuality the Christ gains. (Always the man leads Lawrence, in?)" (Olson 1997, 139).[8] The two neologisms—*penissimus* and *goddessissing*—are formed from the superlative in Latin/Italian (-*iss*-) and the repeated verb ("is," from "to be," but encrypting "Isis"), and both contribute to the verbal energy claimed from a heightened appreciation of sexuality. But the female is made into a goddess, while Lawrence's point, and Olson's, is that the male figure is not a transcendent god but simply a potent man.

For Olson the "actuality" of the female figures fails: Lawrence's Isis does not lose her allegorical status; Olson thereby shows that he was aware of the problem of representation of females and that it made him uncomfortable in Lawrence. However, he could as well have noted this of his own representations. The rendering of any historical woman rather than allegorical/mythic females presents a serious challenge to Olson. This kind of issue is strikingly and repeatedly visible in the Boldereff connection and is played out in debates about female coequality and in visualizations of parallel, equal difference. This debate is hardly consti-tuted of pure ideas only—it is clouded and roiled up by a number of extraordinary factors, including sexual passions and claims, betrayals, demands, and indebtedness between Olson and Boldereff. Olson seems to be testing the idea that women and men are equally (though differ-ently) embodied and equally mind. This nicely critical approach to the mind-body split that had bedeviled Platonism and Christianity does, however, run into serious difficulties.

3. "[M]ultiple, he sd, as a man, or a woman / is (is a woman?)"

This excerpt from an early poem expresses Olson's important baf-flement.[9] Are women multiple the way men are? Do they have parallel traits? Can they claim parallel traits even within obvious sexual differ-ence? Can the poet visualize coequality of the genders even accounting for difference? Can he credit a situation in which he "is bound to enter (as she is) / a later wilderness" and where both men and women kill and "do kill"—this comment equalizing ruthlessness (Olson 1987b, 159, 158; written 23–24 May 1950). The poem "In Cold Hell, in Thicket" asks what to do when the "goddess" (based on an actual female, but mythologized in the poem) "moves off" and will no longer provide mythical nour-ishment for the supine male figure (Olson 1987b, 158). While the poem concerns dilemma in a man, there are palpable twinges acknowledging generative female agency. These hints get lost in the development of Ol-son's work as a whole.

In Olson's shorter (non-*Maximus*) poems, females appear funda-mentally in two related ways.[10] In mythic modes, female figures are vital. Their roles and presences in archaic myth are treated lavishly by the "culture-morphologist" poet as necessary for the "restoration of culture" (*Olson/Creeley*, VII: 70). With that argument, however, Olson is bound to the patterns that he surmised once existed, not to the material and historical as it developed. Olson argues that "culture as force cannot be extricated from man as permanently also archaic," a statement having gender implications as a denial of any structural and historical change in the meanings of sexual difference, gender dimorphism, and female civil rights (*Olson/Creeley*, VII: 71). Frances Boldereff might have provided considerable evidence of female multiplicity. Yet Boldereff's gender binarist thinking reinforces Olson's. From the contradictory plurality of her positions, he selects those quite despairing about the fate of women as always to be the second sex, doomed to unequal otherness. This binarism will come to bolster his own inability, finally, to credit female cultural equality. This important, often-repeated move of masculine self-fashioning mythologizes the female figure, fixing her in nonhistorical time. These depictions of female figures then are granted little or no actual existence, no contemporary purchase in the now, and little historical location of any kind.

In several early works, however, one does see Olson debating this solution. In a test case of his debate between a historical and mythic female, Olson writes the same lively, sexual poem three ways. This work maps the arousing acrobatics and eroticized twistings of a circus performer as a sustained metaphor for sexual intercourse. Olson wavers between a contemporary and a mythopoetic approach to this material, visible in the poem's three versions (Olson 1987b, 48; Olson 1989b, 41–42, 43–44). The first poem—"Ladies and Gentlemen, the Center Ring!"—focuses on contemporary circus and ballet terms at length and only briefly links the figure to ancient materials. The second, "Lalage," makes a good deal of a mythic comparison to Dionysiac rituals and the performer as bacchante. The considerably shorter version in *Collected Poems* marks this debate between the two positions by two stanzas of description based on the real circus act and the third stanza calling her "Lalagea" and imagining that "Horace" has discussed her. Olson here tests out different proportions for his depiction of women in historical and mythic zones.

A second debate on a pertinent topic about the representation of females asks whether females have the right to possess the gaze and to turn it outward or whether they are simply gazed upon, as many poems in the Western literary tradition propose. "For Sappho, Back" attends to these matters while accomplishing the cunning task of being readable as homage either to Boldereff or to Wilcock (Olson 1987b, 160–163; written May 1950).[11] The marked allusion to the syllables and the brother figure in section III are a distinct trace of "Projective Verse" material (readable as "hers" by Boldereff), but the proposition that the female figure of this poem is "the hidden constance of which all the rest / is awkward variation" (section IV) as well as the claim "she /creates constants" (section I) both contain distinct puns praising Constance's first name and her function.

Olson shifts notably in representing the female gaze from outward boldness to the more poetically conventional situation of being gazed upon, from powerful assertion outward from a female body and eye to powerful appreciation of one female (or the other one) framed in a male gaze. "From Sappho, Back" begins with an implacable, unflinching female gaze outward both at the world and at her own blood. Menstruation, abortion, failed pregnancy are all hinted at, as well as "her makings." That word, magnetized by the word "Sappho" in the title, cues female literary production, if also reducing it to blood (Olson 1987b, 161; *Olson/ Boldereff*, 339, 340–341, 18 and 19 May 1950; see Clark 1991, 170–171). By the end of the poem, having continued to affirm "her most objective, scrupulous attention, her own / self-causing [. . .] fresh as is the scruple of her eye" through section II and III as beyond "the reed of man" (alluding, as in other poems, to the penis and punning on a male inability to interpret or read), the final section praises the gentleness and delicacy of her "constance," focusing the male gaze as giving "beauty to her eye," to her bones and skin, made luminous by being "tender-taken" (Olson 1987b, 160, 161, 162). The poem begins as a female gazing on a male and on herself and ends as a male gazing on a female; the poem tries thereby to balance his attention between Olson's two women but also reveals his own debate on female creative power and what to do with it.

The question of viewing females as equals is also a question of keeping the term in the singular: there is a special, selected, uplifted (token) female far superior to many women, argues Boldereff. Her match is a specially selected gifted man. Boldereff's extremist vision of the relationship—"we are perhaps the only two equals alive in the world today"—is a response to an Olson poem sent in November 1949 (*Olson/ Boldereff*, 80, 5 December 1949). Olson's "The Laughing Ones" divides the world in two groups—the more destructive ones who slay also treat women as "things to run with, equals" (Olson 1987b, 95). "[T]heir blood / does not go down, it / races out!" is (or will come to be) a negative remark in the Olson map of the real (Olson 1987b, 95). While the "dark men root in woman as a cave" (this is a good), the light men "want to dance, only to dance / & slay" (Olson 1987b, 95, 96). These negative men view women as "equals" running with them. Olson's opinion of the dangers of dance will shift considerably at Black Mountain when he speaks of dance as visceral embodiment, a solution to mind-body splits; in contrast, his resistance to females as parallel runners will harden further. That kind of female figure becomes dangerous in his oeuvre; a man is not "dark" enough when she runs and can keep up with him.

4. Gender, Jews, and Humanism

The debate with Boldereff in March 1950 about a poem called "Lady Mimosa" offers a flash point for these gender materials and more.[12] This poem is about as close to Eliot's "Ash Wednesday" as anything Olson would ever write, which, curiously, may be why Boldereff attacks it for being "full of hebraic modesty" (*Olson/Boldereff*, 292). Addressed to an iconic female, "Deliver us" is the prayer. From what? Apparently from some kind of cowardice—in order to absorb her tenacity and curiosity and her sense of projected beauty. The Lady is a salvationist figure, worshipped, cherished. When she receives the Lady Mimosa poem implicitly addressed to her, Boldereff (in a rather manic moment—her moments alternate in the letters) is furious. She attacks Olson's pulling back from violence, challenging him "WHAT IS WRONG WITH VIOLENCE?" (particularly the violence of and in sexuality). This topic is not in the poem, which is pleasantly pacific, but it is part of her poetics. Violence, she avers, is a tool of art; it is the tool to "attack chaos" (*Olson/Boldereff*, 293). With an unerring ear, she lambastes the passivity of the poem, its imploring of salvation from a female other—the move is certainly conservative and particularly tends to fix the female figure in prior iconic representations. Finally, she rejects the premises of the poem's male subjectivity and point of view, stating, "I want Lady Mimosa speaking aloud to herself" (*Olson/Boldereff*, 294). This is a very striking moment of critique. By calling for such a female voice, she undermines (with a proto-feminist rage) a long-standing set of assumptions about the place of the female figure in the male imaginary as well as the poem's sentimentality. Boldereff sweeps it all away, offering the response "No female thanks. / I hate its guts" to this poem's worshipful stance (*Olson/Boldereff*, 294).

Boldereff says, in effect, that Olson insults sexuality by his sentimentality; she wants him to speak a new truth about sexuality—something passionate, violent, intransigent: "*hard* language full of *hard* paradox"

(*Olson/Boldereff*, 294). In contradistinction to this apotheosis of "hardness," one of the interests of Olson's language is precisely its meditative errancy, its ability to represent debates and contradictory nodes of information in stuttering and incomplete ways. This, for him, is his male power—an incorporative stoking of the poem with questions and multiple paths. Yet, according to Boldereff, he cannot acknowledge his own passionate sexuality and poetic potential, which she apostrophizes in notably primitivist racial tropes: she wants a "new race" (of physically kinetic poems), "a race with the *blood* the hot hot blood of a black man / And the wildness of Olson—his eye / And the intellect of a Greek" (*Olson/Boldereff*, 294). (A note: Boldereff may feel the complex contradictions of the female position but does not grant equally complex contradictions to black social positions—this romanticized primitivist moment is not the only one in the letters.) The ideal "Olson poet" whom she continuously projects is ideally capable of all this, but here the actual Olson person has failed. And his failure lies in not acknowledging how we are sexually "multiple"—female and male, both equally violent, erotically charged, ruthless, needy. In this letter, Boldereff is close to rejecting the whole position of the apostrophized goddess. But, of course, this position is also tempting, a time-honored position for females in culture. By virtue of her angry, articulate frankness, Boldereff is an exposed place where sex-gender contradictions show themselves most unsettled and most unsettling. She is also, unsurprisingly, sometimes quite gratified by Olson's worship (as in his related work "She-Bear"). Nonetheless, Boldereff often calls for a drastically different sexual culture, sweeping away, by her impotent but aggressive fiat, the culture we have.

Olson responds to the rage of her outspoken letter with a deflecting pun about his "TIGRESS (& EUPHRATES)" and says, with pleasure at their synchronicity, that he too has concluded that "miss mimosa" is not an adequate poem (*Olson/Boldereff*, 295, 4 April 1950). However, the root issues—Boldereff's wayward, enraged, conflicted but powerful desire for sexual and intellectual coequality, mixed with cosmic abasement and her insistent desire for more acknowledgment from Olson of her sexual, relational needs in their affair—have all gone unanswered. Missed and mixed messages on gender materials become part of their overwhelming drama—a relationship cast at a perpetual manic, magic pitch. Not simply about them as a couple, this exchange is symptomatic of their mutual struggles with gender as given and their failed attempts to shift male power. Both had too many investments in that power.

The set of archaic or archetypal patterns that Olson discusses in the parallel letter from which the Mimosa poem emerged involve first "FATHER-MURDER" (the Freudian idea of the horde of sons challenging the patriarch's monopoly of women) and second some damaged root of "hebra-christia[n]" thinking whose god is a male "Eunuch" who neither inseminates nor reproduces (*Olson/Boldereff*, 282). (Note how the Lawrence novella is constructed to reinterpret and replace this asexual god by the Frazerian fusion of Osiris and Jesus.) For the ultimate problem of Jewishness for Olson is the obfuscation of sexuality in the first biblical tales. With a quick overlay from Greek myth and polytheism, Olson asserts that these chapters in the Bible censor the real story that he intuited—about father-murder and father-castration. Hebrew Genesis is an influential evasion of the fierce sexual truths at the heart of religion.

Hence Jews have a rather damaged role in this Olson gender mix. Jews, he says, are overly emotional, masochistic scapegoats and live with the "heavy heart" of sacrificed animals, flesh unanimated by spirit; "it is the slaughter of animals which is the curse behind all judaism [*sic*]" and, by extension, Christianity too (*Olson/Creeley*, VI: 139, 143). It is a curiosity that he can articulate this even while having the example of Pound's anti-Semitism so recently in mind. For instance, it is astonishing that Olson does not stop to consider obvious counterexamples—the ways the Greeks, Romans, and Sumerians also sacrificed animals in their religious activities, as most ancient peoples did. This Semiticized representation seems laden with distaste especially because early biblical Jews were nomads, outside of the polis and the state. For Olson, these traits mark present-day Jews despite centuries of historical changes in Judaism; this is another example of his intensely ahistorical thinking.[13]

Thus (nothing follows exactly; it is all assertion) Jews are central founders of humanism, and this humanism—based in the work of Karl Marx, Sigmund Freud, and Albert Einstein (*Olson/Creeley*, VI: 144)—constitutes the assumptions with which we live. Olson's genuine praise of Marx, Freud, and Einstein is put forth in the hopes that someone will surpass and transcend the damaging "humanism" they embody. It is up to "us" to "prove 'em wrong" (*Olson/Creeley*, VI: 145). This is a volatile stance; these Jews and, by extension, all Jews have formed the hegemonic compact in which we live; the challenge is to get to the next stage (Olson might assume that he is the capable man for the job), from "blood" (and organs such as liver, stomach, heart) to "sun." This is always pure male futurity, compounded of generative phallic pride and male multiplicity, but it involves doubts about whether females have any powerful part to play in this compact, whether from coequality or from parallel but different powers. The "Lady Mimosa" exchange is one of Olson's turning points in his sense of gender. What do women have in the sex-gender regime? Are they multiple the way men are? That is: can they be coequals? Can they be respected even in co-difference and for their kinds of multiplicity?

Donald Wellman has recently made a spirited queer defense of Olson, precisely concerning this question of multiplicity for the male figure. Wellman sees Olson's sex-gender subject positions as "womanly man," as an oedipal son who reaffirms the pleasures of the body of the mother in her geographical or land-forms version, as passive male whose visual text of the father's phallus (a generally accepted interpretation of one page of *Maximus*) plays on the desire for penetration, as someone interested in becoming a "fused figure of uncertain sex," as the imaginary "father of [gay] sons" (Wellman 2007, 58, 57, 55). This study divines the uneasy fusion of "phallic narcissism" (also "overdetermined phallicisms") with an excitingly metamorphic and unstable fusion of genders and family members readable as incestuous, pre-oedipal before castration, queer, masturbatory—a large array (Wellman 2007, 53, 52). Wellman shows with a detailed grasp particularly of later Olson how the poet claimed a sex-gender "surplus"—of multiple modes, forms, images, myths (Wellman 2007, 53). Precisely—this is the position of imperial claim that I have called "patriarchal poetry."

With Boldereff as evidence, however, and with the statistically small representation of females in the *Maximus* poem factored in, it seems that Olson does not perceive female figures as mobile in parallel ways. They are put in mobile positions only insofar as they appear in combinations useful for the male imaginary. The result is notable but "normal" for patriarchal poetry—a totalized imperial ability for males to be positioned at a number of sex-gender nodes or points, even if these are contradictory and even if some positions—like the fantasy of a challenging phallic male who confronts male vulnerability—produce an anxiety that was also somewhat exciting, as in "The Lordly and Isolate Satyrs." Olson's achievement of the condition of "womanly man" from the position of patriarch is reasonably familiar in cultural circles, if hard won in any particular case.[14]

A related issue, as Olson proposes in an essay on D. H. Lawrence, is "the evidence of the connection between sex and the structure of the mind" (Olson 1997, 136). Olson is well able to negotiate a number of subject places for maleness. But the female body stops him: despite many examples in his dual relationships with Boldereff and Wilcock, at Black Mountain and later, he cannot visualize much mind in it. Female mind cannot seem to emerge from female body or from female sexuality. Now, in Boldereff's view and as we have seen historically, females are limited by the ideological framing of their bodies and by the sexual politics of inequality tied to reproduction. Boldereff states this passionately, enraged and resigned in volatile combination. She also sees, in an inchoate way, that the contradictions she constantly presents are made by a sexual politics (a social norm) at the same time that she claims it is an eternal condition. Olson seems to have taken up this eternal, unchangeable part of Boldereff's analysis with a vengeance, missing its particularized historicizing arguments. The debate between a "real"/historical female entity and an allegorical, "eternal" female entity is constantly being solved in favor of the transhistorical. This has the effect of discrediting female mind/body links or the relationship between female sexuality and mind as shifting in historical time.

What Olson also cannot easily credit or focus on is what might emerge from female sexuality and genital pleasure inside female mind, if, that is, one claims that sexual difference creates significant (although nonhierarchical) difference between the sexes. This is true despite the example of at least Boldereff and certainly a number of other quite embodied and intellectually generative females with whom he interacted. And this is something that Olson, curiously, sees D. H. Lawrence failing to acknowledge for females. As he states to Creeley in a long apostrophe: "our own deepest knowledges, loves, these two, the brain and the cock, are what we stand on, more than our legs—are what man is glorious in having, that, he can go so far with each of them and yet, when he gets that far, he knows he is instrument" which he glories in "so long as we still throw words, and our cocks, around" in search of "'beauty'" (which is here accorded a female pronoun) (*Olson/Creeley*, X: 68, 69, 15 May 1952). Writing after the mending of any mind-body split does not get any more explicit than this.[15] For males, precisely. That is, men have both mind and their specific genitals; women simply do not get credit for what they have in that general line. It is not that the human universe rests on human embodiment. It is that the human universe is expressed by male embodiment—and that's it, over and out.

The gender limits of Olson's fervent commitment are symbolized by his binary WOMB/COCK, as in the "kinetic of the human" is "WOMB AND / COCK" (*Olson/Boldereff*, 282–283). The womb is not the particularized organ of pleasure; rather it is the organ of childbearing. Olson's word choices are hardly motivated by discretion: he is perfectly capable of franker, more taboo words like "cunt." Indeed a "cock and cunt" combo is one set of the four "word" groups repeated in three of the lines in his sexual mantra "Hymn to the Word" (Olson 1987b, 8–9, written early 1940s). The "kinetic of the human" for females becomes the female organ of reproduction, not (*grosso modo*) the zone of female sexual pleasure.

5. "[T]he absolute dynamiting of, the PATRIARCHY"?

The "absolute dynamiting" that Olson invoked reveals another notable moment of gender debate, again solved by the normative and conventional.[16] The question becomes: can male and female be imagined to be co-regnant, mythologically speaking? Boldereff and Olson felt that they were enacting some gigantic, ritualized *hieros gamos* of gods and goddesses that would construct a grand transformation of history, the world, and consciousness. "In the dance of this love of ours, in the wildness of it," Boldereff is cast, pretty willingly, as all the avatars of female figures of myth, Olson as all male figures, and their conjunction has cosmic force (*Olson/Boldereff*, 410; the whole run of letters on 409–435). Alas, the "chthonic, archaic thing which we, perhaps more than any two living beings, are living out" must also include the pain of their being constantly separated and having their sexual urgencies repressed as a (rather convenient) cosmic test. The striking element for this discussion is that Olson also sees his "heaving" and his relationship with two women at once (which, according to him, should not be put in some "easy frame" of adultery, jealousy, and simplistic reactions) as "the absolute dynamiting of, the PATRIARCHY" (*Olson/Boldereff*, 413, 13 July 1950). It is unclear what this means or how this functions: in another light, maintaining two relationships in which two women are available to, pursued by, and giving much to one man seems to be about as good as hetero-patriarchy may get, at least in heterosexual terms (*al que quiere*). The only better situation is visible power over other men, with their serious homage. Irony aside, the point here is that Olson sees this "dynamiting" as an important goal.

In history, patriarchy has already culturally and politically tri-
umphed over whatever is meant by matriarchy—male gods do not
necessarily have higher status than female gods, but property rights in
children, male possession of females, and patrilocal marriage and kin-
ship patterns dominate Greek, Roman, and Hebrew civilizations. With
monotheism, goddesses are finally theologically kaput, if also appear-
ing as striking revenants in Catholicism. But this stratum of the archaic
appeals to both Olson and Boldereff; indeed, Olson feels that he has
reached a more archaic historical level simply by absorbing the work of
scholars such as Jane Harrison (for example, in his poem "The Bride,"
Olson 1987b, 340–341). Olson wants to remember "another organization
of human society [. . .] huge and covering the then known world, which
we inadequately call THE MATRIARCHY" (*Olson/Boldereff*, 417, 13 July
1950). By this he means archaic female power.

In the context of this interest in matriarchy, Olson invents a striking
word—the "'patsies' (we can call 'em!)"—for the upholders of patriarchy
(*Olson/Boldereff*, 417, 14 July 1950). This slang demeaning name (a patsy
is someone duped or manipulated, a pushover, coming, possibly from
pazzo, Italian for fool), however, is as quickly dismissed as invented. Almost as soon as that idea of "matriarchy" has occurred to Olson and to
Boldereff, both, apparently independently, come to "distrust this whole
matriarchy business" as "too goddamned sociological"—a suggestive
phrase unglossed by Olson (*Olson/Boldereff*, 460, 31 July 1950). Does this
mean too invested in female political power or too much inflected with
the historical potential of civic equality? Or necessitating an acknowledgment of contemporary social prejudice against females, for example,
as wage-earners (Boldereff's doomed job searches in New York offer poignant examples). The analysis that puts male/female rule together as a
model is "dirty generalizing" and "'soft-headed'"; putting "this man &
woman thing into a parenthesis, matriarchy-patriarchy" abrogates the
strength of individual contact and the will to make a new gender vision
(*Olson/Boldereff*, 460–461, 31 July 1950). This is a very graphic moment.
Leaving aside the already mooted question of historical accuracy, what
is visible is Olson's claim that a political-spiritual system of co-regnant
genders once existed. Almost as soon as he enunciates this, he withdraws
it as an interpretation of history. Olson's discomfort with the rule of both
genders in concert is palpable in his imaginary.

Whenever Olson senses social/political analysis, he sees it as determinism; whenever he thinks that individual will cannot act in perfect

freedom, he balks and resists; whenever there would be room for female participation and contribution to the polis, he stalls (*Olson/Boldereff*, 461). Significantly, this briefly considered vision would put the two genders as cooperating rulers in history and/or in myth. It is this power-sharing vision that gets, yet again, swept to the side. The mythic or archaic is an intellectual space of infinite comfort only as it keeps on validating where Olson is tending: affirmation of males, patriarchal imperium (including androgyny), and homosocial bonding.

An implicit Jungian vision of masculine-feminine polarity and hierarchic complementarity in one person's psyche undergirds Olson's gender terms—he first read Jung in June 1950 (*Olson/Boldereff*, 395–396, 4 July 1950). Boldereff accepts her role as anima, a delivery system for what Jung "calls the 'logos spermatikos' ('the spermatic word'). Jung insists that a woman's creativity reaches only as far as inspiring a man to productive activity," as Christine Battersby notes (Battersby 1990, 7). Indeed, Olson discusses this structure in a poem from 1950 called "The Advantage," in which he resists the "domestic abstract gods / of paled-out humans / father   mother   son" in favor of a theory meant to "call / the sun a male, / and give him back the moon / for wife" (Olson 1989b, 68, 67). He rejects the Freudian "Oedipus complex" and the family positions (with an unspoken sense of struggle to form gender and sexuality, along with "castration," as a theoretical concept policing the son who, with pedagogic wounds, joins the regime of the father) and moves to an organic, always-already Jungian framework for sexuality. This is designated first by the moon (as naturally reflecting the sun) and then by the poem's imbalanced nouns: "male" and "wife." To incorporate and address one's anima, to seek confirmation of current female and male interactions in myth and ancient story, to move to this "basic" or primal level of gender (as if ancient myth—mediated through modern research in cultural anthropology—provided such ground), and to reduce interactions to this type is to ignore any historical shifts in the conduct of gender, sexuality, family, maleness, and femaleness from ancient moments to our common era. Indeed, by postulating a "wrong turn" in Western thought with Greek thinking and "abstraction" (another of his basic arguments), Olson made even more credible his mythopoetic searches to try to reinterpret—and to intervene in—major ideological shifts in the history of human culture. Hence archaic mythopoetic feminine power is one thing; demanding and aggressive females in the historical present are quite another. The one Olson will honor; the other he will avoid or contain.

6. "The derogation of woman"

How was Olson to resolve the question of, and the potential represented by, women and the feminized within a male-female (or male-
male) relationship?[17] The issue remained powerfully unstable and
destabilizing for him. Finally, however, as we have seen continuously,
male figures were granted by their own fiat the capacity to change, shift,
and debate but female figures were held in the social imaginary (sometimes by males and sometimes by themselves) in more conventional and
immobile positions. This outcome generally psychologized (and mythologized) sex-gender politics and muted the active, pragmatic implications
of this struggle over gender ideas.

Olson was all too aware of the onomastics of his name; changing
"son" to "sun" was a clear emotional necessity (Ross 1986, 118–122).[18] In
an evocative letter to Creeley, Olson produced a picture of affective manhood debating itself: "and we, we who are no longer males, but sons,
SUNS are become our bizness, sister, and, if we leap on you without in-
termission, that's the way it's gonna be, for a while, wile away o green
GREEN is the color of the (ambiguous, sd mister Freud, which sex is
which[)]" (*Olson/Creeley*, I: 90, 8 June 1950). This farrago is quite suggestive for sex-gender thinking—especially the claim of joyously aggressive sexual behavior in homosocial partnership with another man,
along with an explicitly evocative placement of homoeroticism or gender
ambiguity as the green (or commons) on which heterosexual coupling
takes place, green at that time being a word coding homosexual. Two
men together will imaginatively leap together on the "sister" who is no
longer an equal sexual partner but a site against which/through which
the minor and incipient (son) becomes major and patriarchal (sun) in
its claim of power. The little frisson of rape or of "gang" sex is palpable
without being resolvable.

Thus one finds that the "archaic or chthonic is not, and never was,
horizontal and history: it is always present perpendicularly in each of
us" (*Olson/Boldereff*, 419). This is Olson's notable idea of the vertical, the
shaft, the tube bored into strata that survive in us, upon which one can
draw or into which one enters. Downward is his shorthand trope for this
zone: "the downward is the place where form is to be found" (*Olson/
Creeley*, X: 113, 25 May 1952). Thus the vertical descent and thrust is important; writing that goes down the page (pictographs, ideograms) is not
considered abstract but embodied and concrete (see Billitteri 2009). A

writing that acts as if it did not use the alphabet but rather used pictographs for its words (cf. Pound's ideogram) is a guarantor of specificity
and concreteness (*Olson/Creeley*, X: 94, 22 May 1952). Each individual
is like her/his own archaeological dig. This sense of the shaft into the
past, active and permanent in everyone, not as residue or traces but as
active still and fully intact, unchanged through millennia, is precisely
archetypal thought. Thought and action get pictured as a phallic thrust
down into the vaginal shaft of vertical time. This is a fairly reductive
sense of historical investigation. But it is also, quite strikingly, a picture
of self-intercourse—one's own male aspect thrusting down into oneself
as female: the eros of poesis scintillates in Olson sometimes as a powerful androgynous narcissism.

In Olson's sex-gender debates, yet another moment of the potential
construction of a new woman to match his fantasy of a new man occurs in August 1950. Olson contrasts two worldviews, one that he calls
heroic and one (from the biblical Moses) that he calls an "ethic." The
difference is in "man's attitude toward woman" (*Olson/Boldereff*, 515, 24
August 1950). The "judeo-christian-european-american tradition [. . .]
rests on the derogation of woman" (*Olson/Boldereff*, 515). "Derogation" is
a legal term as well as one in common use in the form "derogatory" (disparaging, belittling). To derogate is to cause to seem inferior, to detract
from; a derogation of a law is a partial annulment of it or enactment of
something contrary to it. The force of this is clear: the civilization (thou-
sands of years of it) in which we live has a negative, resistant, detracting
view of female power. But the "heroic [tradition] raises itself only on the
recognition of her, of her as the tragic source of joy" (*Olson/Boldereff*,
515). Olson is reconstructing civilization, in his fantasy of the archaic
root below the "ethic," and Boldereff is given the role of "creatrix of a
new root place of woman" (*Olson/Boldereff*, 515). A day later, however,
the excitement sputters with a reality check: "it is not the relation you-
me, that makes me nervous, but, the effects on me-con [Constance], to
put it baldly, and to say no more about it, now" (*Olson/Boldereff*, 519, 25
August 1950).

This is not a scolding comment on biography—all the people involved simply acted as they did—but a comment on subjectivity and
structures: the archaic was a zone of suggestive, refracted history to
which Olson had no temporal responsibility in the now. His powerful mythologizing and synoptic reimagining of civilizations and traditions were ways of veering from actions and choices that occurred in

contemporary time. The female's responsibility was to maintain her archaic/tragic self in the time zone of modernity in which it was out of place or could only with difficulty be enacted; Boldereff's letters testify to the strain. The male's responsibility was, again, worship and a contemporary authentication of the archaic. It was an arena for which "She-Bear" (written March 1950) was the script, for the bulk of this overeager, undistinguished poem, which appears in several indeterminate versions, consists of pages of apostrophes (o this, o that) to avatar forms of the Great Goddess (Jung links the she-bear to Artemis) or to the variously invoked names of the sacred prostitute, who opens herself to many male comers at designated sacred moments (Olson 1987b, 130–131, 651). Olson owed much to Boldereff, but, symptomatically, he could not make this particular poem come out right, although it remained a token and talisman of joy to her.

By September 1950 the published correspondence with Boldereff rounds off.[19] Olson and Boldereff still are in an epistolary relationship but at a different pace. Boldereff becomes sexually involved with a man ("a beautiful young negro [sic]") she picked up on the subway—an act of willful challenge to Olson's reluctance to visit her and to his endless, abrupt shifts of their plans (*Olson/Boldereff*, 539, 3 September 1950). The correspondence continues with sporadic connections over the next years (1954–1964 into 1968) but never with the same verve, although some tempting contact clearly occurred in 1952. Boldereff even tells Olson in September 1964 (after Betty Kaiser Olson's shocking death in an auto accident) that she has found "someone more Maximus than yourself" (Thesen in *Olson/Boldereff*, xvii)—a cunning, mean, and well-placed blow at that time, trumping his intellectual claims, his poetic persona, his six-foot nine-inch physical presence, and their intense relationship.

In a letter to Creeley in May 1952, Olson produces a valuable document for this sex-gender context, ten pages on the depiction of female figures in the work of his most significant authors (*Olson/Creeley*, X: 121–130, 29 May 1952). Quite visible once more is a contradiction between what Olson says about the representation of females and his will to enact these ideas in his own world. The letter outlines (quite obscurely) the ways in which Arthur Rimbaud, Herman Melville, D. H. Lawrence, and Homer depict female figures and/or his speculations (except with Homer) as to how actual relationships with women figured in their biographies (*Olson/Creeley*, X: 123–130, 29 May 1952). The letter is saturated in something unspoken: his apparent recent choice to forego the relationship with Boldereff. This letter is distinguished by outbursts of empathy and by a long discussion of what women may learn from jealousy; he clearly has drawn on recent personal situations. The empathy is striking and may also reflect his close understanding of the tasks of taking care of an infant; set off in white space, he expostulates sympathetically "(jesus, when i think what a deal women get now)" (*Olson/Creeley*, X: 127, 29 May 1952).

How can one read this? It is not clear whether "now" means now in 1952; now with Boldereff after one of his renunciations of their bond; now in the early months of Wilcock's motherhood; now at Black Mountain College where his struggles with female faculty had become notable; now in the literature of modernity about which he speaks; now in the damaging residue of the jealousy that he has provoked in at least one woman.[20] Those bad "deals"—unnamed—that put females in a strikingly different place from males are not ones he feels responsibility for or to. His words offer an appreciative empathy without particular plans for action.

The other statement in this letter that shows particular self-debate about women concerns "nature (if it is fair to call women ultimately that)." A few words later he decides that this (common) position is indeed not fair: "(take out woman as nature: 'taint so: we are both something else than it, however much we are involved with same[)]" (*Olson/Creeley*, X: 129, 29 May 1952). Particularly the remarks about the reductiveness of "nature" are far more decidedly critical of ideological commonplaces than his binarist position that seems precisely to reduce females to nature. Again, Olson had a significant amount of conflict on this point. He also appreciates Fyodor Dostoyevsky's "recognition" of women, his modesty "about them," and—this is interesting—his "never for an instance [*sic*] set[ting] himself above them" (*Olson/Creeley*, X: 126, 29 May 1952).

Yet Olson's debates—about coequality, gender similarity amid specific sexual difference, a sex-gender regime adequate to the postwar period—ebb and sputter. He had also mentioned the Jungian term "individuation" without particular elaboration except to say that women are not limited to being mothers, actually or archetypally (*Olson/Creeley*, X: 126, 29 May 1952). Certainly envisioning sex-gender materials as formed in political and socioeconomic institutions and (therefore) as potentially changeable was not common then. Nonetheless, it is still striking that Olson notes that he can learn from women (particularly crediting the

penetrating insights that their jealousy gives them) and that he can em-
pathize with them without any sense that he could contribute institutionally to their "individuation" through his own personal or professional
choices. He frames a cultural situation; he does not make a particular
intervention toward altering it. That is, when dealing with the United
States and world cultures *in toto*, he wanted to diagnose and alter them
to make a major shift of politics and ideology, but he did not, finally, intervene in the particular sex-gender regimes in which he actually lived.

By virtue of their sexual-intellectual connection, Boldereff could
declare melodramatically, if inaccurately, "forever it will never be possible to separate an Olson from a Motz because my blood is his ink," a
metaphoric translation of the female body through the male into writing, something so visceral, if not placental, that it dramatizes the stakes
that both felt (*Olson/Boldereff*, 184, 17 February 1950). Despite her/his or-
ganicizing dreams of fusion, the sexually passionate, needy, creative, authoritative, and demanding Boldereff became too much. Despite his own
notable energy and complex motivations, Olson could not sustain the
yearning and mutuality that Boldereff exacted, particularly as he might
have had to choose her over or negotiate her presence with his common-
law partner, long-term beloved, and sometimes financial support, Constance Wilcock (Clark 1991, 157). Olson had trouble choosing and acting
when change was going to be a difficult wrenching of the habitual (Clark
1991, 169; there are other sources, including Olson's own self-analysis).[21]
Hence Olson finally transferred the erotics of the poetic connection—
the erotics of mutual instruction—from Boldereff to Creeley. Olson is so
ready for this bond with Creeley that one does feel, simply and directly,
that his readiness slid over from the ongoing but pressured, enthralled
intensities with Boldereff ("THIS IS A TREMENDOUS UP-HEAVING
THING") to this moment of acknowledging Creeley—a relationship intellectually and professionally gratifying but not as "up-heaving" to gender hierarchies, not as challenging sexually or as unsettling to familiar
social-sexual structures (*Olson/Boldereff*, 412).

7. The Projective

The writing of "Projective Verse" (first published in October 1950)
at just this time of transition triangulates Olson, Boldereff, and Creeley
and marks Olson's passage from one to the other, particularly visible in
the five months from May through September 1950. The compositional

back-story of "Projective Verse" includes marks of both Boldereff and Creeley; the first and second versions of the essay began respectively in letters to each. Typography, incest, the hidden female ear, and possibly poetry as performative are ideas emerging from the Boldereff zone. One may see Boldereff's influence in the issues of performance and voice, in the sense that voice may be scored on the typewriter, and in a new use of printed page space (Thesen in *Olson/Boldereff*, xv). The first version of the essay was essentially on open and closed form, rejecting T. S. Eliot's spiritual narrative and finished formalisms. On 3 April 1950 Olson announces that *Poetry NY* has accepted this essay and begins rewriting it. In mid-May he speaks lyrically about subject positions, including incestuous ones, and mentions to Boldereff that women are ears. Boldereff actually addresses her letter of response (27 May) to "Charles Motzson," graphically presenting the familial and filiative motif.[22] After Olson has riffed to her on all the generative positions he takes up in relation to her ("male," "brother-father," "son of, as well as the man of, f.m.," and a "TWIN" of the male he is) on 15 May 1950, he claims a further emergence on 5 June 1950: "a man is being born, right in front of all of our eyes, a male child!" (*Olson/Boldereff*, 333, 361). These expostulations about a second birth are enormously exciting; she is both sexual partner and mother, he, both paternal inseminator and baby. It is a new and, in fantasy, uncastrated oedipal event, but it also marks Olson's shift of Boldereff away from the mixed zone that she had previously inhabited of the affiliative (professional/social) knotted passionately with the filiative (sexual/familial).

In the meantime, the very first letter to Robert Creeley is written on 21 April 1950. By June, Creeley has seen the essay and casually (but importantly) uses the phrase "that form is never more than an *extension* of content" (*Olson/Creeley*, I: 79, 5 June 1950). Three days later Olson capitalizes this and sends it back, in a mirroring move (*Olson/Creeley*, I: 85, 8 June 1950). On 9 June he then cites this sentence to Boldereff, using Creeley's name; that attribution is notable, for a parallel attribution to Boldereff did not occur in letters to Creeley or in the published essay (*Olson/Boldereff*, 371). Also on 9 June he cites this phrase back to Creeley yet again, showing how talismanic this summary mantra has become (*Olson/Creeley*, I: 94). Creeley praises Olson for his formulation that breath defines line (*Olson/Creeley*, I: 149, 24 June 1950) and states that field composition is the "ONLY gig" (II: 54, 5 July 1950). This is the moment when the "pact" with Creeley begins (see chapter 6). Creeley sends Olson an extremely affirming letter, with a number of extracted summaries of Olson's more vatic and exciting thoughts, focusing and annotating them (II: 58–62, 7 July 1950).

Importantly, Creeley makes a significant distinction between Olson's poetics and Pound's. Pound was fond of stating (as in *Guide to Kulchur*) that all key thoughts or principles could be summed up on "a half sheet of notepaper"—in Creeley's memory "on a postage stamp" (Pound [1938] 1966, 369; the aphorism is apparently T. E. Hulme's). Creeley penetrates this claim in one move: "It's the PLAY of a mind, that shows whether a mind is there at all," substituting the processual for what emerges in Pound as demands for static, declarative obiter dicta (*Olson/Creeley*, II: 59, 7 July 1950). This moment contains several shifts for Olson: the first from Pound's current, more "totalitarian" poetics—findings offered as fixed principles; the second away from Boldereff as enthusiast/contributor; the third toward Creeley as fellow cultural worker.

This shift is visible particularly in Olson's choice not to credit or acknowledge Boldereff in "Projective Verse," although the first version of the essay, generated with her help and on her watch, so to speak, had already been accepted for publication (Thesen in *Olson/Boldereff*, xiv; DuPlessis 2006a, 88–89; Rifkin 2000, 51; Davidson 2004, 34–35; Mossin 2010, 37–44). This point has been made severally because it is both symptomatic and galling. It is the second, Creeley-inflected version of the essay that goes into print, in which Olson credits Creeley for his talismanic mantra. Indeed, a strong signal of this coming shift in allegiance is Olson's willingness even at the end of May (*Olson/Creeley*, I: 50, 27 May 1950) to want to acknowledge in print Creeley's contribution to his work. But this is not even a reference to the "Projective Verse" essay; it refers to an understanding of the poem "In Cold Hell, in Thicket" (*Olson/Creeley*, I: 79; see 168, n. 83; Olson's response: I: 85, 8 June 1950; his repetition and slogan-deployment: I: 94). That is, Olson was already inclined to foreground Creeley's name in acknowledgment of his presence and inspiration even before Creeley's key Form/Content statement emerged in early June.[23]

In contrast, although repeatedly inspired by their connection, Olson's use of materials from Boldereff (aka Motz) has no conventional or textual acknowledgment anywhere in the essay, although many points in the essay, in her view, are "Motz points." She is being relegated to a filiative, sexual, and familial relationship even though she had previously fulfilled affiliative, professional roles as well. While concealment of their intimate relationship is a possible motive (although Wilcock absolutely knew of it), such nonacknowledgment had the very powerful effect of erasing the intellectual contributions of a woman to Olson's work. Women were to be "hatchers" of men only: incubators, sexual partners, and nurturers, with whom the normal professional courtesies of affiliative indebtedness and acknowledgment could be ignored: "O Lady down there, / o Hatcher, of men" marks her most memorable contribution, despite her also being "o Sister-Maker" (Olson 1987b, 140). Olson made a serious choice about the ethics of indebtedness, and it had resonant implications both for his career as a whole and for impact on his cohort. He digested the work of female figures with no trace, working to repress them and to repress any knowledge about intellectually generative females in his literary life, in order to credit only real males and allegorical females in his struggles of incipience and in his coming to poetic power.

Six

Olson's "Long Exaggeration of Males"

*Anyway it was striking how there were no females in this generation;
& the first children of the male-females & of Olson & their other
brothers were all males, and there were very many of them because
of their fathers' incredible promiscuity.*

ALICE NOTLEY, *Dr. Williams' Heiresses*

1. "Write as the father to be the father"

The "long exaggeration of males" that Olson acknowledges to his
estranged partner Constance Wilcock in 1952 (Olson 2000, 176) is a historical as well as a personal artifact.[1] "Manliness and hypermasculinity,"
Suzanne Clark proposes, were ideological formations in the American
Cold War era. Yet while manhood "was everywhere invoked and women
were largely silenced," there was a general disinclination to credit this as
a temporary formation in cultural politics (Clark 2000, 15, 203). Further,
the manhoods evinced by rational or economic men, by the "professional
and managerial classes," were in denial that "subjects were marked by
any gender, race, or class at all" (Clark 2000, 203). Resisting this culturally sanctioned blind spot, some white intellectuals and poets responded
by aggressive uses of ethnicity (not necessarily their own), class (not necessarily their own), femininity, and—yes, maleness ("hypermasculinity")
as a self-conscious marker of revolt. It might be counterintuitive to acknowledge "exaggeration" of the masculine as a social revolt, because it
also replicated and heightened social norms, but this position, with its
many consequences, is the focus of an imperium of gender materials
central to Olson.

Maleness and related gender ideas offered topics of tremendous seriousness to Olson. If Olson's self-conscious social affirmation of manhood resonated with his historical era, it is also a politics to which he
migrates after having tentatively proposed alternative sex-gender frameworks. His attempts to negotiate theoretical curiosity about gender coequality and/or equal complementarity (discussed in chapter 5) proved
impossible for him to enact with actual women. Yet multiple female

traces occur in the mythography of his later work, which delivers many rich and contradictory subject positions to men, including feminine or passive ones. Charles Olson's career reveals the limits of any model of a teleological narrative (like Edward Said's) that postulates a passage from filiative relations to affiliative ones as a mark of modernity. Olson's construction of poetic community collapses the familial and sexualized into the professional and social, articulating an influential poetic subjectivity centered on self-consciously gendered cultural politics. This construct is patriarchal: it both assumes male power and polices it, and it also deploys for men an imperial array of conflicting subject positions involved with sexuality and gender.

What does it mean either to write as or to be the father? From his early career to beyond 1956, Olson's variable and volatile patriarchal claims provided a cover for gender performances of all kinds, so long as these were authorized by two features. He asserted that these performances were the work of maleness and of the father, evoking the physical, emotional, and unstinting support of others (both male and female) for love, for respect, for assistance—by sheer force of charm and energetic will. Olson's own relationships included and combined companion, son, "androgyne," and more, yet all were organized by his term "father."

"Big Baby" was among these positions. This is Charles Boer's intelligent term, shared with a delighted, approving Olson, for certain great men (politicians and artists) whose "charm was a lifelong continuation of babyhood and disguised an enormous ravening ego that secretly consumed everything and everyone" (Boer 1975, 35–36). "Big Baby" is hardly Olson's only gender performance; at the same time, Olson claimed Boer (and perhaps other followers) not as his metaphoric "son" but rather as his own "father." "'I'm your son!'" Olson affirmed, a comment that shows how much he desired the mobility of male positions and the narcissistic pleasures of being cared for and cared about (Boer 1975, 88–89). Then, deploying the ultimate binary while also entertaining androgyny, "I am more woman than man. The woman is the creative part of me. All artists are part woman" (Boer 1975, 144).[2] For Olson, the subject position of "patriarch" involved gender-mobile elements, interestingly conflicted, mercurial, generative, and omnivorous. This is patriarchal insofar as the user imperially claims all available spaces and many sex-gender positions and deploys them to subsidize the self.[3] While metaphoric/mythologized femaleness was a delight and a fascination, real women, for the most part, were positioned well outside this imperial multiplicity of sex-gender possibilities and did not have rights to draw upon it.

The feminine of great male figures was of particular interest to Olson, who clearly analyzed it, claimed it, hankered for it, and was trying to work out exactly how to achieve it while also having the right proportion of "hardness." He wanted a "feminine":

> As Melville was, but his difference
>   methodologically it is true, he was feminine,
>   but an altogether different feminine [from Shakespeare's], more that
>   genetic one
>   of a child—tho here one must be very precise,
>   for a child is so quickly gendered, is conspicuous
>   so early—as baby—in those drives we call male
>   and female, those
>   importances
> his differences is the hardness
> as are things when things are properly constituted
>
> (Olson 1987b, 280; written in 1953)

Olson's yearning for a place inside a new concept of gender is moving and authentic; however, the drive was so fierce to alter the nature of genders for men that thinking about the gender issues of actual women was, to him, unnecessary and irrelevant.

2. A Pact with You, Robert Creeley

In the early 1950s Robert Creeley performed several notable functions in the formation of this patriarchal, generative, and imperial Olson. Creeley channeled into homosocial relations the erotic-intellectual energies formerly devoted to Boldereff; he participated in a Them vs. Us, male-to-male narrative about the literary field; he allowed Olson to gain some traction on and solution to his *odi et amo* relationship with Pound; he paralleled Olson's own tepid (in)attention to female professional striving; and he provided an example of a younger man who was not in any supine, "son-like" position, despite being considerably younger than Olson. Olson's relationship with Creeley in its lateral aspects, its mutual expressiveness, and its opening to male emotionality not only created a fraternal bond; it allowed the role of mercurial, omnivorous patriarch to form as a particular outcome of the compact.

The Creeley-Olson letters (ten volumes in only three years), like the Boldereff letters, are an astonishing record of incipience, intimacy, insistence, passion. Writing in 1960, Creeley was to recall Olson's letters constituting "a practical 'college' of stimulus and information" (Creeley 1989, 107). But more was at stake. The cathexis, the desire, the link, the eros of mutual instruction and need are impressive. The letters teem with sparks and mirroring: "we are forward, and it is such gratification, that you are ready to go with me" (*Olson/Creeley*, Olson to Creeley, I: 24, 9 May 1950, only their fourth letter).[4] Soon afterward Creeley produces the words that Olson longed to hear, countering Olson's self-disgust, rage, impatience: "Now & again: someone like yrself: can make me believe that, even at hand, right now, things are happening. Most of the time: slush, slosh, shit" (I: 97, 11 June 1950).

In these letters, women are mainly absent or mentioned as rarely as possible. This is particularly illustrated by the absence of Boldereff, though this gap is not necessarily odd; correspondences, even very intimate ones, always have zones of the unspoken, and exaggerated frankness may intermingle with discretion.[5] The letters contain only grudging allusions to any cultural mutuality with women. The men's propulsive partnership gets established, with heterosexuality as the unquestioned boundary: "what don't come from the ladies / or what dont [*sic*] move from them: is ball[l]ess" (Creeley to Olson, II: 67, 7 July 1950). In modernity, R. W. Connell reminds us, unambiguous "heterosexuality became a required part of manliness" (Connell 2002a, 253).[6] Two key differences are found in the Creeley and Boldereff letters. First, Boldereff insisted that she was not a writer but a muse; and second, the Olson and Creeley letters enacted no sexual passion between the men, except a forceful eros of poesis.[7]

The two men make a pact in July 1950: "Let's you and I, by God, write for each other!" It was Olson who called for that "PACT"—mutual engagement, drawing on Pound but surpassing him, pushing all others away as inadequate. This is, in Libbie Rifkin's career-oriented interpretation, a "strategic" move: Creeley had more professional contacts, and Olson could thereupon draw on them (Olson to Creeley, II: 43, 3 July 1950; Rifkin 2000, 45). It is also a fully needy move of incipience, saturated with poetic eros. Olson's "pact" with Creeley, appropriating Pound's comment on Whitman, reaches forward or "onward," in fraternal comradeship (II: 12, 24 June 1950; for "pact," see Pound 1950, 89, a poem also cited in full in this letter).[8] Creeley's response is cautious: "altogether with you on pact: IF you are sure" (II: 54, 5 July 1950). While quite aware of the tenor of their discussions, Creeley realizes that this tempting bond could thereupon become obligation or hang up, stifling and smothering (II: 54; I: 57, 28 May 1950).

Olson made very large claims for his companionship with Creeley: "that, you and I *restore society in the act of communicating to each other*" and can therefore say "go fuck yrself" to the larger society. Their propulsive erotics of mutual instruction is often signaled by the emphatic expostulation "fuck." In tidier language: they claim a counterhegemonic utopian zone (VII: 79, 9 August 1951). This parallels Olson's earlier appeal to Boldereff—that their precise relationship provides a model for society to come. It certainly impacted the Nation of Poetry. These relationships are similar, in Barrett Watten's words, as "a collective identity formation at a specific historical moment [. . .] in a form of negative solidarity in opposition to a common foe" (Watten 2003, 54). In the shift to Creeley, however, it is not just inadequate males but any affiliated women who are cast away. The men together take on virtually the entire array of gender roles.

Olson and Creeley manifested an empathetic maternal/feminine masculinity between themselves as self-reliant/independent but mutually bonded brothers. Their masculinity does not "avoid feelings" or reject "self-exposure" but is professionally focused on work (Segal 1990, 219). They accepted complex emotion in males, not just the more available and oft-deployed gestures of rage and aggression. Their emotions are frankly, passionately expressed; Creeley particularly praises the importance of affectivity in men. Indeed, Creeley's radical critique of guarded, unemotional maleness offers a strikingly alternative social vision of masculinity (I: 104, 16 June 1950). Creeley mocks acceptable advice to men and boys: "what had so cursed us / as to make these exclamations: 'reasonable' . . . Dont [sic] be emotional. Control yrself. Sentimental. Yr feelings are excessive. Enthusiasm. Childish. I dont want to talk abt it. Now be reasonable. Keep yr head. No use getting excited [. . .] A long time ago: I had read that in Italy, men sing in the streets. I cant forget that. Too, there are countries where men can cry. Nor that either. I want to move there, some of these days" (I: 104).

This passage protests eloquently against normative male expectations: control, rationality, containment. It suggests what is powerful and significant in the oppositional maleness upheld by this cohort of poets. This is a masculinity that ruptures postwar covenants of normativity, especially emotionless stereotypes. Olson and Creeley pioneered a range of possibilities for males; their male intuition and enthusiasm, their vatic comprehension, their passionate hysteria as health, their erotic arousals to knowledge all protested against the "administered world" for maleness ("The Position of the Narrator in the Contemporary Novel," in Adorno 1991, 31).

Creeley claimed "no evidence of seriousness other than hysteria," and of male hysteria there is much to spare (III: 22). Unfinished thoughts, eagerness, intensity, desires to communicate, depression, rage, lust, anger, annoyance, empathy, hopefulness, pride, encouragement, curiosity, explosive engagements with ideas and idea clots are all strongly expressed in these long and involved letters. It appears that each man represented to the other what passionate professional commitment looked like; each could be a sounding board and impetus for the other; each drew upon and was processing the same literary figures. They become each other's crucial audience (VII: 173, 19 September 1951). This generative erotic connectedness is familiar in poets' letters; it is possibly a function of general poetic desire mixed with distance. A collaborative, pleasurable, and sometimes aggressive self-positioning and mutual self-mirroring occur. But their correspondence is also predicated on enormous trust, self-exposure, supportiveness; it virtually never involves misunderstanding, misreadings, or anger at each other.

Why did the Creeley-Olson correspondence, this fraternal-enthusiastic compact, help Olson become an omnivorous patriarch of all subject positions? The men were almost never critical of each other, virtually never focused on moments of debate or difference. It was an affirmative relationship of self-formation a lot like an idealized maternal, nurturing one. In fact, the one time in these letters when Creeley offers serious criticism, Olson explodes with rage. The occasion is a four-line work by Olson, a sentimental poem to his infant daughter, which Creeley criticizes directly and intelligently for its inconsistent poetics and questionable ethics (Olson's poem: X: 94–95, 22 May 1952; Creeley's remarks: X: 116–117, 27 May 1952; Olson's angry response: X: 130–133, 1 June 1952). Olson's intense anger is shattering, even with a subsequent backing off and Creeley's further apology (X: 133–134, 4 June 1952; X: 142, 10 June 1952). It is one of the few times when a strong difference—with implications for their differing poetics—stands out (see Rifkin 2010, 149). For the fifty years thereafter, Creeley never makes any critical comments in print about Olson. For Creeley, Olson was (and after death remained) the undisputed leader of a fraternal "company" and *primus inter pares.*[9]

Olson and Creeley came to their friendship with the homoerotic a taboo position in their sex-gender universe, and theirs is an eroticized but nonhomosexual masculinity. Libbie Rifkin discusses their "intense environment of linguistic intercourse," frankly and openly fueled by the eros of literary desire (Rifkin 2000, 47). Using the frameworks of Koestenbaum and Sedgwick, Rifkin first suggested that this correspondence is a "homoerotic collaboration": a "dismissal of women and [. . .] appropriation of the feminine"; changing positions of "active and passive roles"; "the eroticization of the text as the conduit of intercourse between men" (Rifkin 2000, 46, summarizing Koestenbaum 1989, 1–15). In a further elaboration of this "company," drawing on Barrett Watten, Rifkin proposes that this "'homosocial equivalence'" is related to a fantasy of a primal formation ("androgyne" or "pre-Oedipal narcissism"), a manhood beneath conventional social and oedipal formations (Rifkin 2010, 148; Watten 2003, 78–79). Male subjectivity drawing on this kind of fraternal-maternal cathexis is omnivorous of multiple subjectivities and—in Olson's case—is socially freed to become uncontainable in its demands. This is the stance of patriarchal poetry.

The female figures between the two men are mainly allegorical. Both men confront "language": "ain't she lovely, / our old whore? / god damn // good, / creeley / olson" (II: 46; 3 July 1950). Given this seductive, energetic letter about the homosocial using of that promiscuous female figure who goes with all but whom they can take for their own, one might well again want (with Sedgwick, Koestenbaum, Rifkin) to speak about the male homosocial dyad (or, in Davidson and Watten, the homosocial group) of poetic practice. This explicit bond between two men occurs not over the body of an actual female or fictional woman character (as Eve Sedgwick argues in plots for novels) but over an allegorical female figure of Language or Profession. Olson's always fresh even if despoiled female is somewhat like the sacred prostitute of ancient ritual and the virgin-whore of Williams in both *Paterson* and *Desert Music*. Seeing language as an "old whore" still ready to give pleasure to you and your pal is fond, manly (appreciative of sexually active women, whatever their condition), and innocent of the potential burdens of actual, not metaphoric, sex work. The energy and drive occasioned by the female figure appears in Olson's Falstaffian riff on Mistress Quickly (from Shakespeare's *Henry IV* and *The Merry Wives of Windsor*), ending in the punning vow "I'm puttin' up, at yr INN, mistress / quickly" (II: 44, 3 July 1950). A metonymic linking of results follows: "things like / a good kiss, a good fuck, a good friend" and "suddenly, POP, there's / creeley, in this universe, there's / creeley!" (II: 45, 3 July 1950). It is as if Creeley's very appearance—the fantasy birth of a male companion—results from adequate erotic desires and sexual fulfillment, exposed by Olson.

Olson and Creeley's pact with each other also involves verbal threats to inadequate literary men of their acquaintanceship. Cid Corman, who strikes both men as neither masculine enough to be an equal nor quite passive enough to cede all power to them, is a particularly battered case. Corman is damned if he does (try to assert himself as an editor, act as their equal), damned if he doesn't. They attribute many negative feminized traits to him: "he's twisty, and so fucking coy," for example, "ball-less like a priest" (Olson to Creeley, VIII: 146, 18 November 1951; Olson to Creeley, IX: 41, 17 January 1952). Corman and his new magazine *Origin* always provide a pretext for gripes. Excluding him, noting his pretensions, mocking his ephebic affect, and disparaging his position as a follower are constants in their ongoing snide, bonding remarks.[10] This continuous reviling of Corman becomes an aggressive, taunting ground note in the correspondence; it is the parodic reverse of Sedgwick's thesis. Here men bond by dispossessing another man (see III: 15–17; III: 55). Whatever Corman's actual sexuality, he is trapped inside Olson's homophobia, so willy-nilly he provides the feminine or "capon" over whom Creeley and Olson bond with a fagging, ragging attitude (Olson to Creeley, IX: 41, 17 January 1952). Despite an ongoing correspondence with Corman (1950–1956) and a serious professional bond, Olson says that he cannot get through to him but would "stick my words right up his arse, good" (V: 115, 31 March 1951). Yet Corman is in fact male, so it "comes back to, we have to, lead cid on, eh?" (Olson to Creeley, VI: 35, 2 May 1951). Even feminized males are finally admitted under the big tent of patriarchal poetry.

Their recoil from a commonplace corporate manhood to a hysterical, affectual one is nonetheless woven with affirmations of an enriched poetic, tough-guy manhood. This is a 1950s debate between conflicting qualities of manhood, in which the masculinity of an insecure, alternative maleness (tentative, needy, incipient, countercultural, blocked) must be secured. Consequently "MAN" becomes a repeated term of praise and affirmation. Creeley's appreciation of Olson's poems puts a good deal of emphasis on gender: "in this ICH ['In Cold Hell'; a pun on 'I' in German], you damn well have *possessed* yrself [. . .] you make an entity, a substance, as finely & surely a MAN as anything I've ever got to"

(VI: 151, 18 July 1951). Creeley praises "La Chute" similarly: "it is, male, distinctly, & will, is also, male. Or, to say it better: this is *male will*. Ok! One can't expect the ladies to enjoy it" (VIII: 21, 5 October 1951). The two wives have indeed resisted the terms in which this poem is praised (not necessarily the poem). Ann McKinnon Creeley is cited: "'Sure it's *male*, but does THAT make it good . . . '" In a comic masculinist coup de grâce, Creeley says that even David (born 1947, now four, but a boy) saw its excellence right off (VIII: 21).

Creeley's poem "The Awakening" dedicated to Olson is a serious and complex work in seven quatrains, beginning with a "small" self who, seeing "his size with his own two eyes," may be an image or dream image of a very young Creeley before his loss of one eye, thus at the moment of bodily intactness (Creeley 1982, 205). The interruption (shades of the strangers from Porlock—some sound occurs, a "door bell" or "telephone") by another story from a woman who also sees the morning and its greenness does not complete this dreamy, indeterminate space. What is the "conclusive concluding / to remote yearnings"? It is neither woman nor "God" (making an abrupt appearance). The resolution occurs when a "you" (presumably Olson) is also awakening, as if in a hospital of hurt, wounded, and disabled men but able to declare motion, determination, and propulsion.

> only as I move, you also move to
> the awakening, across long rows, of beds,
> stumble breathlessly, on leg pins and crutch,
> moving at all as all men, because you must.
>
> (Creeley 1982, 205)

The bond around manhood and maleness clearly involved their mutual support to reject that woundedness, vulnerability, even a hint of an amputated leg. Each figure was the supplement, as against the Freudian notion of the "castration" that makes one a member of the order of sex-gender normalcy. The men in this depiction were as if prosthetic for each other in an all-male order.

3. "[T]he old Business of measuring me by Pound"

Creeley and Olson struggle to position and evaluate the modernist male masters, particularly Pound, but also Williams, Lawrence, and Eliot and, to a lesser degree, Crane and Stevens.[11] A short but precise canon emerges: Williams and Lawrence. Their main effort is to declare Pound's work retro and obsolete. Gertrude Stein might be deployed here to make an oblique comment: "Patriarchal poetry needs rectification and there about it. / Come to a distance and it still bears their name" (Stein [1927] 1980, 116). Olson writes about Pound after his twenty-four visits to St Elizabeths over the months between 1946 and 1948, recording the charisma, scattered mind, and stubborn, often scandalous opinions of that incarcerated poet as he awaited a hearing on the charge of committing treason by incitement during wartime (Maud 2008, 59–69). Olson was enraged and stunned at Pound's anti-Semitic and anti-immigrant opinions, as seen in his bitter satiric poems on Pound as well as in the angry, analytic letter about Pound's politics sent to him in 1948 (Olson 2000, 76). Olson's second-generation familial status provided a useful mechanism through which he tried to decathect from Pound. Olson reports that he cited his Swedish ancestors' name, knowing that to Pound the name would "sound" Jewish and would predictably lead to Pound's taunts. Olson alludes to this 1948 incident repeatedly in these letters.

Olson wrote notes about his visits, a memoir centering in 1946, a short coda in 1948, and several poems and essays dating from that postwar moment and the early 1950s. He differed from Pound politically; during his visits he tried to shake himself loose from the charms of that brilliant, impervious, insistent figure, from the attractive charms of another patriarch. Although Olson resisted personal contact after 1948, this correspondence returns repeatedly to *The Pisan Cantos* (1948) and to Pound as a figure. Is Pound now "'behind / the time'" (Olson to Creeley, I: 52, 27 May 1950)? Is he "drifting in the Cantos" (Creeley to Olson, I: 68, 1 June 1950)? Do *The Pisan Cantos* show only "the trillings, rather than the thrustings"?—a perfect little gender trope of feminine/effeminate versus male-coital claims (Olson to Creeley, I: 92, 9 June 1950). In short, and in the typographic pun/accident/slip that plays throughout Olson's letters—is Pound "Ex" rather than "Ez" (I: 92)?

Creeley continually challenges Olson to get over this rage—"YR MOVE, MR OLSON" (I: 107 [repeated on 108], 17 and 18 June 1950), asking "WHY get hung with this pettiness" and stating that Olson is not "cool" to take Pound's demagoguery seriously (I: 119; I: 120, 21 June 1950).[12] Creeley was neither directly enthralled nor revolted; his more temperate and cunning placement of Pound helped Olson disengage. But Creeley also translates the political rage to a family metaphor. Creeley adds oedipal fuel to this political critique by positioning them as "sons against real fathers: us against him, the old man. That's the fucking fight" (Creeley to Olson, III: 74, 3 October 1950). Pound's energy and method are still essential; having a "reaction" against him (still using a Poundian vocabulary) "is going to throw you back to the Georgians" or to general "looseness" (III: 75, 3 October 1950). Hence negotiating one's difference within a general similarity of poetics is a key task—the same challenge that Zukofsky faced. Yet Pound (an unrepentant fascist and one with neo-fascist epigones—but ones, like Darren Simpson, with printing presses) remained a fraught, strained case.

Olson's critique both of *Paterson* and of the *Cantos* focused on their "non-archaic" presentation.[13] In *Paterson*, Williams has (according to Olson) allowed for only "NON-ARCHAIC facts—documentation," and so the work is "thin and quaint" (VII: 69, 8 August 1951; sent to Louis Martz and Creeley).[14] Creeley's critique of Olson's thinking is based on an entirely opposite principle, rejecting the archaic vision on which Olson founded his poetics (VII: 102, 16 August 1951). Creeley lists his three main principles deftly: "1) [. . .] one thing is everything; 2) an attention is the only instrument; 3) nothing remains but what is" (VII: 94, 14 August 1951). Precisely this last principle articulates a counterposition to Olson's archaicism, which is based on the proposition "that something *is* present we have denied ourselves use of, even though we are its last extension" (VII: 94). Creeley states that "to be always here, and never a thing of all times, or places, etc. I can't stand that [latter] thought" (VII: 96, 14 August 1951). This actual, if nonantagonistic, debate about the archaic versus the sense of present presence marks a serious distinction of poetics.[15]

About a decade later a literary history was built to conform to this tendentious version of a break with past poets. Olson convinces Donald Allen, who is editing *The New American Poetry* (1960), not to include any older-generation writers as "smudging the point" and demands the presentation of a major historical and poetical break in 1950 corresponding to the beginnings of his correspondence with Creeley and their careers. No "aunties" or "grandpas" will give the "company" any familial/filiative past; links to older modernists are unexamined in this vision of a historical rupture with Olson as its head (Olson 2003, 59–60).[16] In his 1993 introduction to his edition of the *Selected Poems of Charles Olson*, Creeley also speaks of the year 1950 as an epochal break, symbolized by a shift in gender relations between men:

What changes immensely in the few years separating Williams'
Paterson from Olson's *Maximus* is the literal configuration of that
world which each attempts to salvage. All previous epistemological
structures and, even more, their supporting cultural referents were
displaced significantly, if not forever, by the political, economic, and
technological transformations following the Second World War. The
underlying causes were well in place at the turn of the century but by
1950 the effects were even more dominant. There could no longer be
such a "father/son" disposition of reality as either Pound or Williams,
tacitly, took as a given of their situation. (Creeley in Olson 1993, xviii).

It is hard to know how to gloss Creeley's "epistemological"—a change
in knowledge and ways of knowing might be taken to emerge from Olson's methods of poetic and historical research by a vatic inspiration and
tendentious new historicism, focusing whole eons via symbolic elaboration of specific documents. Both Olson's endless ruminative organicist
poetry (poetry as ongoing meditation) and his mythopoetic historical
ideas might have been the warrant for such a claim by Creeley. The epistemological loyalty to a new sense of vatic, enthusiastic method is visible in the ability of a cadre to continue Olson research well through the
1970s in the ongoing "Curriculum of the Soul" project. An attitude toward the instrumentalization of knowledge also comes through fiercely
in Olson's blistering rejection of the parasitic scholarship of the Melville
industry in "Letter for Melville 1951"—a critique that could be extended
to any professionalization of research on literature, in contrast to a poetic
investment in it (Olson 1997, 233–241).

Throughout his life, Creeley continued to honor and champion the
achievements of Olson's thirty-year poetic career. Further, he continued
to establish (in part in Olson's name but also evoking Zukofsky, Duncan,
and others) what he called, fondly, "the company," a mobile, elastic, and
continually increasing set of (apparently) like-minded practitioners and
critics. Once connected, you could never be expelled from this group;
nor did you particularly want to be. The company—not innocently but
with a latter-day sweetness—might well overlook particular abrasions,
discrepancies, and conflicts among its members, including the demo-
graphics of gender. This company takes shape in the early letters with
bitterness, rancor, some antihomosexual prejudice (mainly from Olson),
judgments of other men's manhood, and an exclusive and expulsive
fervor. Creeley's concept of "the company" modulated dramatically,

eventually including a few women and generally losing its rancor (see Faas with Trombacco 2001, on Duncan and Corman, 86–87).[17] This company is sometimes expressed or fueled by a reading list on which Olson always figured largely (Creeley 1989, 108–109).[18]

Creeley particularly emphasizes Olson's alternative modes of professionalism—Olson was an avatar of the 1960s revolt against powerful invested authorities that drain meaning and liveliness from texts and stances; "such perverse professionalism is a condition he attacks all his life, and in every possible context" (Creeley in Olson 1997, xiii–xiv).[19] This, too, is part of the role of the company—it provided a credentialing system alternative to the norm and, in Creeley's many book blurbs, a genial seal of approval. To understand this gender bolus as a protest against the increasing standardization and bureaucratization of society in the 1950s, the increasingly rigid career ladders, is to offer empathy to males for a loss of what they felt was their (perhaps always mythical) freedom. Michael Davidson speaks of this as a crisis of agency in the 1950s; the compensation was that challenges to the norm helped to shift norms (Davidson 2004, 8–9). Intellectual independence, guerrilla raids on the archives, and alternative socialities—this was the Olson mode in Creeley's presentation of it. The outsider status that these men of the 1950s felt—their marginality, energy, desire, their alternative positions on form (as ongoing activity that discovers its own order), on subjectivity as an energy source, the choice "to move in the field of its recognitions," on content as declared by what was at hand—was a breakthrough of poetics that Creeley staked his career on encouraging and sustaining (Creeley 1989, 94; written 1967).

Hence Creeley's comment on male-male coequality and the loss (in his hopeful view) of patriarchal "father-son" poetic relations among men raises many ancillary questions. First, this shift in gender materials is imagined (and imaginary?) only within male-male relations; there is no comparable curiosity about women and their situation. Second, these male-male relations are now presumably nonauthoritarian, horizontal, dialogic, egalitarian, fraternal, sometimes even maternal, and neither law-bearing nor invested with the issue of oedipal challenge and replacement. This would be completely revolutionary if true. But even if not true, only sporadically true, or rarely true, the statement indicates some of the transformative, utopian gender claims at stake for Creeley. So, finally, Creeley's version of this new egalitarian world for male gender in poetry is proleptically supported by his selection of Olson's poetry, particularly by his exclusion of two of Olson's most important poems: "I, Mencius, Pupil of the Master . . . ," a reading of Olson's relationship with Pound as poetic patriarch, and "The Lordly and Isolate Satyrs," a poem of hypermasculinity and hierarchic ranking.[20] That is, Creeley excluded from his anthology two magisterial poems that would most dramatically have undercut the case he was making and at least would show Olson's own contradictions with and debate about patriarchal plenitude.

4. Rhetorics

Given their exciting and productive fraternal-maternal compact and correspondence, Creeley and Olson yearned to meet each other but did not actually do so (IX: 45, 17 January 1952). As Robert Duncan remarked later, "[I]t was really their adventure, between Olson and Creeley, and it took place in their correspondence" (Duncan 1980, 14). Did their mutual projections produce such an intensely imagined second self that they experienced disillusionment and readjustment when they did finally meet? Or did the sense of intimacy carry through? When the two are together at last at Black Mountain College in March 1954 and confronted with speaking directly to each other, they are at first relatively taciturn and telegraphic; in the correspondence, a different "voluble" rhetoric had been shaped.[21]

So Olson and Creeley were mail-order males, each benefiting from a lively projection of the other. Throughout, their language and rhetorics are enormously streaming, very intimate, and (as George Butterick says) "jumpy" (III: viii). The letters are almost unreadable in allusiveness, in shifts of topic, and in encoded, skitterish, unfinished thoughts, in breathy, stuttering awkwardness, and in emphasis of words by anomalous punctuation, page space, spasmodic capitalization, elision, wildly incomplete enthusiasms and bursts. That is, the rhetorical pulse and the constant emotional volatility and changeableness are feminine by every normative stereotype. The rhetoric serves as an expressive protest against the business letter, the draining of personality and passion that a conventional professional career demanded.[22] This rhetoric is also decisively active—epistolarity as action writing. The language leaves no doubt that this relationship is filled with an erotic, semiotic energy.

The text itself, with its feminine or effeminate "enthusiastic" and expostulary rhetoric, is the zone of gender appropriation and queerness, as male writers engage a breathless, tumbling sound. This is in precise

contradistinction to Olson's rhetorically hypotactic and elegant epistolary bond with Edward Dahlberg, who had formerly assumed the powerful, demanding, and unpleasant role of Olson's paternal mentor.[23] The
rhetorical contrast of the two correspondences is striking: the Olson-
Creeley bond and Olson's letters to Cid Corman are more tonally, rhetorically, and emotionally similar to the Olson-Boldereff letters than to
the Olson of most of the Dahlberg letters. Indeed, when Olson jumps
modes in writing to Dahlberg, in a letter of invective and hysterical panache, Dahlberg calls attention to his protégé's rhetoric with great disdain (Olson 1990, 178–179, 8 November 1950).

At the same time, the local rhetoric and the diction rather than the
organization and general swoop are strongly tough and masculine (by all
conventional stereotypes). Their feelings of anger, hostility, anguish, resentment, and rage are expressed by various seriocomic desires to "fuck
it," "KILL EM," and "kick them where they should have balls" (refer-
ring to the editors of *Nine* and of *Golden Goose*) (Creeley to Olson, II:
54, 5 July 1950; Olson to Creeley, II: 88, 31 July 1950).[24] Whenever any
work is rejected, the offending little magazine editors become instantly,
definitionally nonmasculine, while the poets' pulp magazine macho language makes them supermen rhetorically, if rejected professionally. Bra-
vado, mockery, spitting as expulsion are all at stake. Repeatedly using
a (then) taboo word casually in a fond, emphatic manner also projects
maleness; it helps that "fuck" is etymologically close to "strike" (Easthope
[1986] 1990, 94–95). Another favorite Creeley epithet is "damn"—an all-
purpose expletive, interjection, adjective, phatic cheer, or disparaging
put-down (depending on context), a word both thoroughly expressive
and quite indeterminate. It is often an expression of anger, impatience,
a shrugging off of hurt or meanness. It is a word without precision, the
expression of a feeling without an acknowledged cause, and in many
ways it is perfectly poised between male toughness and the risk of a self-
disclosure and trust: because the actual feeling is unspoken, the affective
content remains oblique.

"I believe a man talks best straight and going out to another," said
Olson to Creeley (Olson 2000, xv, 5 July 1950). Straight?—this is heartfelt and double. The path is straight; and, of course, this erotics of poesis
needs to affirm its conduct through frank, honest talk, but its "straight
talk" is the first protection, against any homosexual implication. One sees
in their epistolary rhetorics an attempt imperially to claim all the available gender territory—feminine and effeminate excitements, masculine

(and hypertaboo) diction—but some care is taken to disparage and re-ject homosexual inflections, despite their rhetorical presence.

The fates of these rhetorics indicate gender shifts in Creeley's later processing of his bond with Olson. "Nor his disciple ever," Creeley says in 1997 about Olson and himself, not "sidekick or straight man." He con-tinues, "We had to be equals, which is really what Olson here says to all who read him" (Creeley in Olson 1997, xi). To experience the call of poetic citizenship or affiliative coequality in "Projective Verse," however, one had to ignore the exhortation to boys, to identify as an honorific boy, or perhaps both—all stances that put an interrogative twist in the invita-tion to active poetic vocation that this seminal essay incited.

The only hint of any defensive feeling from Creeley about Olson comes in 1997, upon the occasion of Creeley's (easily) thirteenth essay on Olson, the introduction to the *Collected Prose*. The first sentence is "I have no apology to make for the friendship with Charles Olson that, veritably, changed my life" (Creeley in Olson 1997, xi). Why, in the event, even evoke the word "apology"? There is a related verbal-ideological change. At this point in his reception of Olson, Creeley was more prone than before to emphasize Olson's word "human" and the "fact of our common humanity" (about Olson's reception and his readers' position), to state "what we've made humanly of the experience of living" (xv), and to evoke "men and women" together, carefully adducing both Duncan (cited a good deal) and Elaine Feinstein (xii). These verbal choices con-trast with those made earlier by Creeley—the Creeley of many of the other twelve essays, who is insistent on the use of the word "man" in both its ambiguous (human) and unambiguous (male) senses.[25]

That is, when Creeley writes about Olson throughout his career, from an essay in 1951 to the introduction to Olson's *Collected Prose* (1997), any discussion of maleness and gender materials is almost irrelevant to him. But the term "man" is continuously and unself-consciously used, with very few exceptions, to mean everyone, but especially men (mainly because that's who "everyone" is).[26] This was, of course, common at the time. Very few people in 1953 would have pointed, with any rhetorical emphasis, to the relevance of a certain work in poetry ("In Cold Hell, in Thicket") "for any man, or woman," but Creeley in fact did (Creeley 1989, 100; written 1953). This rare example of bigendered diction was some-what authorized by the expressed anguish over females and the verbal articulation of coequal genders in this early Olson work. These two gen-ders ("any man, or woman"), however, are in the position of receiving work as readers; the makers of such work are more often denominated as "men."[27] That is, in Creeley's early writing on Olson, poems are "the modulation of a man's attentions"; parts of the outside world "can come into a man's own body"; a geographical "place in a given man" may be articulated so it may be made "present, and actual for other men" (Creeley 1989, 104–105; written 1953); that this essay concerns *The Maximus Poems 1–10* bolsters the gender insistence.

5. Olson's –Ism: Phallus Is This

Olson is generally considered to have concerns with the "polis."[28] But Olson was a disenchanted New Deal liberal. He rejected the left and was contemptuous of Communist thought and of the residue of Popular Front thinking that could be traced among friends such as Ben Shahn.[29] Yet he came of age in the era of the Popular Front, with its cultural efflorescence and radicalism. Olson took and personalized or privatized (and, in a nonce word, "genderized") the broad goals of Popular Front thinking about a "cultural front." He retracked that concept to a far smaller group of forward-looking, spirited male artists who were pioneering cultural analysis, making anticommercial art products, intervening in social and stylistic debates, forming parallel institutions with "ways of seeing and judging, canons of value," and affirming a community-based aesthetic (Denning 1996, xx). The Olson formation rejected "the 'corporate' or 'multi-national' liberalism of Roosevelt's historical bloc," particularly as it was downgraded to Harry Truman as a figurehead and to the first moments of postwar neo-liberalism; Olson also has some inchoate sense of working-class radicalism, particularly as personified in his father's labor struggles against bureaucratic impositions (see Denning 1996, 464).

Yet Olson claims that he is antihumanist, anti-Communist, anticapitalist (the list becomes overgeneralized, but he rejects both the Popular Front and its opponents). For example, he avers that communism is another version of humanism: "all summaries, consolidations, generalizations, all things drawn off from the particularism which is local to the time of its existence" (VII, 25–26, 30 July 1951). His New Deal ethos, as Robert von Hallberg exactly notes, meant his respect for "executive leadership" (von Hallberg 1978, 12). It is consistent with the political "ism" that he claimed: that "extraordinary individuals will produce a new society" (with the Boldereff letters now known to scholarship, saying "extraordinary [male] individuals" might be more accurate; von

Hallberg 1978, 124). Olson wants to generalize from physical maleness into political power by claiming organic or physiological warrant.

Olson was visited by the Federal Bureau of Investigation in 1952, both as a former employee of the U.S. government and as the rector of Black Mountain College. The FBI agents were trying to investigate the possible leftist associations of those with whom he had worked; he thought, in contrast, that he was being vetted for a Fulbright Fellowship to Iran, and his fear that he might now be "restrained inside" his own country gave him a resentful, yet heroic frisson (IX, 71). His government portfolio had included organizing potentially volatile immigrant communities into support of the war effort on the U.S. side. He might have known leftists or Communists in government service (such affiliations had been legal, of course, until the 1940 Smith Act). He was also suspect as an administrator of an arguably left-wing, certainly countercultural college.[30] Yet his protest against this intimidation in the guise of investigation was not socially or politically oriented (as political resistance) but seen metaphysically within gender politics (IX, 69–77, 1 February 1952). Therefore he does not allude to feeling any common cause with others against this political pattern of antileftist harassment. He registers the menace of J. Edgar Hoover's department to freedom of association and freedom of thought; however, the specificities of any political struggles against this investigative intimidation are not in his arsenal of discussion. Olson maintains a me-against-them heroic analysis: he has met "perjorocracy" face to face; his rights to freedom of thought have been violated. That is accurate, but he does not go further.

Indeed, Olson feels that he was "called (on) (for) I WAS CALLED" in the sense of manifesting his vocation, to face "these two lies, COME TO MY DOOR!" (IX: 73, 76, 1 February 1952). And he analyzes this visit as further exemplifying that rupture in U.S history, just before the Civil War, in which "the MALE principle did itself in" by believing in two "LIES" (precisely personified in these FBI agents)—the fatedness of nature, by evolution, and the fatedness of the state, by modernity's versions of total systems, whether capitalism or communism (IX: 73; also by "perfection, & progress" VIII: 216). To understand this, one must appreciate Olson's resistance to any philosophy of (in his terms) social or psychological determinism. Freud is placed with Marx—as (Hebraic) overgeneralizers and determinists. In their theories limning how men/people act in general, they offer no account of exceptionalist genius beyond system: they are inadequate to the particular "single human person's act" done out of "PARTICULARISM" (VIII: 217, 216, 1 December 1951; see also 213–214). Olson tried, by radical individualism, seriously to escape necessity, the sense that subjectivity is variously mediated. Any tinge of determinist thinking or control over individualist freedom of thought or "conjecture" is, for Olson, a violation of "MALE energy" (IX: 74).[31] Further, since men are "metaphysically creative" but women are creative "physically" (they give birth), any passing thought that these different creativities imply positions that do not necessarily mesh with "corresponding sexual parts" is quickly overridden (IX: 74, 1 February 1952).

Hence for Olson the FBI visit is not so much an act of political violation based on an unconstitutional misuse of state power as it is a sex-gender violation of male energy and creativity.[32] It is also a violation of the "act & art" of the poet, who is the only cultural (and national) force going "forward" (IX: 86, 2 February 1952). This is interestingly reductive, or monofocal, showing the degree to which sex-gender regimes and poet "as hero" were at the center of his thought at this time (IX: 81, 2 February 1952). Hence Olson wanted to affirm an -ism that would replace the general and controlling aspects of politics in contemporary culture and reinterpret both history and human agency, an –ism alternative to "the biggest shit-piles modern life offers: racism, fascism, collectivism, 'Americanism,'" and of course humanism (IX: 141, 19 February 1952).

This -ism was "phallicism." It was not simply a sex-gender affirmation but operated for Olson as a political ideology. This political philosophy is set forth in a letter of 19 February 1952 (IX: 135–144). It is beyond sexuality, beyond sexual satisfaction in both genders, as being more "inclusive"—which I take simply to mean pro-eros (IX: 136). Any religion (like Judaism) or any civilization (like "the Hebraic") that "lacked any phallicism, or at least any phallicism of interest to me" is problematic (IX: 137). "[T]he PHALLIC is / ALL we are & do, & SEX / that PART itself only" is his oblique notation (IX: 141). So the phallic is (male) will or individual agency driven by a powerful desire akin to sexual arousal but beyond it; it cannot be (female) will by default of its name and the female cultural position, not to speak of Olson's own striking ambivalence to female agency, but it can be human will, insofar as a metaphor from maleness stands in for all.

Olson made a transition between collective social action and resistance, affirmative ideologies, and political programs and a position that depended on that erotic potency that he recognized as the root of all creative action (from Lawrence on), the male-based communities that could be built by affirming this power, leading to personal affirmation and creative transformation. It is as if a purely sexual (sex-based) politics could stand in for and replace a sociopolitical politics. The organicism and archaic structures of sexuality validated this position, in his world-view. In this Cold War and McCarthyite context of binary positions, it seems a gigantic substitution of a mythopoesis for a political response, a way of avoiding serious social contradictions and public debate.

The phallic is a totalizing system—but in what does it consist? Having no "sexual deformations," no "sexual failings" (IX: 137, 136), is certainly important; it is a cheering thought to be, by definition, anti-impotence (the potential for physical potency compensates for political *échec*, one might venture). A sense of heterosexual manhood goes absolutely without saying; indeed, homosexuality is probably the "sexual deformation" that he notes. The phallic is a zone of authenticity, of actuality, of the real and the ineffable at once (IX: 167, 25 February 1952). And finally it is the guarantor, as Barrett Watten noted in 1985, of "a psychologically elaborate topography"—"a kind of 'dream time'" in Olson's poems, fabricated from an endless ongoing sound of continuous self-creation. It cannot be based in or finished within thetic statement but posits the seminal pulse of male-poet creativity as the pulse of history and time itself (Watten 1985, 127, 131, 134). Olson's oeuvre's mesh of fragment in projective incompletion is guaranteed by the actual phallic body of the poet himself; that is where form is found.

This thinking on "phallicism," vague as it is, becomes one of a piece with the proposal of a "redefinition of the reactivation of THE HUMAN CONSCIOUSNESS" that would avoid all "dogmatic" and subservient relations to existing –isms (IX: 207, 208, 30 March 1952). This consciousness authenticates "authority" through the body and through affectual sensation, particularly led or given credibility by a platonic ideal of the penis. This vaguely delineated attitude (to which I have applied Olson's term "phallicism") is poised bravely (unbelievably?) against all the political -isms of the historical moment (IX: 210, 30 March 1952). No position except phallicism allows men to exercise free will, energy, agency, and—this is remarkable—freedom from social, economic, biological, historical, psychological constraints. It is a libertarian position. For all the historical claims he made, in this particular, Olson sought some primal element of validation beneath history and its effects.

This articulation of political phallicism is a step back from a rather more self-critical set of thoughts on the same issue in a ten-page letter

written in October 1951, just a few days before the birth of Olson's first
child. This letter offers an intellectual but also ineffectual credo, because
it is a credo on which he, finally, did not act. Olson claims that the mind-
body split, Plato's partitions, and intellect separated from both sexuality
and our embodied gender all are false. Olson is trying to stand for embodiment, yet not for the overvaluing of (again another binary) either
sexuality or mind. Thus he proposes that Lawrence makes "an overstate-
ment of the phallic" to state his case for embodiment overly strongly but
that "it is now necessary to be as chary of separating the phallic as it has
been the custom of the enemy [abstract thinkers] to separate sex" (VIII:
75, 20 October 1951).[33] So he presents a theory of embodiment that does
not belong only to men but to all. Abstract thinkers have done humanity
a disservice with the mind-body binary. An investment in maleness (the
phallic) does humanity a disservice by investing in one gender's eroticism
only. Unfortunately, his undoing of one binary (the mind-body split) did
not carry over into an undoing of another binary (male-female) under
the overarching rubric of eros. This is yet another moment of ideological
possibility and loss.

For Olson did not end up with this position; finally, sex-gender difference meant sex-gender hierarchy, not total human eros. Certainly the
bond in these letters with Creeley avoids hierarchy; it is a lateral, fraternal, frank, emotionally and intellectually generative exchange with few
disagreements or power plays. Further, in Olson's sketchy restructuring
of Western intellectual history, he has some very critical words for "the
master-disciple biz" and for "the 'great man' not as leader of the state
or of society but as leader of ethical, metaphysical, intellectual & religious sects or movements—and I have this feeling, that all this, too, is
WRONG" (VIII: 70, 20 October 1951). The abstractions and systematizing of a "Confucius" are as problematic as "Dionysus, or Priapus," that is,
as pure sexuality or lust (VIII: 75, 20 October 1951).

Yet at the same time, there is a fundamental, riven contradiction between Olson's ideas and Olson's behavior on the topic of master-disciple
relationships. This is another moment of possibility and loss. What made
Olson's actual behavior so out of line with his announced propositions?
Perhaps it was power—a minipolis of his own at Black Mountain, a zone in
which he could flourish, make suggestive and wide-ranging claims, experiment intellectually—all with a high-flying sense of expansive possibility.
That is, the zone of power in which he became a charismatic star undermined his principled rejection of hierarchy in "the master-disciple biz."

For in his pedagogy Olson generally created the kind of hierarchical structure with which he had already announced serious ethical
disagreement. Olson's resistance to men with a system, to their analytic
abstraction and their charisma, seems to have transformed itself just a
few years later at Black Mountain into exactly the opposite—into Olson
the patriarch, Olson the charismatic leader to whom a person surren-
dered, Olson the colonizing authority (Duberman 1972, 213, 214, 295,
320, 368). Olson encouraged, created, and sustained a cult of personality,
a court, in which his approval mattered, his anger was transformative or
devastating, his temperamental shifts kept attention focused on himself,
where his interests were defining and his agendas central (Duberman
1972, 347; see Levertov in Duncan 2004, 504, letter from 1965). Michael
Rumaker also remarks the degree to which Olson has made his Black
Mountain teaching the apogee of a paternal malehood, with himself cast
as the Wise Man in a Jungian map of types, "spiritual father" to "the
lost sons" (Rumaker 2003, 141). Students sought Olson's approval, even
his "love," by remembering his obiter dicta, by tracking his reading and
his enthusiasms, and—more ambiguously for the role of the teacher—by
following his conflicted and hierarchical attitudes to women.

Not only is this actual master-disciple relation different from Olson's
announced theory for such bonds, but this structure exists in further
contradistinction to his critique of key ethical leaders (Christ and Bud-
dha) who have wrongly "come to the notion that they must reject woman
in order to take on god!" "Their overt demon is SEX (woman, when you
come to it, the thing they must degrade[)]" (VIII: 71, 20 October 1951).
Here Olson saw and theoretically rejected a ("wrong") structure of feeling in which he participated and which he even championed. Degrading
women was one of Olson's pedagogic practices. As Michael Davidson
and Charles Boer have already documented, women were hyperchal-
lenged and regarded with extra suspicion in Olson's classroom (Black
Mountain College), were explicitly barred/taunted or treated to sexual
innuendo (SUNY-Buffalo), were chased away with harassing/hazing remarks (University of Connecticut).[34] Olson was hardly alone in his era
in the university—there are plenty of parallel exclusionary or harass-
ing allegations about other (famous, infamous, or fatuous) professors
from many other institutions. Yet Olson's cultural leadership undoubtedly had a chilling effect on people who were not male, even after his
death. For example, Marjorie Perloff, trying simply to underscore that
Olson's stance "is just pretty hard for women to take," has been attacked

for explaining this (Perloff 1995, 36).[35] Females were cast as the Oedipal "prize" in the Crackerjack box, rather than being autonomous participants or actual protagonists in a cultural community. The interest of this particular point about sexist pedagogy, already made several times by several commentators, lies for me in the contradiction between Olson's principles and practices, his notable debates and yet his inabilities to put his more civic gender ideas into practice. For in Olson's case, the contradictions between his claims to critique those male leaders who "must reject women" and his actual actions as a male leader are startling. His emphasis on (male) will is thus a curiosity, an assertion, not an actuality. His ideas did not go into action.

At the same time, Olson was fascinated by the "sexually marginal" (that is homosexual) students—mainly male, for lesbians had a particularly difficult time at Black Mountain, according to Rumaker (IX: 62, 29 January 1952; Rumaker 2003, 445). The oddity here is seeing what Olson calls, in early twentieth-century terminology, "the Third Sex deal [as] just too goddamned EASY" (VIII: 185, 27 November 1951; he is speaking about Duncan). Given contemporaneous legal, political, institutional, and social strictures against homosexuality, the term "easy" is politically naïve. Olson's immediate evocation of the "Puritan" in himself suggests that he felt that a personal struggle for repression of that sexual impulse was what was hard; in contrast, giving in to that sexual/relational temptation was "easy." Homosexual men were a site of intensely contradictory feelings for Olson, who sometimes acknowledged his complex sexuality and a sense of queerness (as to Boer and to Rumaker) but just as often regarded homosexuality balefully. It was important to him that the "hermaphrodite" (or male homosexual) was mainly dishonorable; he was interested in the complex "androgyne." Olson used shifting terminologies for this point, and the terms are quite hard to track, but generally "androgyne" is a term of considerable approval for him (it emerges from both Melville and Jung). As "the potential for homoerotic pleasure was expelled from the masculine and located in a deviant group" (Connell 2002a, 253), the "purging" of masculine sexuality to uniform heterosexuality had a number of consequences for individual desires, fantasies, and their policing. Women as figures were the easy scapegoats for this irreconcilable set of conflictual, semiacknowledged sex-gender stresses as well as for Olson's specific pleasure as the cynosure for others, in the male-male erotics of poetic and intellectual community (cf. Rumaker 2003, 153). Olson's repression of women and his claims of power over actual women are measures of his resistance to the fascinations of the feminine, the androgyne, and erotic yearning around male epigones.

So we now know yet again the many ways in which Black Mountain under Olson was an exaggerated mirror of the 1950s, "a replica of the hierarchical and patriarchal order" (and homophobic order), "more so as Olson took over"—it just had more "wiggle room" than the society at large (Rumaker 2003, 188). Where gender hierarchy was concerned, where sexual preference was concerned, critique was sparse or absent. And we also know that somehow the imprint of Olson—his ideas, his rhetoric, his presence, his writing—is not "so much *read*, then, as *absorbed*, is not so much *interpreted* as *internalized*"; Carla Billitteri's words seem to be a very accurate description of Olson's visceral impact—what Barrett Watten named "the affect of presence" (Billitteri 2009, 134; Watten 1985, 125). This general framework has larger meanings for art and culture. If absorbing Olson did mean a profound realignment of one's sense of being and of thinking, reading, and writing, this realignment did not easily or idiomatically extend to reconceptualizations of sex-gender, particularly once Olson's own contradictions on those matters were resolved as they were. The introjection of Olson has been a fact in some alternative poetry, even a condition of its formation. This fact becomes part of a several-pronged ideology within poetic institutions: the repression or denial of female capacity for artistic and intellectual work combined with an appropriation to men of this capacity; accompanying this was a gigantic blind spot on the contradictory gender thinking of male figures, as if it had to be unspoken.

Olson's critique of classification systems in favor of "particularity" thus has this enormous contradiction: Olson himself assiduously deploys one of the most primary systems of classification—gender binarist divisions, a metaphysical division, in Julia Kristeva's terms.[36] Presumably, for him, absolute gender divisions were not the result of the errors of Greek systematizing but of a human reading of "nature." Yet it is interesting to focus on such a denial of specificity and particularity, despite the claim that, as Creeley articulated, Olson's "intelligence [. . .] cannot propose the assumption of content prior to its experience of that content" (Creeley 1989, 123; written 1966). Olson's thought about embodiment and "active and definitive engagement" with the real and his refusal of any closed system do not extend to the hierarchic system of gender difference, the disdain for female cultural participation, or the political system of homophobia (Creeley 1989, 122; written 1966).

In Page Dubois's description of what happened with genders in Greek culture, in the Socratic, Platonic, and Aristotelian ideological universes, man "stands for all human beings" and thereby "becomes the subject of philosophy and all intellectual life, rather than [simply] one half of the human race" (Dubois 1995, 93). Olson's vaunted critique of the negative cultural effect of Greek rationality, abstraction, logos, and intellectual generalizations is in fact inconsistent; he himself enacts the same arguments that it did, arguments that he claims to deplore and criticize. As Carla Billitteri incisively articulates, in his formulations about sex-gender, "Olson himself falls prey to *logos*, universalizing male experience and abstracting from it laws applicable to all forms of art or action" (Billitteri 2009, 126).

Olson helped to create and perpetuate a male separatist world in the Nation of Poetry. Such a world can be erotic, charming, and productive and give rise to notable art products, although such products may also be stylistically and ideologically marked and qualified. The male separatist community can also have problematic effects in the historical world in which people are brought up and educated, work, create, and form bonds. Olson certainly created a functioning community with his enormous and interesting cultural power, but he made it gender exclusive. He solved many of his intellectual and ideological contradictions about gender and sexuality with that exclusionary model. Olson hardly invented these matters, and (as I have noted repeatedly) he sometimes debated and self-questioned gender assumptions. However, he emphatically resolved all topical contradictions (and particularisms) by creating a monogendered universe of cultural action and by engaging in a charismatic performance of this monogendered, imperial, and patriarchal poetry, from which others learned, which others evoked—and which others sometimes eventually resisted.

6. Coda: Resisting "Patristic" Literary History

A key contemporaneous practitioner proposed a talismanic—and also vatic—alternative model of community. It would be a long task (not attempted here) to take up the historical turns of the conjunctures and clashes of Robert Duncan with Charles Olson, given this model of what Duncan called "an entirely patristic world" (Duncan 1995, 26).[37] Although he was admiring of Olson and his thought in many particulars and on many occasions, Duncan finally describes that world as involving first archaic/phallic energy rather than the energy of "the community of meaning that I [Duncan] see language as being"; it involves, temptingly, playing with the "enraptured" sound of poetry, dangerously and interestingly close in Duncan's imagination to rape (or, differently imagined, to penetration). Duncan's vision of Olson also gave rise to a pitiless critique of Olson just as he was dying, dismissing as delusion the sense that women (and his "live-her" cancer) belonged to his "interior schema." Olson thought that "his anima, his own feminine character," was troubling him, not a disease or, in Duncan's view, his lived relations with actual women (Duncan 1995, 41). While it is true that Duncan's *The H.D. Book* began in 1959 with a commission to honor H.D. from Norman Holmes Pearson, the work is inflected with a generally antimasculinist poetics of vulnerability and transformation that recontextualizes many male modernists. While engaged with Duncan's work of vatic cultural history and poetics, it is impossible not to contrast the contemporaneous Olson-inspired abjection and erasure of female cultural influence and potential that emerged in their shared poetic community. Duncan's picture of community emphatically and fundamentally includes female practitioners.[38] Hence *The H.D. Book* veers orthogonally from *Maximus* and from Olson's increasingly "entrenched masculinism" (Keenaghan 2009, 89). Olson's thought can be counterpoised against Duncan's as differing in its major gender assumption—though both poets are, of course, encyclopedic, sublime, metapoetic, engaged in vatic claims of cultural discovery.

Duncan weaves Olson into his visionary work, but on Duncan's own particular terms. Olson is mentioned repeatedly within the great collective project of poesis that *The H.D. Book* articulates: a rejection of normative masculinity, a refusal of a monogendered culture, an intense rewriting of literary history, a heterodox collage of romance, quest, and spiritual striving beyond any monotheistic covenant. Duncan poses comparabilities and juxtapositions continually: H.D., Williams, and Olson; Olson, H.D., and Jean Cocteau; Olson, Moore, and H.D.—his rhetorical segues write Olson in didactically among a peer group including female cultural actors. It is not a domestication of Olson but an act bringing Olson into a configuration under alternative premises. These premises rest on "mothering language" and "The Great Mother" (Duncan 2011, 525, 526). These are hardly secular premises, of course, and they point to a world different from modernity, with its extractive, materialist, exploitative realities.

The first chapter of Duncan's book is a *Bildungs*-narrative as portal to these concerns. Duncan reads a lyric of H.D. through the intellectual generosity of a female teacher in high school. Drawing on this source, he passes to a carefully articulated allegorical turning point. It is the moment when, buoyed by two female stereotypes—the scintillating Jew and the generous Italian—and while responding to a poem by James Joyce that he reads aloud to them on the lawn between college classes, the young Duncan finds the courage to reject many hegemonic aspects of male subjectivity. He refuses to march in a required Reserve Officers Training Corps (ROTC) exercise mustering at that very moment. He thereby questions society's preparation for and his participation in that always-already future war. Along with the critique of state militarism and its "compulsory authority," Duncan refuses a "prescribed [professional] career" and "caste" in favor of poetic authority. He resists all the elements of masculinity that moved one to the "seizure of power" in contradistinction to a less defined sense of inspiration, aesthetic-spiritual joy, and "true community" (Duncan 2011, 64, 66, 68). He refuses the staging of these social imperatives, particularly "War"—"as if only there we would prove our manhood" (Duncan 2011, 65). He has found another kind of "authority"—that poetic authority whose avatars included several women. His female friends, from these two cultures, certainly sentimentalized variously, were his "nurses" for that defining moment; this is his explanation of one of the multifoliate poetics of the book, as stated immediately in chapter 2: finding his life in poetry through the "agency of certain women" (Duncan 2011, 63, 69). This work of a sublime social imagination as a critique of normative masculinity may be counterpoised to Olson's narrower vision of communities of practice that also attempted imperially to transform masculinity but into a monogendered universe. Neither poet, however, grants full historicity to women; in both, a metaworld is idealized. In Olson, that metaworld of intellectual originality and synthesis is male property (despite Jane Harrison, Frances Boldereff, and others). In Duncan, the metaworld is pan-gendered, if also grandly, powerfully narcissistic. So while there is a mythologizing of women in Duncan, his attitude does not rest on a denial and eradication of their historical and cultural presence and power.

Seven

Wieners and Creeley after Olson

> *Patriarchal poetry partly. In an as much to be in exactly their measure.*
> *Patriarchal poetry partly.*
>
> GERTRUDE STEIN, "PATRIARCHAL POETRY"

1. *WOMAN* in "A Curriculum of the Soul"

In 1972 the poet John Wieners published his contribution to "A Curriculum of the Soul," an Olson-inspired project continued by Jack Clarke,
Albert Glover, and George Butterick after Olson's death in 1970 and centered on key Olson topics.[1] The Wieners pamphlet is called *WOMAN*;
later it was called "Women."[2] The differences between a title in the singular (including capitalization) and a title in the lowercase plural are
enormous; the title in "A Curriculum of the Soul" (1972) is definitional
and generalizing; the title in *Cultural Affairs in Boston* (Wieners 1988)
offers one particularized and personal account. That the Olson-cenacle
"Curriculum of the Soul" pamphlet on woman was written by a gay man
is either the *reductio ad absurdum* of masculinist cultural separatism or
a proto-queer gesture without portfolio—or even both. It is certainly a
moment when, in Judith Butler's terms, "the binary system of gender
is disputed and challenged, where the coherence of the categories are
[*sic*] put into question"; but it is not clearly a moment that challenges the
"binary system of gender," because it is not backed up by a community
which desires "becoming otherwise" (Butler 2004, 216, 217). Wieners's
WOMAN therefore offers a fascinating, multifaceted, and also suspect
moment. The fact that access to the feminine aspects of "woman" occurs
through a sometimes transvestite homosexuality, not through women,
is a provocative proposition, if notably incomplete; it is obvious that access to cultural thinking on "woman" could plausibly come from women
themselves.

Homosexual men like John Wieners, with their legal and personal
vulnerabilities, are assigned and assume the expression of male vulnerability in general in a group of men who were themselves generally
nonhomosexual.[3] This was part of their fascination in a homosocial but

straight cenacle. When Creeley comes to praise Wieners (in his 1988 introduction to *Cultural Affairs in Boston*), he glosses Olson's remark about Wieners's "'poetry of affect,'" speaking of intense and articulate feelings, and "primary need" (frequently sexual materials, often gay encounters, a lot of drug activity, mental health questions, and the pain of addiction) (Wieners 1988, 11). So Wieners's intense emotional vulnerability and need are spoken of positively—the survival of a man-of-feeling being so rare. Creeley does not talk about the laws about gays (or about drug users or transvestites) but rather shows Wieners in the 1950s up against the atomic age without "shelter," as a way of indicating his danger and his defenselessness within a life of personal suffering. The dangers of the 1950s national political realm thereby get intermingled with (and serve as a metaphor for) sexual politics. Sexual and gender politics as such are alluded to only obliquely.

That the feminine and vulnerable have survived—in Wieners, in a man—is a cause for great celebration. To say it another way, vulnerability, struggle, pain, and challenge can always be stabilized rhetorically by words like "man"—such a word provides the assurances that can help authorize a man even of great woundedness. One begins to see how actual females are somewhat excrescent to this system of praise for male sensibility. Thus in such circles a gay man might be viewed as the person best equipped to discuss women as a general caste or group. It was a torqued way of acknowledging female vulnerability in their male-based system without directly confronting another zone of information—actual women speaking about themselves.

The early 1970s incipient moment of feminist cultural critique was probably not accessible to the progenitors of this "Curriculum" when they came to assign the pamphlet on *WOMAN*; the worlds of feminist analysis and poetics are now slightly more interwoven. After Olson's death in 1970, his world, still drawing on 1950s masculinity and 1960s critical propulsion, did not intersect, with one exception, with the worlds of early feminism. Catharine Stimpson was the exception; she explored the Olson world with a 1973 essay in a special issue of *boundary2* on Olson that pointed to his "domineering patriarchal bias" and went on to become a feminist scholar, editor, and administrator (Stimpson 1973–1974, 152). Early feminist critics, from about 1966 and through the 1970s, had proposed a serious critical approach to women/woman in cultural institutions—including narrative, authorship and the reception of women writers, debased Freudianism and the consumerist framing of women, the conflict between the historical position of women and the fixity of Woman, the ideologies of masculinity, the psycho-social construction of women, economic, legal, and political issues facing women, the institutions of everyday life like street harassment, and the rediscovery of neglected examples of female cultural work.

So it does seem symptomatic that the author of "A Curriculum of the Soul" pamphlet on WOMAN was John Wieners, though it is not that he does not have things to say. This assignment allows us to locate one late "end" of 1950s construction of masculinity—by which I mean both a marker of its chronological end or termination and a marker of its aims or goals. The pamphlet's authorship says that a woman could not write a general statement on WOMAN (or possibly that females in the Olson aura were asked but refused what might have been construed as a ghettoed assignment). Therefore, however interestingly "queer" this assignment is in our terms (and it emphatically is by accomplishing gender crossovers and by separating biological gender from mental constructs), still the authorship of the pamphlet is hardly an intentional prefiguration of the gender critiques of queer theory. It represents a homosocial compact between Olson, dead for two years, and Wieners as a gay author, made on the "body" of WOMAN.[4]

The camp tone of knowing inside out and outside in alludes constantly to the "device" of this pamphlet: a gay man (in both the drug world and the drag world) investigates WOMAN by assignment of the (unself-consciously) masculinist Olson circle. As Wieners says archly, "Working without guidelines here, I abjectly suspicion retrograde aspersions as to why I do not accept this Assignment as an insult" (Wieners 1972, 12). To call a man feminine or womanly is possibly an insult; to call a gay man feminine, Wieners plays as a compliment—and as a complement to the masculinity of others of interest both to himself as a man and to himself as a "woman." The joking about this assignment suggests a male terrain in which certainly women are not imagined as having analyses on their behalf, but where a feminine and femme man can be an important researcher into "woman."

The women eulogized by Wieners are dancers (Melissa Hayden, Vera Lorina), models in high fashion venues (Vogue and Harper's Bazaar), stars (Marlene Dietrich, Judy Garland, Greta Garbo, Lana Turner, and Ingrid Bergman—some, incidentally, lesbians), dancers, performers, all with a general aura of dynastic glamour, celebrity, and some sexual scandal. He also mentions female leaders (Senator Margaret Chase Smith), political figureheads like Queen Elizabeth and "Jacquelaine [sic]" Onassis, and a girl next door (Nancy Callaghan). The rich and the famous, those who marry for money but also have class and elegance, come in for praise, but the paraphrasable "message" of attitude or analysis is cast in a strange double-talk. The general tone is a tongue-in-cheek "adoration," the breathless identification and half-catty upstaging that we know by the name of camp. The "Curriculum of the Soul" "woman" is herself in female drag or camped up; this work generally does not concern women in daily life or the working world, except the world of high performance. Woman is more iconic than quotidian. The prose is a wry mocking of gossip column prurience, fashion magazine rhetorics, and romantic novels: "she has retained her lithe figure, lissome coiffure and marvelous charms, above and beyond any teen-school model" (Wieners 1972, 11). The fascination with woman is with the discipline of physical dressage (to use the exacting term of Susan Griffin 1978)—the training in a kind of bondage to the discipline of parading oneself and looking excellent; Wieners admires women's "meticulous control of private gestures," as if women are in a closet all their own (Wieners 1972, 3). Appreciating this closet of the female playing herself as "woman" does not extend to a critique of that closet or that performance.

Indeed, at times the pamphlet seems to be written by a gay "queen" figure who can barely aspire to the level of performative inauthenticity achieved by women who themselves "play" the part of woman with panache, possibly for the reason (covering their urgent wishes for masculinity) that Joan Riviere theorizes (Riviere [1929] 1989). This is probably the most interestingly convoluted moment: "the various aspects of women cause shimmering auras I would never arouse, from their odes, ballads and opus," displacing Wieners's own poetry to them as superior manipulators of performance and desire (Wieners 1972, 9). The work is ventriloquized by a subjectivity merging a "young prince of the United Kingdom" and "a president in the United States" with a "revered, though backward impression of woman, and especially women, who have pleased me, in public and, or in private" (Wieners 1972, 1). While that president has a JFK aura, it is also possible that Wieners intended the poetic community to understand Olson by that honorific: Olson was about to "run" for (or to be drafted for) President of Poetry at the Berkeley Poetry Festival.[5]

So what is this short pamphlet? It is a send-up of woman. It is a substitution of a gay man for a woman. It is a queering of woman or a queering of man. It is a devoicing of woman. It is the strange findings of a participant-observer researcher in verbal drag who simultaneously plays a woman. It reaffirms generally patriarchal poetic institutions by not having a "real" woman speak. It is an antihomophobic sucker punch on a masculinist poetic formation. It is simply a convenient, innocent, yet sly assignment by the coordinating committee. Men are somehow better women than women are themselves. That is queer enough but leaves men still superior in gender range, women as deficient once more.

As Wieners notes: "Dangerous, when a young man attains [women's] princeliness, pricelessness and precociousity" (Wieners 1972, 9). "Precociousity" imbeds "precious" and "precocious" and even "cock" in one summary portmanteau gesture. The coy "danger" is apparently his feminine, tempting pan-desirability to all gender sides. My less coy sense of the "danger" differs—it is the unconsidered sidelining of women speaking on the sex-gender system, on sexuality, and on themselves. The other danger? Patriarchal poetry is destabilized, perhaps ending, because it is so unevenly, so provocatively, so flirtatiously upheld by Wieners. Having a man perform a woman and having him say that women also perform themselves are positions that emphatically destabilize any illusion of natural gender.

The desire for impersonation and the possible female "princeliness" set forth make this essay a somewhat innocent but interesting precursor of another kind of gender crossing, the kind that motivated Boston feminists Roxanne Dunbar and Dana Densmore from the group Cell 16 to show a film in 1968 about female impersonators as a fund-raiser for the early women's movement (Densmore [1998] 2007, 77; Dunbar [1998] 2007, 99). Similarly, Wieners's work can function as a precursor of queer thinking, even if unintended as such. But it is also a symptom of the fact that masculinities may be remade in alternative poetry, "masculinities" could be ephebic, could get feminine, could dress in drag at will, could appreciate female performance; but "woman" was to be the same and was, in a sense, to be anywhere but in women, anywhere but from women. Indeed, the gay voice is mobile, precisely queer, more sardonic about the feminine yet more desirous of some of its effects than even a sample nonfeminist woman might have been in 1970–1972, for this work has something in common with the camp excess of female gameplayers like Helen Gurley Brown. Wieners speaks, finally, like any queer postmodern, from a transvestite sensibility about *WOMAN*, without the social cost of actually being a woman who functions inside systems of male privilege and masculine ideologies.

2. The Hole: Death, Sexual Difference, and Gender Contradictions in Creeley's Later Poetry

In *The Disorder of Women*, Carole Pateman discusses the parallel, unmeeting tracks of political theory (her field) and its feminist critique (her position), locating, again and again, political theory's blind spot to the struggles of women and to their analytic findings. Pateman argues that "citizenship has been made in the male image"; analogously, citizenship in the poetry community has been made, by the activities detailed in this book, in the male image. Hence my argument that, similar to political theory, poetic practices need "radical transformation" (Pateman 1989, 14). It is interesting to identify a little glimmer of this possibility in the latter part of Creeley's career.

Creeley had a long career and toward the end showed some tendency to begin to consider other sex-gender materials and materials on male embodiment beyond his work in the 1950s and 1960s. Vulnerability is still an important ground note, but Creeley modulated from the privileges of male vulnerability into something a little different and critical. The books *Life & Death* (1998a), *Just in Time* (2001), and *If I Were Writing This* (2003) reveal that Creeley, at about the age of seventy-two, started thinking hard about the ways it feels to be on the downward side of his life; he would die at seventy-eight after a writing career of about fifty years, but still too soon. With that consummate spin on colloquialisms for which Creeley is famous, "just" in that second title means living precisely, exactly, simply, certainly, come as you are, in time—poised in time, as Creeley was always poised and in motion in the poetry. Creeley's meditations on death and its surround involve reiterated questions, extensions of the ethical questions about time that he asked continuously throughout his life—how to use this time; how to be situated in time; how, in his particular offbeat way, to catch the beat.

"Common," a term in Creeley's later lexicon, expresses a contradiction between masculinity and personhood. "Common" signifies human; it is implicitly a critical view of gender binarism. The word "common" offers a position beyond gender polarization but retaining some male privilege—or just the accrued privilege of being a rather important poet, which is a status itself achieved with some deploying of maleness (and a lot of exquisite writing). In his last years, Creeley articulated feelings about entering the common place, the common experiences, being "just" like everyone else. He brought to this meditation all the twists and turns in consciousness for which he is well known, the semantic images, the deictic pointing, his sense of the forthcoming thereness of death (which is blank) and the present hereness of life (which is full)—affirmation and anxiety, plenitude and suspicion, all together. There is "I'm here / I'm still here," and there is "he counts his life / like cash in emptying pockets. / Somebody better help him" (Creeley 2001, 141; Creeley 1998a, 4). The poet announces the depression and the acceptance, the reluctance, the fore-knowledge, and the jaunty denial—"Not me's going!" (Creeley 1998a, 73).

Creeley also brought to this task his continuous checking on the body, its placement in time, in space, and in syntax (which served to summarize both of these others together), and his account of the body's function-ing and intactness—intactness and vulnerability being his long-standing themes.[6] As always, Creeley was precise, frank, and not squeamish about tracking shifts of consciousness and feeling, in the oscillation, pulses, and the balance/imbalance of syntax, line break, diction, and semantic image. Thinking was words, it was not contained in words: he concentrated on substance in the instant and instance of its articulation.[7] Far from being morbid, this recursive focus on age and even death is a triumph of secu-lar meditation; he had always thought about what his body was doing. Throughout his career, with all the perceptual turns, line break hinges, notational intimacies, Creeley tried to articulate the particularities of em-bodied experience and the intensities of proprioception (bodily aware-ness). These late books also contain many gnomic aphorisms, reminding us that epigram, epigraph, and epitaph are strangely related words. These genres call upon a very "Creeleyesque" Greek preposition, *epi-*, which seems, depending on the root/word it precedes, to mean on, upon, over, above, around, covering, to, toward, close to, next to, besides, in addition, after, and among. That (thanks to the dictionary) pretty much covers the territory of space and positionality in Creeley.

With these feelings about time, space, and writing, Creeley thereby practiced an art to "*undo* the alienation of the corporeal sensorium, to *restore the instinctual power of the human bodily senses for the sake of humanity's self-preservation*" (Buck-Morss 1992, 4).

This is a citation, a pretty apocalyptic one, actually, about Walter Benjamin's goals in "The Work of Art in an Age of Mechanical Reproduc-tion"; it comes from Susan Buck-Morss's analysis of the misrecognition in the concept of "aesthetics" itself. She argues that this term does not indicate the sublime triumvirate of Art-Beauty-Truth, and, in its damag-ing extension, the self-contained, untouched, often male body. Rather, she produces and affirms the original meaning of the term "aesthetic": the sensitive, the suffusion by feeling and sense perception. The return to the sensible/sensitive allows her to propose an aesthetic of receptivity that foregrounds the joining of subject and object (and other deictic locations—inside and outside, perhaps) in an artwork.

This anti-Kantian argument can frame three striking features of Creeley's poetry. First, he returns us to the local sensorium, thus resisting the organization of the body in modernity (but particularly in fascist and totalitarian modernity) that makes the body a cog in all-over, aestheticized design. This local and *sensible* is one value of poetry in general, one might argue, and Creeley's mode resists and rejects the realm of the "techno-body" to which Buck-Morss alludes, the body "divorced from vulnerability," the "statistical body," "the body enduring without pain," all linked to figurations of the male body, theorized as insensitive, unfeeling, armored (Buck-Morss 1992, 33). This part of his oeuvre (recall his letter praising male emotionality from the early 1950s) manifests a respect for vulnerability, extending his praise of male vulnerability in Wieners.

Second, given Marx's concept of phantasmagoria—a world of attractive commodities constructed to conceal every trace of the labor and social relations it took to produce them—Buck-Morss's analysis could point to Creeley's hesitations, his negotiations of syntax, and the simplicities of his word choices as rejecting the blandishments of phantasmagoria (Buck-Morss 1992, 25). Creeley unconceals poetic and human labor by tracking the particular; this is his ethical, aesthetic, and political goal.

Third, Creeley attends to smallness, to intimacy, to the little words. He rescales away from monumentality whenever he can, even while his most notable companions—Olson, Duncan—do not, or certainly do not overtly. He wanted to stay within the pitch of the minor, the trivial, the connection of one to one.

On this topic, Creeley says something quite witty—not to speak of commenting on many of his boon companions such as Edward Dorn, Olson, Duncan, and others of epic scope—by calling one of his later poems "Epic." The poem is also a proleptic account of his own death and absence. "Save some room / for my epic," the poem begins, and it produces that epic briefly but generously.

•

Absence makes
a hole.

> •
>
> Any story
> begins somewhere
>
> and any other story
> begins somewhere else.
> •

(Creeley 1998b, 78)

Here is the hole of loss, absence, and death. And now we need the story—or at least part of a story.[8] To be a self is to be a gendered self. Yet what does that mean in practice? And how, as a writer, does one practice this? I have noted that Elspeth Probyn proposes that "a gendered self is constantly reproduced within the changing mutations of difference. While its sex is known, the ways in which it is constantly re-gendered are never fixed or stable" (Probyn 1993, 1). She is talking exclusively about women, and she does so to construct "alternative feminist positions in discourse," especially in cultural studies, a project of great importance. However, if females are gendered selves, produced and reproduced and regendered, so are males. I have tried in this book to explore some re-gendering mechanisms and their qualified outcomes. Probyn's terminology tells its own qualified story. The preposition *re-* has two opposite meanings. One points to something happening, with the implication of its being refreshed, seen anew. Another points to restoration and reiteration. This tension between these alternatives seems particularly apt for the difficulty of really altering gender materials. Is the normative restored yet again? Is it jostled, seen afresh and perhaps changed? For this book, one question is particularly vivid: did anyone really change yet?

Creeley's insistence on the small, the common, even the trivial brings me, by cultural compact and association, to the gender-laden ground of oedipalization. The male story of the oedipal plot is a constitutive, conscious mythography for Creeley, not only a biographical drama but a site for poetic exploration. Creeley paid the ultimate price for whatever oedipal fantasies we must fantasize (following Freud) that small boys have: he got a sliver of glass in and lost the sight of his left eye (age two). He thereupon lost his father (to an early death in 1930; he was then four) and soon after (age five) suffered that traumatic kind of trickery formerly practiced on children—he was taken to the hospital without knowing why, and the blind eye was excised in order to save his sighted one (Creeley 1984, 206). These oedipally inflected narrative events occur in somewhat the wrong order—his eye was gone as if twice, his father was dead, but he then lived in the company of women.[9]

In Freud's striking, frightening formulation, little boys fear the loss of their genitalia (for Sophocles, their eyes) to punish their desires (Freud calls this castration anxiety); this makes them give up their taboo sexual desires for the mother for potential rights in all other women. Generally this narrative produces a sword of Damocles—nothing actually happens; there is only a vital patriarchy-producing anxiety in relation to the father and sublimation in relation to the mother. In contrast, little girls have "nothing" in the genital area—or so this story goes—and thus "nothing" whose loss they fear. Hence they escape the punitive regime of castration, because in Freud's immortal words they are "already" castrated. Thus they will be haunted by lack but rather more polymorphous in their attachments.[10]

But for Creeley something did happen; he really lost his eye. That is, because of the blinded eye, the dead father, and the excision, we can argue that Creeley had an exaggerated relation to the oedipal; he was put in the "feminine" subject position with relation to castration because a symbolic/metonymic loss had been literalized on his body through the empty eye socket.[11] But because he had paid the ultimate price and had "nothing" more (theoretically speaking) to lose, those losses provoked several intricate outcomes: a sense of freedom, an early absorption into a woman's world, a stark compensatory binarist sense of sexual difference along with bouts of gender vulnerability—and a multiplex image: the hole. This symbolic and somatically evocative image was his intimate; in thinking about "the hole," he proposed dynamic gender contradictions. He returns to and remixes aspects of the powerful oedipal story of coming into one's gender and makes outcomes and elements of this narrative unstable, ambiguous, deepened in odd ways.

One striking site is the four-page ballad called "The Finger," a work (from 1968) whose emotional and cultural freedom was provoked (but is hardly explained) by an LSD trip (Creeley 1993, 99–100). "The Finger" dramatizes the (arguably) oedipal desire of a male figure to see and to touch a female along with the more ambiguous possibility of pleasing her. It also manifests a subplot with a notable twist on Freud—the vision of women as whole (uncastrated) while males are split and wounded. Thus one may "enter" a woman as into a temple of totality.

Creeley claimed strong identification with and even dominance by females. He said this in answering a question that I asked him when he visited an undergraduate class in creative writing that I taught at Temple University in 1984. In *Creeley*, a film made by Bruce Jackson and Diane Christian (fifty-nine minutes, released in 1988), I am the off-camera voice querying his (biographical, cultural, poetic?) relationships with women. His answer paralleled the argument of "The Finger." He was raised by women; he was nurtured by women; he was, in effect, overwhelmed by women; he identified with them to a degree that seemed defining for him; and he could never be as large and encompassing as they were, never have that power. Therefore he could not possibly be sexist or exclusionary in his attitudes—something that did not and does not logically follow, though it may follow emotionally or affirmatively.

To signal male smallness and vulnerability, Creeley uses the striking word "manny," which means tamed or domesticated creature and is used in falconry but has suggestions of "manikin" and little man. This "manny" dances to try to please the great composite Woman in her laughing, overwhelming nakedness. But pleasure is to come, with the deictic finger, the poetic finger, the phallic finger pointing to the whole visionary experience. This dynamic poem combines and alters materials from the oedipal narrative and from the "Great Goddess" mythography of Robert Graves. Unlike the taboo sight of nude goddesses punished in much mythology with death, in this poem, naked or exposed goddesses (Aphrodite and Athena) have been viewed recurrently yet without any punishment at all. Instead the male is "the lover" but not the "victim" of the mother goddess "in her poetic or incantatory character" (Graves [1948] 1978, 393). This is a poem of escape from punishment into pleasure. The female is protean and auratic; the male is aroused by her labile qualities; he too is many-mythed and metamorphic. The poem's imagistic shape-shifting represents both the female and male figures and desire itself.

The main character learns, expansively, "my / fate would be timeless" (*Pieces* [1969]; Creeley 1982, 384). What is this fate? "Had they faced me into / the light so that my / eye was blinded?" (ibid.). The punishment comes first; the "possession" of the female comes later, and the epiphany or dazzling "light" of that interaction, its blessing and terror, the necessity for male performance, and orgasmic potential are constant and defining. Oedipality has been trumped—or at least narratively reorganized.

At key moments of intensity, Creeley affirms a vulnerable manhood in the loss of normative maleness and the gain of something else. In "The Finger," when the main character says, "I [. . .] / was neither a man nor not one, / all that," we have one of the seminal moments of sexual difference in Creeley (Creeley 1982, 386). It is a moment of intensity and exposure: the speaker evinces both a loss (a fear) and a gain (an advantage) by having more than one should, in having less. Given the aroused, "elated," metamorphic quality of this poem, one reads this line by naming as many options as possible, given that the points made are relatively unsummarizable or irreducible (luckily).[12] It is a point in Creeley in which one sees the evanescent potential of "non-phallic masculinity," defined by Daniel Boyarin as "a masculinity that *knows* of and perhaps even *enjoys* its heterogeneous, inconsistent make-up" without imagining that as "*femininity*" per se (Boyarin 1997, 85). This kind of intellectual exploration is consistent with Eric Keenaghan's discussion of male vulnerability "appreciated as an ethical relation to one's world" and Rob Halpern's discussion of George Oppen under the queered categories of "receptivity, vulnerability, penetrability" (Keenaghan 2009, 1; Halpern 2010).

The line layers the possibility that the speaker is both male and female in an unusually negative, roundabout formula (neither a man—i.e., a woman—nor not one—i.e., a man). Has he added another gender with a Tiresian flair? Is he proposing an imaginary intersexed subjectivity? Is this prefiguring a queer poetics of vulnerability and penetrability? Creeley gives the reader access to the possibility of both vulnerability and androgyny (cf. Watten 2003, 79). The line may mean the hero is the impotent male (a man, but "not a man," in sexual failure or sexual anxiety). Not a man may also mean "a boy": the hero visualized as the male boy (for there are at least four genders in the world—girl, boy, woman, man). This could be the "manny" precisely—a man-boy, "neither a man nor not one"—too small and oedipally forbidden to this luscious maternal goddess figure whose naked body, whose lust, whose sexual autonomy (and anatomy) he witnesses, in desire for both her body and his poetry.[13]

Yet the forbidden resolves by a kind of possession. The whole is an epiphany of double desire to please her body—"let / me touch you / there" (where she pointed, it is vague but loosely resolvable) and to please her spirit—"let / me sing" to and for her (Creeley 1982, 387, 388). So the poem seems to do the forbidden oedipal deed in described fantasy and in the rush of its changes (it is very sexy and sexual) seems to possess that overwhelming goddess-woman. As the aftermath poems in *Pieces* state (very ambiguously, but interestingly as readings proleptic for a whole career):

> One thing
> done, the
> rest follows.

-

Not from not
but in in.

(Creeley 1982, 388)

This suggests, unmistakably, that the possession of this sublime female has occurred and is defining, despite its being somewhat taboo. Some permission has been given; there is a decisive rejection of "not," in favor of "in." This poem is a portal to one major theme in his career, and Creeley knows it: "To go on telling the story, / to go on though no one hears it, / to the end of my days?" (Creeley 1982, 385).[14]

In certain particulars, this argument resembles the observations on the male poetic career that Catherine Maxwell offered about John Milton through the British Victorian poets. She traces a mythic and ideological topos deep inside the formation of the male poet that "co-identifies blindness, castration and feminisation as the necessary loss" that brings the male poet into being (Maxwell 2001, 1). Feminization is then not a matter of the social history of maleness, of biographical particulars, of differential and historically formed ideologies of masculinity or of their contradictions, but rather a mythic narrative of wounding or "disfigurement," a "symbolic castration" in which the male poet experiences a "disfiguring sublime, imagined as an aggressive female force which feminises the male" in a way that is overwhelming, ravishing, penetrating, transforming (Maxwell 2001, 1).[15] This argument almost corresponds to the rapture of "The Finger." This poem, however, argues that the main character, the "manny," is both overwhelmed by and capable of giving pleasure to the female. So the terms do not entirely match up, for Creeley's poem concerns a sublime sexual and poetic joy, a new epiphanic seeing via sexuality, and both male vulnerability and male or "manny" power.

Maxwell argues that gendering processes are vital to the poetic career and that intricate involvement with ideologies and mythologies of feminine, masculine, maleness, femaleness, gender crossovers, the anormative and transgressive, and sexual difference, along with the fantasy materials of gender and related concepts of power and sublimity, intimacy, and inspiration, must be tracked with a full recognition of the cultural meanings proposed. Although her gender processes are alluring, they are also mythopoetic, transhistorical generalizations; in contrast, I would emphasize particular somatic, biographical, and sociocultural matrixes in which these materials take shape.

A critic must credit the degree to which poets of this postpsychoanalytic and theoretically informed generation already knew the theory and self-consciously appreciated its potential for explaining—or exploring—their psyches. Most contemporary poets are not innocent of psychoanalytic explanations and materials; these helped them sharpen their poetic propositions. When Robert Creeley jokes in 1951 to Charles Olson that his toddler sons will someday commit parricide, we are in the realm of a double formation. Creeley clearly knows, or has read about, Freud's mythic history in *Moses and Monotheism*. This "parricide" narrative is not only a theoretical model for and imported "explanation" by the critic of something in the poet but a theory of archaic maleness and fraternal bonding with which the poet was already cozily familiar and which he was deploying in a specific relationship to explain maleness to himself.

So psychoanalytic narratives around the horde and kingship, transhistorical narratives of mythic repetition, are not an explanation that a critic can use innocently. Some poets are implicated in various psychoanalytic or mythical prototypes—seriously or teasingly—and already interpret their experience by using this framework. For them, psychoanalytic explanations are a tool in their own sex-gender toolbox, supporting the gender practices that they wished to employ or enjoy or that they felt they were experiencing. A critic cannot use psychoanalytic or mythic sex-gender terms as a one-dimensional discourse without understanding that the poets were also self-consciously engaged with some of these terms and at least semiseriously and knowingly using them as an explanatory mythology.

If, as Elspeth Probyn argues, "a gendered self is constantly reproduced within the changing mutations of difference," certainly it is not mythic permanence (even if "The Finger" also affirms it is!) but a biographical, historical, and social calling forth that allows gender manifestations, performances, and ideas to be renegotiated (Probyn 1993, 1). Tropes are never transhistorical; even if they carry over across time, they are always appropriated and reinterpreted in specific matrices. That is, even if this decisive wounding occurs for men and for male poets, it does not do so by the agency of "mythoi" themselves or by the necessity of poetry imagined as a force, but because poets and aspirants rearticulate certain gendering processes in their own way, perhaps in part by chosen adhesion to poetic tradition. In Creeley's case, he grasped and struggled with some things that actually, literally happened to him and that—by acts of poetic desire and will and some bravery—he chose to face within his poetry.

In this account of oedipality, men have to imagine something that might be cut from them and something already cut from the unfortunate female. What is left is the hole of absence. This may be feminizing, but, narrated in Creeley's mode, to be a woman is always already to have a "hole." A man, entering that sheath, somewhat compensates for his own vulnerabilities by what he brings to intromission. Creeley consistently uses his metaphor of "the hole" to indicate the vaginal opening and the birth canal and death, the loss of the self, the grave. "The hole from which we came // isn't metaphysical. / The one to which we go is real" (Creeley 2003, 42). When the vaginal "hole" is in play, that hole is culturally loaded with absence and lack, whose potential banality is not avoided in Creeley's poetry.[16]

When death enters, Eve and the Fall hover in the background. That is, the "hole" of death is a secular version of the conventional fairy tale of hegemonic theologies in which women are responsible for bringing death into the world. In this evocation of sexual difference in the imagery around death, Creeley is playing with that theology, but he is not making a critique of it. So too the stark Freudian narrative: in the time of Creeley's early career (1940s–1960s), this had the status of dogma and was memorably invoked, even intoned, to define inevitable, unmovable psychosomatic gender fates. If these sets of claims (theological and coarsely psychoanalytic) manifest sexual difference at its most binarist, it remains true that Creeley found this material staggeringly generative, part of the ontological ground on which he stood.[17]

The title poem in *Life & Death* compares the boy or youth-situation of not really knowing about the mechanics of (heterosexual) intercourse, and thus not understanding life itself, to the situation he is in now, not really knowing about death.

> The first time couldn't
> even find the hole
> it was supposed to go in—
> Lonely down here
> in simple skin
>
> (Creeley 1998a, 69)

Then with an evocative citation from Zukofsky that Creeley uses several times in this book he explicitly compares the holes of sexuality and now death:

Born very young into a world
already very old, Zukofsky'd said.
I heard the jokes
the men told
down by the river, swimming.
What are you
supposed to do
and how do you learn.
I feel the same way now.

(Creeley 1998a, 71)

Creeley's late poem "Conversion to Her" is a four-part work beginning with the speaker's birth from the mother's body and moving quickly
to his life in an aging body. Based on a suite of paintings by Francesco
Clemente, the imagery evokes materials very fundamental to Creeley about the complex "hole" of oedipal punishment, vaginal entrance,
and death. In the bulk of life, the part hardly narrated, the speaker asks:
"Who was I then? What man had entered?" (Creeley 2003, 40). This is a
question perhaps about his father (whom he hardly knew and, to his sorrow, barely remembered), about himself (uneasy or vulnerable maleness
being a major topic for his work), and perhaps about what one might,
stolidly, call "a male subject position" that one faces and introjects.[18]

At any rate, in this poem, the body, now aging within one quick quatrain, is "crossing over": to death, absolutely, and thus images of physical
destruction abound in the next quatrain, but also, startlingly, to being
made female by some wounding. The quatrain is about being hurt, cut,
wounded, "castrated," and full of desire--to say this luridly, but no more
luridly than the poem.

Knife cuts through.
Things stick in holes.
Spit covers body.
Head's left hanging.

Hole is in middle.
Little boy wants one.
Help him sing here
Helpless and wanting.

(Creeley 2003, 41)

A second part of the poem "wonders" at the fact of gender and responds to the gender binary and its stereotypes:

Being human, one wonders at the others,
men with their beards and anger,

women with their friends and pleasure—

(Creeley 2003, 42)

"Human"—the common life and the position of the speaker—seems,
importantly, to differ from these strange gendered figures. However,
"one cannot say, *Be as women, / be peaceful, then*," perhaps because the
speaker has a whole history of existing within maleness (Creeley 2003,
42). But also because (as noted before) "The hole from which we came //
isn't metaphysical. / The one to which we go is real" (Creeley 2003, 42).
The third part ends with two rhyming couplets announcing proverbial
gender wisdom. The rhyme (a formal feature) both mocks and affirms
ideology—the statements are simultaneously "true" and "truisms":

Women are told
To let world unfold.

Men, to take it,
Make or break it.

(Creeley 2003, 42)

Then the speaker says in italics, "*All's true / except for you*" (Creeley 2003,
42). This "you" could be an addressee who has escaped these truisms; it
could be addressed to the self as you. What happens if one does not really
conform to or confirm these truisms? It appears there is a space—it could
be life, it could be the looming of death, "in which a man still lives / till
he become a woman" (Creeley 2003, 43). What might this mean? First,
that death, like all other insulting losses suffered, is the ultimate "castra-
tor" and feminizes a male. (We will then all become [like] "women" in
death?—an odd thought and certainly hard to prove.) The poem may be
said to rest upon a word in the title—"Conversion"—and a word at the
end—"become"—perhaps a subjunctive form of the verb "becomes."
    In his 2003 interview with Leonard Schwartz (online in *Jacket
Magazine*), Creeley makes clear the double direction of "Conversion to

Her"—back to sexual difference (men are not women) and forward to some intersection of the two genders into one, as the title of the poem says (Creeley 2004). Men are, in some sense, converted to women. Conversion means a change—adopting a new religion, a change of belief or practice.[19] To convert to woman is to change into another form, substance, state, or product. Or to change in ways that credit her ideas and notions. So he "becomes" a woman in that hypothetical, subjunctive fashion. But he also might "become" a woman, which means to be appropriate or suitable to or to show to advantage. If he is an ornament that enhances a woman, he is something small and subordinate to her gloriousness—the "manny" again. Although the terms are still couched in the binarist gender words (man, woman), the poem seems to propose the human, the common life, as a new path beyond (and a conversion from) polarized genders.

When Creeley talks about "Conversion to Her," a number of contradictory ideas about gender are simultaneously proposed. To Leonard Schwartz:

> You're quite right that it [the poem] certainly all goes back to the insistent sense in Graves' own concerns, the whole *White Goddess*, and that sense of—again I will take it from Williams—"the female principle of the world [which] is my appeal in the extremity to which I have come . . . " But here I'm actually thinking of the conversion of a male "principle" that would somehow be like that "female principle."
>
> (Creeley 2004)

This statement is filled with gender ideas with fundamentally colliding impacts; this is not a consistent "position"—it is a series of semi-contradictory vectors of interest for Creeley's debates concerning sexual difference.

White Goddess is a work in which Robert Graves lavishly discusses the archetypes of female power as represented in myth. This iconization of the female principle is not inconsistent with the segregation of, rage at, hyper-contemptuous "respect" for, and sense of taboo around women—they are so powerful that one has to control them, even violently. But in its best-case scenario, this position maintains spiritual/visceral awe of somewhat mythologized women for their power, aura, and force (thus, "The Finger").

In Creeley's work, a continuous reaffirmation of strong polarized gender binarism (or sexual difference), with an extreme sense of the largeness and hieratic sublimity of women and/or female figures, is sometimes coupled with striking imagery of wounding and loss that is both exacerbated and cured by repeated addresses to the same sublimity. In this argument, males are "converted" to the female principle by recognizing, as converts or epigones, the Mana (and manna) of these goddesses, and they desire to "enter" them in some way, even together in experiences with other men, in order both to be inside their powers and to be protected from those powers by the company of male partners. Lyrics by male writers in general resist the opportunity to depict or neglect the question of depicting the speech or reactions of the generally female "other" even when they flirt with that possibility.[20] One might then note that "Conversion to Her" is the poem in which Creeley tries to make some kind of halting amends for the position articulated at the end of *Pieces* (though surely not making amends for the poem), a position in which women are not coequal humans, although they may be auratic goddesses.

The statement that Creeley cites from Williams in the Schwartz interview might say that women or goddesses (embodying "the female principle") will rescue men; it even appeals for that rescue. Like the role of African Americans in many representations (in Toni Morrison's analysis) the favored narrative role for black people is to save some white person. Similarly, women are not "for themselves" in existential terms, but "for another." Clearly this sentence returns to female bigness and male vulnerability. The salvationist role, the role of offering care to someone in "extremity" or need, is presumably a human function. Hence when faced with the notion that this ethics of care is based solely on the *female* principle, I think one must refuse and critique these blandishments: of conceptualizing such excellence as exclusively female; of seeing females as without aggression and irresponsibility; and of assuming that care is given only by males who have assumed a female aspect.

Finally, Creeley and Schwartz continue by evoking a sense of androgyny or an increase in the sense that any person is two genders.

RC: But here I'm actually thinking of the conversion of a male "principle" that would somehow be like that "female principle."

LS: Virginia Woolf [in *A Room of One's Own*] did suggest early on that the good writer has to have an androgynous mind, so certainly, for us [men], it would have to be a question of becoming women in order to write.

RC: Yes, I feel that.

(Creeley 2004)

Here we see the potential for a "recognition" (to evoke the now long-ago term of Carolyn Heilbrun [1973]) of the androgynous self, gender multiplicity, a position that seems to leave interesting spaces for females as well as males to undo gender binarism.

One response of Creeley to male vulnerability and male power is the continuing affirmation for himself, and appropriation to himself, of elements of a feminine subject position. This is also quite familiar to his poetry and rather fascinating as at least double-crossing gender binarism by playing with a certain bi-ness (we see this in "The Hole"). His interest in a feminine position sometimes led Creeley to some empathetic identifications. For instance, in his intellectual and emotional frankness, in his care at anatomizing inner and outer, memorable yet generally unmentionable body parts (like the bowel, bladder, and prostate), in his sensitive attention to the pulsations of thinking inside real time, and in his selectively framing colloquial and spoken language, Creeley dissolves certain binary formulations that have often been mapped onto gender stereotypes.

In particular Creeley tried to erase and flatten the force for *male* subjectivity of the mind-body "split" which has served our culture so notably as ideology and which usually maps on woman as body, man as mind. Creeley appropriates the female materials to himself and denies, by his own maleness, the hegemonic force of that particular gender binary. In this he can be (but is not always) critical of cultural clichés about gender and revisionary about manhood. For if males take femaleness into themselves, making it part of themselves as men, this produces the potential for appropriation: men now possess all standard available genders in their psyche. More is thought to be better than just one, and this claim may certainly make males more powerful, more gender-mobile or gender-various.

As noted, Barbara Johnson has proposed that a male poet (Charles Baudelaire is her example), entering a feminine subject position, has a good deal of cultural privilege. He has "both" gender positions and can negotiate them, in part imperially ("Masculine privilege is enforced precisely by male femininity"; Johnson 1998, 127). I have continued her discussion of this culturally powerful move; it is the imperial gender claim of the patriarchal, even the pleasantly provocative patriarchal that I have spoken about repeatedly in this book. One might even argue that this creates a new "universal"—a souped-up version of the human. And once more, as is culturally normal, males are in charge of this new universal. It is rare for someone granted much power and latitude to affirm the potential for proliferation of gender possibilities for whatever figure (often female) that he needs to hold static in order to constitute his range (cf. Butler 2004, 219).

Yet the arguments about the common life and humanness that Creeley makes continuously from 1990 on cannot encourage very fervent binarist thinking about men and women. These arguments run the danger, of course, that the new "universal" human is simply an upgraded translation of the old word "man." But there is a possibility that the "common life," the sheer human about which Creeley talked, is a position beyond gender polarization—or at least tolerant of proliferations of desires and practices. Of course, his interest in gender and women did not extend to feminism. Creeley voiced his discontent and annoyance with the phenomenon of "the feminist proposal" as not accounting for "the functioning substantive fact of a male in a society which males equally, I presume, would like to alter"—the fact of violence, for example. The question "how do *males* now find a place in a common world of men *and* women" is unanswered, but it haunts, and not just Creeley (Clark 1993, 68). His discomfort is, in fact (and ironically, given Olson), with the separatist proposal. His particular discontent seems to focus on Adrienne Rich's work from her phase of strategic separatism, to use Gayatri Spivak's exculpating term (Spivak 1993, 35). Creeley is annoyed that Rich's title *The Dream of a Common Language* is actually gender-exclusive and thus an inadequate use of the word "common."

Yet as we have seen, the term "common" was evocative for Creeley, though he did not much like Rich's claim on it (Clark 1993, 97–98). Some of Creeley's positions among gender materials involve a few attempts to undo sexual difference, to critique gender binarism, to identify with a wounded woman. In these attempts, he also entertains "another" rather more human and common hole. Creeley is particularly memorable in at least two poems, "The Hole" and "Age," about the anus. "Age" discusses the anus as a "common" hole, a bodily site held in common by the genders. "The Hole," an earlier poem, can be read as a streaming meditation exploring taboo or untoward erotic temptations, an attempt haltingly to open the unspeakable by violating some boundaries, particularly by some meditations on passivity and penetration.

"The Hole" intermixes eroticism, shame, and curiosity, along, arguably, with a depiction of orgasm or a mental meditation before orgasm: "I want / to, now I / can't wait any / longer" (Creeley 1982, 345). This poem may concern anality in its current critically melodramatic

(Bersaniesque) sense of the "self-shattering [. . .] *jouissance*" of sexual penetration and passivity (here imagined or actual), although the exploration of the anus depicted in the poem is either the speaker's or a woman's and the mode of *jouissance* seems nervous, not satisfying (Bersani 1988, 222). "The Hole" is a scattered, uneasy poem, empathetically contemplating a variety of semitaboo materials as well as (with some relief?) evoking the penis, for it is book-ended with two penises, both revealed while their possessors are swimming.

As Catherine Waldby argues, "anal eroticism carries disturbingly feminizing connotations" by its acknowledging of the penetrability of the male body (and the consequent "abandonment"—is this indeed a consequence and for whom?—of any purely phallic vision of sexuality). Then there is also the fact—precisely interesting to Creeley—that the anus is a common orifice; everyone of any gender and sexual claim has one (Waldby 1995, 272).[21] This circumstance need not be called feminizing (it is merely convention to equate feminine with receptive). Yet the poem conforms to Waldby's outline only in part. "The Hole" concerns the question of penetration and forced receptivity, proposing a woman as penetrated object, and it has a pensive yet scatty quality, because of the quick pace of associated thoughts which generally lead to a taboo space. At the same time, the evocation of anality hardly has this poem "abandoning" the penis—reaffirming it is more accurate.

"The Hole" (from *Words*, 1967) contains set of frank images, identifying with a girl (anally, vaginally?) raped with a Coke bottle, feeling this situation on and in himself, both as rapist and as raped person.[22]

> later,
> felt there,
>
> opened
> myself.
>
>   (Creeley 1982, 344)

"There" is a complex place, most likely the anus, but possibly the exploration of a vaginal opening. It is a poem in which intimate openings cross and which manifests a lot of unease and fascination about one's position in this array of possibilities.

Is the speaker the subject perpetuating something upon another person—"opened [there] / myself"? Is the speaker the object of another's

sexual act or of self-exploration—"opened myself"? It is Creeley's brilliance to produce in the four lines cited above just those words that
propose both these alternative positions simultaneously and undecid-
ably. What it would feel like to be raped (for a male, let us posit anally
penetrated) is half-considered, and what might a woman feel who was
raped anally, or vaginally, but who also (according to the poem) semi-
consented? What might it be to note all this in a poem? The poem becomes a streaming set of associations of "holes" (orifices, really) and
things available to fill them.

The work seems to consider or to confess a scene or scenes of sexual
penetration that involve anxiety-laden acts, rape perhaps, semiconsen-
sual intromission, or perhaps anal penetration.[23] The very equivalence
and relationship of these possibilities in the poem's repertoire shows
its studied, somewhat breathless amorality; the speaker carefully holds
himself in a nonjudgmental position, to see how far he gets with the
thought that "[e]verywhere // there is pleasure" (Creeley 1982, 345).[24]
For example, after the fascination with a raped woman (and possibly the
confession of a rape), the speaker remembers his mother and sister seen
naked. One taboo—or pleasure—meets another without comment. This
is a poem of double—multiple—positionality, as the speaker not only
is the possessor of a penis and possessor of at least one orifice but is
meditating on the curious ways of pleasure and, possibly, guilt, shame,
masochism, sadism, release. Certainly with the imagery of the anal hole,
the intimacies, uneasiness, and frankness are mobile and polymorphous.

Such somatic exploration of a "common" hole modulates into the
unambiguous consideration of the anus, human aging, and the continuum between insideness and outsideness, substance and emptiness.
Creeley's poem "Age" in *Just in Time* turns to the hole of common humanness, the anus, with a terrific pun on *annus*, the word "year" in Latin.
"Age" is a meditation as if "during" a colonoscopy, a diagnostic examina-
tion involving a light and a camera at the end of a tube up the back end
of a sedated but possibly twilight-awake person (Creeley 2001, 146–149).
Written in thirty-four couplets, in several self-interrupting parts, looping, with very subtle transitions, it is a pretty antipoetic poem. The un-
flattering, fond mention of the snoring lover, the colonoscopy, and the
use of the word "anus" plus other terms in the realm of "ass" all challenge
elevation and sublimity.

The main figure, a patient, is isolated and fears the diagnostic outcome of the procedure, finding it difficult to wrap himself around the

"other side"—illness, death, old age, common humanness. He appeals to a "you" for loyalty and empathy during these bad moments, the "whimpering" times in which a person feels thoroughly isolated. The poem ends with an ethical proposition that to be listened to and heard is crucial, but the self will, in any case, keep talking.

Many semantic images concern the discomfort of being in the wrong position. All those words ("implosion," "prolapsed") have a secret bottom in the thing that this poem tries to avoid saying—death. The poem travels a distance, then jumps a bit, but keeps returning to the same general topic. It begins with the wedged self, in a narrowing tube of time itself, precisely not (the choice is striking) in a hole but in a narrowing cone. The wedged trap is the possible path to death—no one knows where or when. This idea of "death" is then avoided with a jump to the word "quite" pronounced variously. There is an interplay between the American and British (and/or New Zealand) pronunciation "quite," which is one of those phatic terms indicating a general agreement. By sound association, this word links to "quiet" but also, as a crypt term, to "quietus." That famous word concerns the deathblow, so we have not avoided the hidden topic at all.

It is very odd to be scrutinized from behind and from inside—it is not one's best face, so to speak—yet Creeley makes the most of this strange (not totally uncommon, but usually unspoken) position, showing again how positionality has always been crucial to him and what brilliant use he made of it.

> [N]ow you see the
> two doctors, behind
>
> you, in mind's eye,
> probe into your anus,
>
> or ass, or bottom,
> behind you, the roto-
>
> rooter-like device
> sees all up
>
> (Creeley 2001, 147)

The anus is associated with the eye, but as the subject of scrutiny: "see," "eye," and "sees" alternate with "ass," "anus," "bottom," and the preposition "behind" (another ass word) repeated twice. Later, with punning exactitude, the poem proposes: "The world is a round but / diminishing ball" and "butt" is punningly palpable with that line break. Here, there, where, now, then, and when, inside and outside, are all "sites," deictically variable, powerful locations in which the paradox of meditating on one's insides goes forward, but so does the power of forward-pulsing time.

A colonoscopy should not be painful, but it can be uncomfortable, to use that euphemism (if too little sedation is administered—something less common now in the procedure). And, if one reads the medical release form carefully, one finds that there is always the slight danger of a puncture. This discomfort enters the poem in its sound, through the two long vowels (*o* and *oo*) of the image/descriptor of the long tube with a camera: "roto-rooter." Suburban homeowners in particular may recognize that this is not a medical term but the brand name of a plumbing company specializing in this device used to clean out pipes, such as sewer connections, blocked by tree roots.

"Roto-rooter" is a pool-word that condenses and focuses many of the vowel sounds of the poem. In this context these are sounds of pain/discomfort and emotional vulnerability, and a lot of the poem's words emit them. The *o* sound is heard in "narrowing," "cone," "probe," "no," "old," "prose," "joke," "echo," "alone," "close," "over," "glowing," "approaching," "retro"; the *oo* sound occurs in "into," "whom," "you," "two," "concludes," "cube," "do," "crucial." It is a poem in the keys of *o* and *oo*. Another repeated sound comes in the key of *j/ch*: "age," "wedge," "gesture," "joke," "reach," "touch," "approach," "judgmental," and "just," and these words function as reiterations of the title sound—the ultimate *reductio*—"age." The sound functions as well, perhaps, as a sound of commiserating sympathy: tch, tch, tch.[25]

The poem finally names its hidden topic, but only gingerly. The allusion to Keats is torqued, not speaking about fears when I may cease to *be* (as in the great sonnet), but about

[. . .] the approaching

fears when I may
cease to be me, all

lost or rather lumped
here is a retrograded,

dislocating, imploding
self, a uselessness

talks

(Creeley 2001, 148–149)

The three emphatic adjectives at the end of this poem all emphasize major shifts in positionality of that "self." "Retrograded" means moving or tending backward, retreating, opposed, contrary, and opposite to earth (in motion). "Dislocating" means shifted out of the usual position, and the similar descriptor "prose prolapsed" in the middle of the poem refers to the ordinary, commonplace *proversus*, to turn forward--a description of the intestine, poetry, the line break, life, and this poem. "Prolapsed" is a slippage or falling out of place, said particularly of an organ. It also contains the fears of one's lapsing past one's shelf life. Not only death is a fear but also a really bad disability, where one is precisely "not oneself."

These physical meditations on a body first of all acknowledge un-heroic male humanness in all its poignancy. This is a poem in which strong maleness is eroded, unmentioned—the work concerns the worn-down human. Taking this poem and its hole as a key late work, one might propose that male subjectivity is a bit more mobile and critical in later Creeley than in earlier Creeley. One may well see, in poems and their discussion, the affirmation of gender binarism yet again, but sometimes in Creeley's thinking and his work another position emerges: that both male and female dissolve into the human, the common place.

The force of any one poem does not do away with sociopolitical power or cultural assumptions. Nonetheless, a poem may jostle assump-tions and may destabilize deeply embedded gender materials. Some of these cultural explorations of gender occasion powerful debates in Cree-ley's later work. This is a magisterial and poignant part of his oeuvre, whose contradictions and dilemmas carry forward into our time and place.

3. An Ending of Sorts

This book has had many through lines and proto-thesis statements. The eros of poesis. The test of such a utopian passage as Said claimed between filiative and affiliative relationships and modernity. The ways in which males performed gender and its debates in modernisms. The ambivalence as to what patriarchal means—the interests of many in its charms and powers. Its clearly "sublime" importance to literary creativity. My use of the term "patriarchal" to indicate imperial claims to enter all subject positions, no matter how contradictory. The simple power privilege of this possibility, one that not all men took, but which all were protected and buoyed by.

This imperial, all-sexes-and-all-genders subject of patriarchal poetry shows the utopian ease of making a solution to social contradictions by appropriating significant, affirmative cultural sites. No need to choose; this is an innocent imperial subject who fuses all sex-gender contradictions into himself and thereby solves them simply by being. This subject negotiates within himself the strands of sexuality and gender (and perhaps other social locations) without having to account for political, economic, and historical issues that would confront him, were he in fact an embodied and material and not an imaginary female or an actively homoerotic person. This imperial male subject of patriarchal poetry becomes one central type of modernist masculinities.

This book tracks one general genealogical poetic "line" and does not even include everyone in that line. So yes, not every male poet of that era is discussed. Would the findings be different with a different cohort? If Frank O'Hara and John Ashbery were included, if Jack Spicer and Robin Blaser were included, if George Oppen was included, and so on? If Robert Duncan was elaborated? Well, it is plausible that the book would be different. But would the findings be significantly different? My brief excursus on Duncan and his mythographic study is meant to indicate that this era sometimes reveals critical changes, some differently inflected versions of a situation of cultural inequality, some attention to actual historical gender situations for men and women, some rectification of sex-gender hierarchies. Duncan opens one door to a full literary history, perhaps to a full literary culture. The glance at later Creeley indicates that changes of material and stance are possible, if also slowly and tentatively negotiated. This may be true of other poets (Oppen, for instance). The finding that sex-gender systems in literary institutions are a site of significant, sometimes rancorous cultural and ideological struggle for all involved would not change.

And I would also offer some self-criticism about this analysis. Why did these relations occur? Because there was some intersection of the specific biography of the male writers with the general social ideology regarding men and women—this despite the poets' "radical" stance.

Because most men showed little or no critique or self-consciousness about male benefit from these relations. Because women had some (but not ever enough) professional, economic, and political leverage. Because the eros of poesis was so enchanting in its single gender modes that extending it was unthinkable. Because once imperial claims of patriarchal poetry in all sex-gender places were critically and institutionally reinforced, women were somewhat excrescent, quite unevenly appreciated in what they brought to any aesthetic community. (And with all chilling effects melodramatically, bitterly, comically deflected, and/or tragically registered in their careers, as feminist critical studies of women have repeatedly argued.) But I do not actually answer the question *why*, in general or with overarching psycho-social generalization. The book is deictic. I am mainly saying "that": that this was, that this happened, that this showed some of the debates and strains I analyze, that this had the following outcomes.

Is the patriarchal era of poetry over? Can we postulate that this era is over in U.S. poetry at least? This book exists because I literally wanted to write poetic culture beyond patriarchy (as if!): by pointing clearly and analytically to all the twists and turns and strategies and contradictions of (some recent enough) patriarchal poetic relations, I might help incite a change in the present or reinforce the changes that may be occurring. Thus it was important to me to show that there was real, active, concerted debate upon points of gender equality or the value of difference, otherness, proliferation of positions, diversity. And I also showed that time after time the male writers spoken of here could move neither themselves nor their cohorts to acknowledge coequality, especially in realms of sexuality and gender (or even sometimes in related materials of religious culture). For them there was no multiple sex-gender universe where women were concerned and sometimes where gay men were concerned or (abruptly) Jews; generally they saw only a binary (hierarchical, unequal) universe. The male poets discussed here could see coequality as a possibility, sometimes even an end that they could enunciate, but female coequality/difference in coeval community was not, finally, something it was in their interest or in their repertoire to pursue.

I wanted (imperially?) to declare the end of the patriarchal era of poetry by the sheer force of these sometimes negative examples and by the temperate if also suspicious empathy that characterizes most of my analysis. I wanted to declare (by showing the distasteful outcomes of the options discussed here) the end of any part of femaleness and the feminine as a disabling—if also occasionally idealized—condition, whether this is ethnically signified (male Jews as feminine and thereby qualified), signified by sexualities (gay men as feminine and thereby undercut and women as female, feminine), or just plain negatively affected by gender. The "feminine" is only good when it helps rupture category; it is only any good when women are given/possess/can claim the same rights for any and all gender mixes, when the particularities of those mixes are critically and poetically legible by all, and when women are (when everybody is) seen as 100 percent human—coequal, coeval, social partners with all civic and cultural rights. Including, perhaps, the right to reciprocal care, including, perhaps, the imperial claims of any and all sex-gender positions in culture. And even another possible end: fully beyond gender as a hierarchical marker but not as a multiple human condition. It is a fairly straightforward end, after all. Isn't it?

Notes

1. Manifesting Literary Feminism

1. This book is indebted to Peter Middleton and Michael Davidson on maleness and poetics; Barrett Watten, Charles Bernstein, Gail McDonald, Libbie Rifkin, and Wayne Koestenbaum on maleness and the institutions of a poetic career; Andrew Epstein, Andrew Mossin, and Maggie Nelson on gendered cohorts; and Sandra Gilbert and Susan Gubar for a vivid depiction of modernist gender relations.

2. Edward Said, notably dubious about feminism, nonetheless evokes its shadow presence by using the phrase "men and women" whenever he speaks about this "horizontal affiliation" (Said 1983, 18).

3. The ventriloquism and mastery of positions that "personae" involve, Peter Nicholls argues, are chosen in opposition to passive/receptive reveries on the indefinable, the queerish form in which inspiration was depicted in the nineties (Nicholls in Davis and Jenkins 2007, 54).

4. "Errancy" is Colleen Lamos's useful catchall term for the effeminate, hysterical, sadomasochistic, homosexual, homoerotic, voyeuristic, or matrisexual in male writers (Lamos 1998).

5. A reminder from Tony Lopez: authorship "can be made of competition, hatred and envy"—the aggressions of eros, not its nicer side (Lopez 2006, 44).

6. The erotic force of specific relationships is not the only zone of the erotic in poetry. Stephen Fredman has argued that in the post–World War II period formal features like assemblage/collage (by practicing juxtaposition, decontextualization, and recombination) had poethical (Retallack 2003, 3) implications, modeling "new [erotic] energies" via "visionary psychoanalysis," "liberatory anarchism and [. . .] sexual mysticism" (Fredman 2010, 7). Fredman's book excavates, from a literary historical perspective, the erotic-visionary analyses and art products of a network of West Coast figures, including Robert Duncan, Norman O. Brown, Harry Smith, Wallace Berman, and Jess (Collins) as well as the impact of this material on figures like Denise Levertov, Allen Ginsberg, Jack Spicer, Jerome Rothenberg, and Robert Creeley. He emphasizes the centrality of Brown's psychoanalysis of culture to an "erotic poetics." Jeanne Heuving is also reinterpreting the love-beloved "troubadour" bond as a mediating form prior to the achievement of poetic language. That is, any of the modern poets' relationships to language as possession are analogous with the ways that poets such as Pound and H.D. play out being possessed by love (Heuving n.d.).

7. A good overview of Pound's influence in constructing a countersublime tradition is found in Christopher Beach (1992); similarly emphasizing choice, negotiation, and dialogue with mentor figures and deemphasizing "oedipal" replacement, it is also notable in treating some gender issues.

8. How and whether men could contribute to feminism or be feminists was a question in the era represented by the Alice Jardine and Paul Smith anthology *Men in Feminism* (1987). In contrast, I apply a "feminism of reception" to male figures and to their ideologies of masculinity.

9. Queer theory, as Michael Kimmel proposes, helps a critic to "theorize masculinity as a system of power relations among men as well as a system of power relations between women and men" (Kimmel 2002, xi).

10. "Company" is also apparently Robert Duncan's term. This mix of countercultural and hegemonic evocations recurs in chapter 4.

11. Babbitt was T. S. Eliot's professor at Harvard and a noted traditionalist about whom Eliot wrote approvingly on several occasions (see McDonald 1993, 123–133). A climactic antiromantic passage: "To set color above design, illusion above informing purpose, suggestiveness above symmetry, is to encourage that predominance of the feminine over the masculine virtues that has been the main cause of the corruption of literature and the arts during the past century" (Babbitt 1910, 249).

12. "Theoretically informed close reading," Calvin Thomas avers, can contribute to the "political project of intervention into power relations that animates cultural studies" (Thomas et al. 2000, 5).

13. This critical practice scrutinizes what Theodor Adorno presents in his essay on Friedrich Hölderlin: "das Gedichtete," translated as "that which has been composed poetically" in the medium of language and its rhetorics (Adorno 1992, 112).

14. Feminist study of aesthetics also avers that there is no "universal, generic spectator" for a work of art and thus no neutral critic (Korsmeyer 2004, 54, cf. 50).

15. This position is indebted to many anthologies from the 1990s and later, most particularly Gardiner's 2002 anthology and her introduction to it (Gardiner 2002b, 2002a). By "pan-gendered" I mean omni-sexual, omni-gendered, participating in critical gender studies.

16. Some critics have analyzed male writers according to the degree of their sympathetic depictions of females, their identification with women, their femininity, even their feminism. This is not quite the critique I had in mind, but it was sometimes helpful.

17. For instance, Griselda Pollock's work in *Differencing the Canon* (1999) reads important modern male visual artists with a feminist eye. Lisa Tickner's related position: "The proper study of womankind is not always or necessarily

women; masculinity is a problem for feminism (as well as for women and, arguably, men)" (Tickner 1994, 56).

18. I can also appreciate that one might attempt, as a strategy or a tactic, to withdraw one's political consent to various forms of patriarchy via separatism or transgender identifications, but this will not bring the current sex-gender system down, though it may destabilize it somewhat.

19. Beyond the male body, add to that list male attitudes to female bodies and embodiment as well as to female careers and female literary production.

20. Or in Ian Gregson's words, innocently echoed here even before I read them: "masculinity has been, as it were, hidden in plain sight—so difficult to see, paradoxically, because it is so pre-eminently there" (Gregson 1999, 10).

21. Homi K. Bhabha reports, following Peter Middleton, that the universalizing practices associated with maleness, as internalized by male persons (and of course also by numerous female persons), mean that it is hard for males to see what they do as inflected by their maleness amid other social locations and variables; but once they do, in his view, definition or taxonomy does turn into (should turn into?) critique (Bhabha 1995). Many contemporary anthologies on masculinity studies have that "plot." One of the more moving formulations is Joseph Boone's: "a community with phalluses, rather than the community *as* Phallus, need exist only as a threat to the existing patriarchal order" and not to feminism or to women (Boone in Boone and Cadden 1990, 25). This speaks precisely to cooperative investigation of these materials.

22. It is striking how many of these feminist, gay, and queer literary studies examine only narrative—in film, in novels, in memoir. Poetic texts and poetic institutions are very rarely discussed.

23. Judith Fetterley's title phrase from 1978 is still irresistible.

24. Indeed, Charles Olson's resistance in "Against Wisdom as Such" to Robert Duncan's work came from this magical, mage tonality and its dictions, his notable derivation from Stein and other women writers, like Edith Sitwell and H.D. (Olson 1997).

25. Incidentally, I do know that pink and blue make lavender (can't help that).

26. Although the theoretical framework and the interpretations offered exemplify what I have called "feminist reception" (DuPlessis 2006a, 64–66), only three female practitioners are treated concertedly in the book: Gertrude Stein (briefly), Mina Loy, and Frances Boldereff. Nor does this book attempt a survey of all the arguably important United States poets in this time, homosexual writers beyond Allen Ginsberg and John Wieners, or even all the writers, male and female, who dealt variously with maleness.

27. For "desire" in "labour, power and desire" (Segal 1990, 96), I have substituted the term "eros."

28. To borrow a title from Regina Barreca and Deborah Denenholz Morse (1997), this eros includes "the erotics of instruction."

2. Pound Edits Loy and Eliot

1. The subhead of this section is a citation from Stein [1927] 1980, 122.

2. For both Pound and Eliot, Robert Browning is a more complicated case.

3. Pound's loathing of the Gertrude Stein and Natalie Barney circles and the Bloomsbury group occurs in some measure because their work was both formally radical and sexually transgressive (heterosexuality and homosexuality were both accepted).

4. The affirmation is all the more amazing since a good deal of Lentricchia's subtle study of Stevens finds the poet pulled toward a feminine sense of interior space, the creation of a kind of gender mix that the critic calls "transvestite" and that sometimes turned "patriarchy against itself" (Lentricchia 1987, 775).

5. Ronald Bush importantly notes that Pound's gender ideas emerged from and sometimes returned to a sexual liberalism characteristic of feminist pro-sex thought in the teens (Bush 1991, 74–75).

6. Koestenbaum cites brutalist examples of Quinn's misogyny—re micturation and menstruation and concerning the female editors of the *Little Review*—from the Beinecke Library materials (Koestenbaum 1989, 119).

7. *Rappel à l'ordre* is a term alluding to political conservatism and to a neo-classical artistic and ideological turn after World War I; it may have come into the Poundian lexicon from the title of a 1926 book by Jean Cocteau. One place Pound evokes this term is in his self-proclaimed postfascist career periodization: "the sorting out, the *rappel à l'ordre*, and thirdly the new synthesis, the totalitarian" (Pound [1938] 1966, 95). The critical assessment implied in the term *rappel à l'ordre* is associated with Pound's memory of his collaboration with Eliot in the 1920s, in the following quite interested literary historical account from 1932.

"That is to say, at a particular date in a particular room, two authors, neither engaged in picking the other's pocket, decided that the dilutation of *vers libre*, Amygism, Lee Masterism, general floppiness had gone too far and that some counter-current must be set going. Parallel situation centuries ago in China. Remedy prescribed 'Emaux et Camées' (or the Bay State Hymn Book). Rhyme and regular strophes.

"Results: Poems in Mr Eliot's *second* volume, not contained in his first 'Prufrock' [(]*Egoist*, 1917), also 'H. S. Mauberley'" (Pound 1932a, 590).

The occlusion of Loy's influence on "Mauberley" and of Pound's praise of both Moore and Loy for intellectuality and impersonality (see note 8 below) has been completed here.

8. Pound praises both for their intelligence, their dryness, the shock of their almost entire want of "emotion": a prime example of what he thereupon names

intellectual diction or "logopoeia" (originally in *Others* [1918], cited from *Instigations* [1920] 1967, 233, 234; DuPlessis 2001, 38–39).

9. Contrast *The Pisan Cantos*, LXXXII, and its regretful "Swinburne my only miss" (for contact) (Pound [1948] 2003, 101).

10. The subhead for this section is a citation from Stein [1927] 1980, 146.

11. This poem was written after Loy's separation from Haweis (1913) and after her affairs with both F. T. Marinetti and Giovanni Papini (Italian futurists) in approximately 1914. Roger L. Conover dates the poem ca. 1915 (Loy 1996, 185). It was published in *Others* in 1917, was noticed by both Pound and Eliot in 1918, and is now in the 1996 Conover edition; Pound's redaction is now in B. Scott 1990, 247–248.

12. Marinetti's 1909 "The Founding and Manifesto of Futurism" proposes both "contempt for women" and the destruction of feminism (Loy 1996, 182). In his notes to the poems, Conover produces brilliant small essays about futurist sexual politics and Loy's various intellectual not to speak of sexual provocations in that milieu (180–183, 184–186).

13. Pound also cut a stanza from the section he cited, removed a few lines, changed a preposition, and put in some periods, so even the material he cited is not an exact account of Loy's poem.

14. No mention of this redaction by Loy or Pound has yet been unearthed.

15. In *Instigations* each poem is cited in its entirety. For the one that is not—Williams's "The Old Men"—Pound uses ellipses for the last five lines. The *only* work not given in full is Loy's.

16. Nicholls's claim that Loy's work was "pivotal" to Pound focuses on stylistic issues such as abstract words and her internationalist verbalism and on ideological issues such as her critique of romantic fantasy (Nicholls 2001). The issues I raise are not discussed.

17. It is striking that this redaction occurs in a book that Pound titled *Instigations*, for this very word is arguably taken precisely from Loy's description of Gina—"an instigation to the reaction of man." The title thus avers that Loy has served precisely as "instigation" to Pound's "reaction." His book title again both credits Loy and muffles her impact.

18. This critique of marriage did have some currency with Pound. In an appreciative review of Allen Upward published in 1913 in *New Freewoman*, Pound (echoing Upward) notes: "Modern marriage is, apparently, derived from the laws of slave concubinage, not from the more honourable forms of primitive European marriage. So much for the upholders of 'Sacrament'" (Pound 1973, 404). His ethnographic irony against the sham pretensions of organized religion resembled some feminist interpretation of marriage as legal prostitution—an exchange of sex for a living. Pound's tacit approval occurred before his own marriage in 1914.

19. The eccentric Dunning (1878[?]–1930) emerged as Pound's protégé in the mid-twenties, with poems published through Pound's good offices. It is an

aesthetic shock, for those saturated in modernist poetics, to hear this work. "Where did you learn that smile? From what dead lips / Of little children and a queen's disgrace / Rose the immortal butterfly that sips / Upon your mouth and flits about your face?" (Dunning 1925, 7). Dunning is also remembered in *The Pisan Cantos* (Pound [1948] 2003, 76).

20. Dunning uses "a verbal system almost identical with the verbal systems of Swinburne, Dowson [. . .] and a strophic form like those employed by the 'nineties' and the Victorians"; he nevertheless constructs "musical phrases; their freshness and precision are not less remarkable because they are not set out in fancy type, broken lines, hosiery-ad fonts, valentine wreaths or other post-Mallarmé devices." This is from Pound's proleptic review of an as-yet unpublished book by Dunning. Pound's attacks on both *vers libre* and the visual mannerisms of modernists (alongside high praise of Dunning's world-weary poetry) qualify his normal avant-garde insistences (Pound, 1925, 342).

21. *Profile* is a pedagogic and literary historical anthology, with 100 poems prefaced by historical and stylistic notes about their representativeness of the era from the 1890s to 1920s. Pound also writes himself emphatically into literary history—underlining his presence, noting his participation in all the manners or styles available. Based on his choices, one sees Pound's willingness to continue to champion his list of male and female writers, even his willingness to extend a brief welcome (mediated by *New Masses*) to some political writers and to anonymous African-American blues and ballad makers (Pound 1932b, 127–142).

22. Michael Levenson has shown the ways in which these were contradictory poetics (Levenson 1984, 126–148).

23. The same pattern had occurred in 1912. Pound's simultaneous appropriation from and reduction of a creatively active woman (Florence Farr) to a deficient muse figure in "Portrait d'une Femme" (1912) is also a gesture of dehistoricizing, despecifying, and even deprofessionalizing active female cultural producers (DuPlessis 2006a, 122–136).

24. The subhead for this section is a citation from Stein [1927] 1980, 143.

25. In 1953 Pound notes to Margaret Anderson that Eliot "allus threateded AXshun if anybuddy reprinted Eeldrop"—as she had just done (Pound, 1988, 304; see also 322–323, 326).

26. For this era of the Pound-Eliot bond, Richard Badenhausen proposes one poet as "authoritative," the other as "acquiescent" or even claiming roles of "domination" and "submission" (Badenhausen 2004, 10, 63).

27. I am alluding to the surface problems with sexuality and his apparently mixed desires (see Gordon 1999); however, Koestenbaum makes the striking argument that Vivienne Eliot and T. S. Eliot were deep collaborators in their mutual hysterias and pathologies (Koestenbaum 1989, 117). The couple had married in 1915.

28. The Pound/Williams correspondence (Pound 1996b and Williams 1996) is cited as *Pound/Williams*.

29. "Bigotry" is unglossed, but perhaps it refers to the cut "Dirge for Bleistein"? Or the satire on women, the cut Fresca section? Here one must respectfully note that "bigotry" has hardly been extirpated in early Eliot (there is plenty left in the quatrain poems); nor is this extirpation a reasonable demand to make. Further, "bigotry" is on a different order than the other elements listed and needs a quite different critical apprehension than "urination" and other offenses.

30. Narrative lines about men on a drunken bender precede "April is the cruelest month," which now begins "The Burial of the Dead." Lines at the beginning of "The Fire Sermon" depict a pretentious but lively female writer—Fresca. Lines at the beginning of "Death by Water" concern sailors on a bad—even doomed—voyage. This last has many echoes of boys' adventure books like Rudyard Kipling's *Captains Courageous* as well as Samuel Taylor Coleridge's "Rime of the Ancient Mariner."

31. Jack Stillinger notes the total of more than 400 lines cut or changed by Pound, reducing an almost 1,000-line draft to 434 lines. Thus his provocative claim of the poem's "multiple authorship" or co-authorship (Stillinger 1991, 133, 134, 136).

32. The possibility that Eliot was not (fully, subtly?) conscious of his (original?) intentions is unprovable; further, the reason Stillinger adduced—his precarious mental state in 1921—is insultingly problematic (Stillinger 1991, 138). Eliot did authorize this poem, assessing what was there, what was cut, what remained, and how to complete it.

33. Drawing on and extending Wayne Koestenbaum, Michael North also demonstrates how works both by more realist novelists (Willa Cather/Ernest Hemingway) and by more experimental writers (Stein/Eliot) have very similar goals in a "reorientation" and "destabilization of gender" and sexuality, in a transgressive attitude, and even in a "feminine self-identification" for some males, masked for them by a displacement averring resistance to conventional women (North 1999, 192).

34. *Cassell's Dictionary of Slang* gives "fly cop" as an alert policeman. There might be a pun on fly (a flap covering an opening on clothing), however.

35. Colleen Lamos efficiently sums up the evidence for the "homoerotic implications" of this passage from a series of critics, from John Peter to G. Wilson Knight, John T. Mayer, and James E. Miller, and how it is dealt with in the poem (Lamos 1998, 113–114).

36. Fresca's literary pretensions and preening social climbing owe something to parodies of the smart set such as Aldous Huxley's; her friends resemble characters in Eliot's saturnine poems on Grishkin or Mr. Cheetah or, in fact, the cosmopolites of "Gerontion," among whom the name "Fresca" appears.

37. See Sandra Gilbert and Susan Gubar for a sense that Fresca, whether present or absent, is thoroughly symptomatic of modernist male misogyny (Gilbert and Gubar 1994, 418, n. 29). Maud Ellmann observes that "the misogyny is

so ferocious, particularly in the manuscript, that it begins to turn into a blasphemy against itself," becoming "enthralled by the femininity that it reviles," a deconstructive explanation for the sex-gender veerings of the poem that also points to self-division in the poet (Ellmann 1987, 98).

38. The only lengthy narrative—the monologue with Ellen Kellond as its originator—could not be traced to its source and thus could not be criticized as unoriginal. Indeed, it was not until "The Waste Land" manuscript was published (1971) that she was identified by Eliot (Eliot 1971, 127; DuPlessis [1990] 2006, 50–51).

39. Peter Nicholls proposes pertinent distinctions among allusion, citation, and intertextuality within modernist poetry (Nicholls 2010, 11–19).

40. In contrast, Peter Dale Scott discusses the "Dantean" and universalizing quality of "the Tiresian voice which Pound had helped liberate" from the draft "Waste Land" (P. Scott 1990, 103), seeing this as one of Pound's main achievements.

41. Just a side remark on gender hierarchies: in our culture, note that this question is structured as greater and lesser, not as different versions of a parallel pleasure.

42. Calvin Bedient views Tiresias as one particularized character and the speaker beyond him as "the performances of a single protagonist—not Tiresias but a nameless stand-in for Eliot himself" (Bedient 1986, ix).

43. The subhead for this section is a citation from Stein [1927] 1980, 143.

44. Granted, one interaction was a negative, apocalyptic review of Stein. Eliot's interaction with Djuna Barnes and his editing of *Nightwood* were to come slightly later.

3. Succession and Supersession, from Z to "A"

1. Hugh Witemeyer cautions that Williams's letters from 1907 to 1920 were lost; hence Pound sounds like the dominant (dominating, domineering) partner (*Pound/Williams*, 5). In the Creeley-Olson correspondence (Olson 1980–1987 and 1990/1996 and Creeley 1980–1987 and 1990/1996, cited as *Olson/Creeley*), George Butterick notes the loss from water damage of some 1951 Creeley letters (*Olson/Creeley*, V: vii).

2. Quoted from Bök's notebook, with thanks for his permission.

3. Epstein delineates individual similar-age friendships with tensions, angst, and negative investments, specifically as these are visible in poems and other documents (Epstein 2006, 4, 7–8).

4. The fraternal—familial/filiative but also affiliative—is the relationship showing the most contradictory pressure in this bilateral model.

5. The Pound/Zukofsky correspondence (Pound 1987 and Zukofsky 1987) is cited in the text as *Pound/Zukofsky*.

6. Freud: "the libido (entirely or in part) has found its way back into regression and has re-animated the infantile imagos"—one might well see the teasing father-child verbalizations as a way of indicating some transference (Freud [1912] 1963, 108–109).

7. Only seven years after fraternal interventions with his editing of "The Waste Land," Pound assumed the role of paternal figure for the younger Zukofsky.

8. Achieving literary status via Pound had its risks, marking Zukofsky "as something of a footnote to Pound," as Bob Perelman and others have noted (Perelman 1994, 177).

9. Pound's long letters are dated 24 October, 25 October, and 28 October 1930; the three responses by Zukofsky, 5 November, 6 November, and 9 November 1930.

10. Both Pound and Monroe manifested much wishful thinking about this. In January 1931 Monroe announced Zukofsky in *Poetry*, calling him "for several years a prominent member of a group of writers interested in experiment in poetic form and method"—about as close to saying the word "movement" as one could come and still veer off (Monroe 1931a, 231).

11. Zukofsky admired Eliot's "Marina" and solicited Eliot for his issue (*Pound/Zukofsky*, 71, 9 November 1930).

12. The Williams/Zukofsky correspondence (Williams 2003 and Zukofsky 2003) is cited as *Williams/Zukofsky*.

13. Williams benefited from Zukofsky's literary editing and advice (indeed, he actively sought it), and Zukofsky benefited from Williams's support and friendship, dinners, and other nurturing offers (Quartermain 1992, 90–91; Scroggins 2007a, 90–103; *Williams/Zukofsky*, 140, 169, 181, 186, 208, including medical advice).

14. The importance of the Shylock reference is discussed in Stanley 1994, 67–68; Perelman 1994, 176; Scroggins 1998, 125; DuPlessis 2001, 166–172; and Scroggins 2007a, 55–59.

15. "Wimpus" is not in the *Oxford English Dictionary*.

16. "Wimpus: n. A patented device intended for use by men suffering from impotentia erigendi, or incapability of tumescence. This mechanical splint, when placed on the member, gives the assembly sufficient rigidity for penetration. It is made of flesh-colored rubber in the form of a long section of a cylinder shaped to fit the lower side of the member, from the root to a little short of the corona glandis, and reaching about one-quarter of the way around the circumference of the organ. At each extremity there is a thin rubber ring, attached to the main body, through which the member is inserted, thus holding the device in place. The long portion contains some sort of stiffener, probably a thin piece of spring steel. Enough of the organ is left exposed for sensation" (2008; http://www.findalay.com/rc-sex-dictionary-W.htm). The dictionary has been removed since my original use of this website, and the site has significantly changed from

one generally informative about sexual matters to one that gives specific information about sex tours, strip clubs, escorts, and the like. See note 17.

17. Unfortunately, the pictures of the similar-looking devices found in contemporaneous ads in *QUACK! Tales of Medical Fraud* do not have sources for
magazine or year (McCoy 2000, 216). But the wimpus was an actively debated
item in the 1920s. Readers who want somewhat more verification about the
wimpus in the 1920s than a now-untraceable citation (see note 16) should look
at *Journal of the American Medical Association* 87.18 (30 October 1926), 1497,
jama.ama-assn.org/content/87/18/1497.full.pdf.

The brief article called "The Wimpus Fraud" contains a summary of an investigative report on various devices on sale "alleged to be for the purpose of
making it possible for those in whom the erectile power was lost to perform the
sexual act." One of these was called the "Wimpus," made, in this case, by Higrade
Specialty Company and sent through the mails. "The 'Wimpus' consists of a piece
of reenforced rubber about 3/4 inch wide and from 3 to 5 inches long, with elastic
bands at each end for the purpose of holding the device on the penis of the user."
The report cites from the advertising: "'So long as a man has the desire to cohabit
it is a prime indication that the glands are still active, but cannot properly function without the aid of the necessary rigidity; [it is claimed] that the "Wimpus"
supplies the rigidity necessary to make the male sexual organ properly function.'"
The fraud order was issued in October 1926 by postmaster general Harry S. New.

18. John F. Kasson's analysis of white American manhood reminds us that
in the period 1890–1914 Anglo-Saxon men often suffered from the modern, recently uncovered disease of "neurasthenia"—"nervous weakness and fatigue"
(Kasson 2001, 10–11).

19. While still seeking some advice—would Pound show him where to cut
"A"?—in 1931 Zukofsky repeatedly claims his originality or at least coequality as
a poet and possibly his superiority to the recent work of Eliot, to the work of e. e.
cummings (from whom he states he now has nothing to learn), and to Pound's
early "slight" critiques of "A" (*Pound/Zukofsky*, 112–113).

20. In contrast, Williams admired "A"—at least in its early moments. He
praised "A"-1–7 directly to Zukofsky in 1932 but made mild comments (both encouraging and critical) all along from 1928, while the early parts of the poem
were being written. Williams also praised the work to Pound (19 October 1929)
for its "quality of scholarliness and extreme skepticism" along with a lack of sentimentality (*Pound/Williams*, 97).

21. Perelman has also remarked on Pound's "volatile" mentorship, involving
"aggression," "indifference," and praise (Perelman 1994, 178–179).

22. After Pound's inclusion of two sections and part of another from "Poem
Beginning 'The'" in his 1932 anthology *Profile* (five and a half pages of Zukofsky),
Zukofsky would have found there Macleod's section from *The Ecliptic* called
"Libra, or, The Scales" (also five and a half pages).

23. Keith Tuma also discusses Macleod's work (Tuma 1998, 131–139).

24. On the aphorism from Brancusi, see *Guide to Kulchur* (Pound [1938] 1966, 59).

25. At times Williams also tried to give editorial advice to make Zukofsky be more explicit and make his work clearer (*Williams/Zukofsky*, 332, 334). Williams indicated that sometimes he felt "restless" in contemplating Zukofsky's critical position; the pressure it put on him resembled the effect of Pound's work (*Williams/Zukofsky*, 315).

26. This was despite Pound's adducing of Zukofsky several times at the end of *Profile*'s literary historical notes as well as anthologizing his poems there—for literary critical articles and for his editing (Pound 1932b, 142). And also despite the serious, striking generosity of both Pound and Williams: both men gave Zukofsky a sum of money in 1933 that would allow him to go to Europe (*Williams/ Zukofsky*, 1155–1156).

27. Scroggins discusses Zukofsky's divided loyalties and dilemmas when faced with Pound's anti-Semitism. He does not note the gender materials (Scroggins 2007a, 167–170).

28. *Intra-* means within (within the vagina); *inter-* means between, but Pound seems to intend a person protected inside the uterus who needs to "come forth by day" (*Pound/Zukofsky*, 158).

29. In his citations Zukofsky makes few efforts to contextualize or to pick material long enough to give a sense of the source text. He generally takes a few discontinuous words from a long source passage and joins them together. The sound of the citation, the look of the letters, the drastic extraction, and the rearranging transform anything he cites into something *sui generis*. Zukofsky rarely seeks the essence or thesis of the cited work—he engorges the bits and puts them through his writing process until they come out as written by him. It is a contrarian, nonextractive mode of scholarship.

30. Burton Hatlen addresses the Poundian aspects through "A"-12 in a brilliant reading of the family quartet and the complex fours organizing this poem; the fourth member of the family is Pinchos, Zukofsky's father, for whom "A"-12 is both an elegy and, in its own way, a Kaddish (Hatlen 1997, 227–229).

31. Peter Quartermain attributes modernist disjunctive language to those writers—Williams, Stein, Zukofsky—whose first language was not American English or who were significantly bilingual in their early years (Quartermain 1992, 10).

32. This retrospective interview occurred when the poem was not yet completed. Only after the 1968 musical ending was assembled by Celia Zukofsky—and only after the Dembo interview in 1968 (Zukofsky 1969)—did (could?) Zukofsky write sections 22 (1970–1973) and 23 (1973–1974) of "A."

33. My sense of the Pauline Zukofsky is indebted to Ben Friedlander's provocative discussion of Paul as an antinomian Jew (Friedlander 2010), drawing on Daniel Boyarin (1994).

34. A complex tracking and coordination of dates and claims, not catalogued here, has led me to the forensic conclusion that (whatever he might say) Zukofsky was well aware of Pound's long poem from the very first moments of his own literary career but perhaps at first thought it would not deal with modernity. See also Perelman 1994, 177. Zukofsky had projected the number twenty-four in one of his earliest letters to Pound (*Pound/Zukofsky*, 24, 12 December 1928).

35. Indeed, this pattern of cultural struggle might also illuminate Zukofsky's sour allusion to *Four Quartets* in "Poetry/*For My Son When He Can Read*." In the essay, Eliot's name is not even mentioned, but Zukofsky is disdainful of the mythopoetic and religious imagination represented by Eliot's emphatically Christian poem, widely viewed as a cultural triumph.

36. Pound seems to have lost this wager, which is why the lines "i.e. it co-heres all right / even if my notes do not cohere" are so often cited (Pound 1996a, Canto CXVI, 27).

37. As Bob Perelman reminded me.

38. According to Jewish tradition, there are three main units of Hebrew scriptures: Torah in five books, Nevi'im in eight, and Ketuvim in eleven. Thus the total number is twenty-four. In the Christian tradition, however, which calls this text the Old Testament, these books are counted individually, bringing the total to thirty-six.

39. Further, Zukofsky's comments in essays about *The Cantos* in 1929 and about Williams in 1928 get replayed in "A"-24 (594–607), minus any mention of either poet's name. Zukofsky's summaries of the work of both mentor figures—paternal or fraternal—have been rearticulated; in the context that Celia Zukofsky created, the several citations appear to pertain to "A."

40. Pound's *Drafts & Fragments of Cantos CX–CXVII* was published in 1968; he died in 1972.

41. See also Perelman 1984, in which the insoluble challenge of treating words as if they were notes in time functions as a critique of the work. My intuitions about the performance were confirmed by Peter Nicholls and Peter Middleton, who both attended the Sussex event (separate e-mail communications to me, 2 February 2009).

42. This information comes from Mark Scroggins, to whom I am quite indebted for the factual basis for this analysis (Scroggins 1998, 41). Celia Zukofsky was apparently the chief compiler of this index, although Zukofsky was a co-worker; it was completed by 1976 (Scroggins 2007a, 440).

43. Because it is decontextualized and information-bearing, an index is normatively viewed as an unpoetic genre and tactic. It has minimum "poeticity"—at least in theory. Zukofsky could have known Marianne Moore's index to *Observations* (Moore 1924). In contemporary work there are Bernadette Mayer's index for her essay-poem *Utopia* (Mayer 1984); Lisa Jarnot's *Some Other Kind of Mission* (Jarnot 1996), with a page of a visual text called "Index"; Joshua Clover's index to *The Totality for Kids* (Clover 2006); and Craig Dworkin's index to *Parse*

(Dworkin 2008), constructed (indexically) of the abstract names for all parts of speech in the source text, an 1874 book called *How to Parse*.

44. "H" is the sign for B natural; "B" for B flat. Many composers, among them Felix Mendelssohn, Robert Schumann, Franz Liszt, Ferruccio Busoni, Arnold Schoenberg, and Anton Webern, have made such an homage.

45. This being an unassimilable gesture is symbolized in Zukofsky criticism by the fact that the main website devoted to Zukofsky (http://www.z-site.net/), which discusses every single section of "A," trying to track the allusions (painstakingly creating a dictionary/encyclopedia of the poem), does not have a section devoted to this index. It was thought of as extramural.

4. Poetic Projects of Countercultural Manhood

1. Spahr's work is made of found language from a review of Tim Gardner's show at 303 Gallery in New York City, Art Forum, March 2000, arranged in sonnet form by Spahr.

2. Robert von Hallberg reminds us that Olson importantly fused a political and a cultural vision (von Hallberg 1978, 10–21).

3. Suzanne Clark has pointed to "a male gendering elevated above all questions of marked gender"—taking "whiteness and maleness, together with American authenticity, as unmarked, neutral positions of superior reason" (Clark 2000, 3). In two of these three particulars, these poets were critical; in one, they were not.

4. The subhead for this section is a citation from Stein [1927] 1980, 126.

5. For social historian Warren Susman, Disneyland was "the mythic essence of what life was supposed to be like in the 1940s and 1950s" (Susman with Griffin 1989, 31).

6. Shoah in "Howl" emerges in "who broke down crying in white gymnasiums naked and trembling before the machinery of other skeletons," although this is more overtly about military induction or hospitalization (Ginsberg 1984, 127). Ginsberg's religious affiliation became Buddhist in the post-"Howl" period.

7. The Federal Bureau of Investigation (FBI) reciprocated with a file on Ginsberg and others that he later received under the Freedom of Information Act (FOIA), selected, photocopied, and distributed to many people (including myself) for information and dispersed safekeeping under the title FBI**Narcotics Bureau**CIA files, "Exemplary Shockers & Smoking Typewriters, 1968–1970" (Ginsberg n.d.). The files reveal the many tactics that the FBI used for "disrupting political minorities" (with informants, disinformation, anonymous letters, and spying). While this group of materials is dated later than my time frame here, it is typical of FBI tactics and collections throughout the 1950s.

8. The proleptic first poem in Ginsberg's *Collected Poems*, "Queertalk" (1947), is an allegory about the male voice: alternative modes (queer, hip, messianic) all seek domination; their correlation and fusion is accomplished by

the speaker's uncompromising judgment of a woman, dismissed with an insult (Ginsberg 1984, 3).

9. Fanny Howe comments devastatingly on the contradictions for women: "It was a man's world, even out there on the edges beyond convention. It was the men who broke themselves at the margin. It was the men who were loud and famous. The women I knew then shuffled barefoot at perhaps a farther edge—the edge where anonymity either creates subversion or self-annihilation" (Howe 1985, 199).

10. The subhead for this section is a citation from Stein [1927] 1980, 134.

11. Creeley's construction of masculinity in the 1950s differs somewhat from his later work; see chapter 7.

12. Many of Creeley's early poems—"The Whip," "The Way," "A Marriage," "Damon & Pythias," "Sing Song," "The Wife," "Song"—are set precisely, explicitly in the marital bed or allude to that bed and its events (Creeley 1962).

13. Davidson makes a related point of great acuity: "In both Beat and Deep Image movements, greater sensitivity or vision is purchased at the expense of women, even when her gender [. . .] is invoked as a positive value" (Davidson 1995, 199).

14. This is my way of saying what Barrett Watten proposed thus: "The halting, indecisive style of Creeley's work masks, here, a profound strategy of recuperation" (Watten 2000, 289).

15. Compare Olson's response to such female markers. When Olson's first poems appeared in *Harper's Bazaar* (1949), he made "boobie" puns on the name of the fashion magazine: "Boozoomzar" "or Bra-sar / or Bubsie-zar / or Boob-zar/ [. . .] or any equally brazen offence" and seemed to be somewhat startled at his appearance near an ad for emphatically capitalized "MODESS" (Olson 1999, 19).

16. Kimmel proposes that although men were "in power," nonetheless "this power did not translate to a feeling of being powerful at the individual level" (Kimmel 1994, viii).

17. Note Tania Modelski's terse summary in *Feminism without Women*: "How frequently male subjectivity works to appropriate 'femininity' while oppressing women" (Modelski 1991, 7).

18. This has particular irony, given the remarks of Bobbie Louise Hawkins (formerly Bobbie Creeley), whose encouragement for Creeley's novel-writing drew upon her sense of open-field poetics (Creeley 1993, 92).

19. The subhead for this section is a citation from Stein [1927] 1980, 145.

20. Chapter 6 continues this discussion.

21. Note the gay male frankness in central poems of masculinity in the 1950s: from Robert Duncan's "cocksuckers" in *The Venice Poem* (Duncan 1949, 31; written 1948) to Allen Ginsberg's frank and noble gay sex poem "Many Loves" (1956; Ginsberg 1984, 156–158), to the vatic sublime sexuality of "Howl" (1956), discussed above, to Jack Spicer's coterie judgment poems in *Admonitions* (1957; Spicer 2008, 157–168) and elsewhere.

22. In the 1950s centrist manhood spoke its name in *The Organization Man* (Whyte 1956), a new kind of socioeconomic type of large national (now global) corporations. No longer were the small town, local elites, small bankers, businessmen, journalists, and producers in small-scale production central; they were superseded by a corporate male identity to which one was obliged to conform in dress, attitude, choices—a standardization and flattening of "independent" manhood, just as Levittown, also from the 1950s, homogenized housing styles to impose efficiencies of scale.

23. The encrypted "bitch" indicates both female figure and male sexual recipient.

24. This poem is astonishingly not one that Creeley selected for Olson's *Selected Writings* (Olson 1966), or for his edition of *Selected Poems* (Olson 1993), perhaps because of the fullness of its discussion of fathers. Creeley seriously downplayed any father-son materials in Olson. See chapter 6.

25. This pleasure and eroticism extended to Olson's appreciation of the first publication of this poem, in *Evergreen Review* 4 (Spring 1958). Praising with rich sexual and narcissistic language editor Donald Allen's photograph of motorcyclists on the cover, Olson writes in a fashion that cannot have been innocent of erotic overtones, "Did anyone tell you how it is to be put out there by another man who has covered you like your own skin?" (Olson 2000, 273; also Olson 2003, 33).

26. Recall that "Howl" was written in 1955, published in 1956. According to Tom Clark (1991), Olson was quite jealous of the Beats during the later 1950s, as they emerged into public notoriety. Again priority and belatedness are patriarchal motifs, although not exclusively so.

27. In support of this thesis, Olson cites and extends a stanza of a poem by Melville from *Timoleon*, about the tragic splitting of the integral human—a male-female androgyne (Olson 1987b, 282); he cites it accurately in *Call Me Ishmael* (Olson 1947, 103). The lines, from Melville's poem "After the Pleasure Party," based on Plato's *Symposium*, mourn the splitting of the human form into two warring sexes who are slaves to each other and who may never meet their true other half of whatever gender (see Melville 1947, 219).

28. It only lacks homosexual panic, self-divided "victimized" maleness, and mythologized, ahistoric females.

5. Sex/Gender Contradictions in Olson and Boldereff

1. The in-print correspondence with Boldereff (Olson 1999 and Boldereff 1999, cited as *Olson/Boldereff*) runs from November 1947 to September 1950; it overlaps with the correspondence with Edward Dahlberg (Olson 1990), not treated here (1936 through 1955—the last years in acrimony). The ten volumes of in-print correspondence with Creeley (*Olson/Creeley*) run from April 1950 to July 1952. A five-month overlap in 1950 between Olson's correspondence with

Boldereff and with Creeley is visible in the printed sources. In the five months of the Olson-Boldereff correspondence from December 1949 to May 1950—which are the five months before the first letter to Creeley—the exchange with Boldereff is almost 250 printed pages; the next unit of Boldereff letters (11 May 1950–19 July 1950) at about 100 printed pages parallels volume 1 of *Olson/Creeley*, which is about 140 pages. These rough statistics give a sense of the overlap but also of the shift of Olson's attention from one correspondent to another.

2. In a 1982 lecture, Duncan called Olson's poetry "a record of our times [. . .] a deep record of a hidden man's house from which this poetry comes. Something more than the picture is that society is patristic, but Olson's was in an entirely patristic world. I mean, the figure of his father is huge in his mind and then Maximus and then the huge father figures that appear, bigger than all that, are amazing in his poems" (Duncan 1995, 26). "Patristic" means specifically relating to the fathers of the early Christian church and their writings as establishing canon, interpretation, and institutions. It also may be Duncan's way of playing with "patriarchal," a word prominent in feminist cultural analysis in the 1970s. The Olson-Duncan relationship is discussed variously in Rifkin (2000, 25–26) and in Mossin (2010, 44–49).

3. Creeley is referred to in one Olson letter to Boldereff (*Olson/Boldereff*, 392, 28 June 1950). "Bigmans" is possibly an allusion to Gilgamesh/Bilgamesh and Enkidu—bonded male heroes. The Gilgamesh story and later the Inanna story in Samuel Kramer's scholarship (which she knew from Kramer himself) are two of Boldereff's significant contributions to Olson's poetic arsenal (*Olson/Boldereff*, xv, 34, 487 n. 25).

4. Olson never wrote his projected book about the human body as the fundamental organic premise we live in—"as object and function," precisely as our embodied reality, "no soul stuff" invoked (Olson 1975, 82).

5. Actually, this is bibliographically complicated: the 1936 notebook is not available (*Olson/Boldereff*, 21); the letter sent to Boldereff is Olson's selective typing of those remarks on which he wanted to comment or which he thought were important enough to signal to her (21–31).

6. Boldereff's enthusiasm for both Lawrence and Whitman influenced Olson's interest.

7. Lawrence's story exists in two versions, *The Man Who Died* (1931), which Olson owned, and *The Escaped Cock* (1929), in the Black Sun edition, which Ralph Maud speculates that Olson knew (Maud 1996, 224 n. 26). Olson's title "The Escaped Cock: Notes on Lawrence and the Real" suggests that he did.

8. Frieda Lawrence's name mixes with the name of a Lawrence character (Constance Chatterley) and thereby with the name of Olson's partner, Constance Wilcock, suggesting Olson's emotional identifications.

9. The subhead for this section is a citation from Olson's poem called "The Story of an Olson, and a Bad Thing" (Olson 1987b, 177, June 1950).

10. Incidentally, in *The Maximus Poems*, nonmythic female figures virtually never appear in the 635 pages of text, in notable contrast, of course, to historical male figures.

11. Tom Clark has analyzed poems from this time as encoding Olson's two partners, though he does not treat this "Sappho" poem (Clark 1991, 167, 171, 174).

12. "Lady Mimosa" is not included in the *Collected Poems* but printed almost verbatim from the letter to Boldereff (Olson 1999, 283–286) and in *A Nation of Nothing But Poetry* (Olson 1989b, 69–71); Andrew Mossin also discusses this poem (Mossin 2005, 30–32; Mossin 2010, 58–60).

13. Maud (2008, 115–117) is kinder than I am in his consideration of these materials, for he changes the topic abruptly to Olson's courage in breaking through a taboo: that as a non-Jew he talks about Jewishness. This is hardly the point. It is what he says about Jews and their animal hearts that is at issue, not his particular religio-cultural affiliation.

14. In Wellman's essay, my work comes in for particular attention, when he notes my apparent "antipathy for the psychological cost (to him and to others) of [Olson's] struggle to create something in the way of an 'open form'" (Wellman 2007, 51). Open form is not the real issue; I also think he means my "analysis," not my "antipathy." This is my argument: at every turn Olson grants male figures the largest part of cultural possibility (whether mythic, historical, psychological, political); Olson resists (sometimes after debate, as outlined here) parallel coequal possibilities for female cultural actors.

15. The same Olson letter contains an interesting unpursued corollary: that in the vertical or "perpendicular" "there ain't nothing to say except as you penetrate your own damn self" (*Olson/Creeley*, X: 71, 15 May 1952). The autotelic metaphor for the sex act of writing does pose the male writer as specifically a heterosexual "androgyne."

16. The subhead for this section comes from the Olson/Boldereff letters (*Olson/Boldereff*, 413).

17. The subhead of this section is a citation from *Olson/Boldereff*, 515.

18. According to Olson's daughter Catherine Seelye, editor of the Olson-Pound materials, in 1948 Olson was writing very self-consciously and self-critically about his father-identified "'amours'" and the tremendous temptation to remain "a mere son" even at age thirty-eight (Seelye in Olson 1975, xxiv, xxiii).

19. Editors Ralph Maud and Sharon Thesen have made this choice of cutoff date, framing the correspondence at its years of greatest intensity.

20. Remembering Black Mountain College, reflecting back fifty-plus years, Michael Rumaker points out the "radicalness" and educational "innovation" he experienced, its relative openness to his gay self, but notes that "despite a bit more wiggle room," the college was "a replica of the hierarchical and patriarchal order outside the gates"—adding that this was "even more so" when Olson became its titular center (Rumaker 2003, 188). This is confirmed by one of Vincent Katz's

interviews in which artist Dorothea Rockburne ruminates: "It was a strange and wonderful place, but it was very sexist" (Katz 2002, 188).

21. Olson sometimes finds it difficult to make a choice to act when he is called on at a critical moment. An example is his convoluted response to Ralph Maud's straightforward political question: would he help lead a protest against a SUNY-Buffalo loyalty oath in 1963 (Olson 2000, 300–304)? The short answer is no, but the justifications and stories of past political actions, backpedaling, claims, and finally the choice to declare poetry a new political commitment and his need to ask Maud to sign on to *that* are a masterpiece of rhetorical equivoca- tion (or party-of-one individuality, depending on your point of view).

22. While this letter was returned by a post office unsympathetic to such generative renamings (i.e., it may not have been read), it indicates that ideas of incest, later incorporated into the essay, were already understood by both as "their" motif.

23. Creeley's specific modesty and care for Olson's reputation is seen in an essay from 1960 when, in listing the generative principles of "Projective Verse," he does not mention that one was formulated by himself (Creeley 1989, 107).

6. Olson's "Long Exaggeration of Males"

1. "Write as the father to be the father" is Olson's note to himself in 1945, cited in Seelye (in Olson 1975, xvii) in the plural ("fathers"), cited by Butterick (1980, xxvi) in the singular. "My long exaggeration of males" is a phrase in a let- ter from Olson to Constance Wilcock in 1952, during a trial separation (Olson, 2000, 176).

2. All these citations of Olson speaking from Boer (1975) date from 1969; Olson was teaching at the University of Connecticut, Storrs, briefly before the symptoms of his final illness declared themselves; he died on January 10, 1970.

3. When a female figure (like Marcia Nardi with Williams) attempts this volatile and metamorphic multiplicity, she may be viewed as a hysterical pre- tender to these positions.

4. Henceforth citations from *Olson/Creeley* in this chapter include only vol- ume and page numbers.

5. There is a lacuna in the correspondence from 4 to 27 July 1950 so marked that Creeley complains of it; almost nothing that he proffers (including praise from Williams for a draft of "Projective Verse") gets a response from Olson. In that three weeks Creeley wrote eleven letters, including his own notes on "Projective Verse" (notes on II: 58–62; II: 54–80). At this very moment Olson was writing incredibly passionate, overwhelmed, seductive, and manic letters to Boldereff and beginning his notable cultural theorizing in an intellectual burst of protean proportions. But he can never reveal this fact to explain the gap in letters to Creeley.

6. "From the point of view of hegemonic masculinity, in modernity, the potential of homoerotic pleasure was expelled from the masculine and located in a deviant group" (Connell 2002a, 253).

7. Rumaker also states that these were "love letters, eros [being] the taproot of so much human energy and endeavor" (Rumaker 2003, 183).

8. Creeley invokes one key word for himself and Olson, the talismanic "ON-WARD" (*Olson/Creeley,* I: 106, 17 June 1950), a word that Creeley repeatedly used as a general blessing throughout his life. Olson uses the variant word "OUT-WARD" for Creeley as the dedicatory glyph in *The Maximus Poems* (1983). The contrast of these two related words is a contrast between a future time evoked in specific quests and general readiness (Creeley's position) and a spatial-geographic expansiveness in Olson.

9. However, Peter Middleton reveals "that Creeley did not encourage Olson acolytes" (observation from 1977) (Middleton 2010b, 159).

10. "20 Questions with Robert Creeley" in *Milk Magazine* modifies this fifty years later—a good example of temporal change at work in the literary field. Asked what magazine was most influential for him, Creeley responds "Cid Corman's *Origin*—that's where I found my company" (Creeley 2002).

11. The subhead for this section is a citation from Olson to William Bronk, on George Oppen's omnibus review in *Poetry* (August 1962) (Butterick 1980, 495–496).

12. For hints of the rage, see *Olson/Creeley,* I: 110–111; for Creeley's cooler discussion of the stakes, see I: 98. Creeley, however, is a forerunner of the position that deflected discussion of the ways in which Pound's political opinions integrated with his poetic tactics, an avoidance that reigned in literary circles for many years.

13. In the *Cantos,* "the morphology is not taken back any further than, approximately, Athens" (VII: 70).

14. Almost two decades later (ca. 1969), Olson is still sensitive/aggressive on the point of genealogy, stating to Boer "'I got nothing out of *Paterson* [. . .] I owe that Bill Williams nothing'" (Boer 1975, 83). In a remark about ten years earlier to Donald Allen, he is more generous about the link between their projects (Olson 2003, 49).

15. Creeley's way of coping is to turn these words over facet by facet, not concentrating on the actually large differences between them. In the meditation that follows, he comes to agree with Olson more (VII: 107), and Olson with him (VII: 116), indicating again their stake in avoiding conflict as well as their powerful dialogue.

16. Olson's "aunties" with their scare quotes are male; he puts no women writers on his list of contemporaries (Olson 2003, 60–61). Peter Middleton outlines this erasure of influences with attention to its emphasis on generational discontinuity and critical rupture in the building of this anthology (Middleton 2010a, 183–185).

17. The section in Creeley's *Collected Essays* called "The Company" contains eleven essays on Olson, three essays on Robert Duncan, a synoptic overview with much on Olson and Duncan, three essays on Edward Dorn, one on Michael Mc-Clure, one on Paul Blackburn, one on John Wieners, and a few multiplex reviews, like one on Denise Levertov, Joel Oppenheimer, and Zukofsky together. The whole book of essays contains one on H.D., one on Stein, one on Diane di Prima, one on Hilda Morley, and a consideration of Madeline Gins and Shåusaku Arakawa. One might contrast this with Duncan's *The H.D. Book* (2011).

18. Olson also contributed to the practice of the "company" by mentions of living male poets—helpers, disciples, and friends, listed in *Maximus* III; some of these men were still alive in 2010 (Olson 1983, 533, 540, 557, 575). One can barely imagine how thrilling and gratifying their appearance would have been in a poem in which many had put so much hope, and in Jeremy Prynne's case, to which he had contributed information and documentation; Prynne is mentioned three times.

19. The sloppy, wayward (albeit suggestive) moves of Olson's scholarship elicit a good deal of critique from any number of writers on him—even George Butterick (quietly), but certainly Andrew Ross, Libbie Rifkin, and others.

20. See chapter 4 for an analysis of "The Lordly and Isolate Satyrs." These poems are also excluded from Olson's *Selected Writings*, edited by Creeley and published in 1966. In 2008 Peter Quartermain noted to me that perhaps Creeley felt these poems were overexposed in 1993, but this does not explain Creeley's similar exclusion in 1966.

21. Olson remarks (to Corman): "Crazy, to have Creeley here. Crazy, that we never talk (in any large sense). It's great: all fast, like telegrams. And what a contrast to the volubleness when we are 500 [corrected: 5,000] miles off!" (Olson 1989a, 137, 6 June 1954).

22. Indeed, whenever one does run into a normal business letter to Olson from some of the helper-figures in publishing, it is a tonal shock (as in Olson 2003, 88–89, 149).

23. Paul Christensen notes the shift from Olson as needy victim of Dahlberg's capricious, even sadistic assaults and Olson as "master" in relation to Creeley and Corman (Olson 1990, viii–ix). While this presents a nicely structured chiasmus, Creeley is not a "son" or epigone figure but fraternal coequal; Corman may be a different story. For Olson, Dahlberg was a paternal mentor who had grave difficulties when Olson became intellectually independent. Dahlberg was enraged at the disloyalty and deviousness that Olson showed in never publishing a review of Dahlberg's long-awaited *Flea of Sodom*, which he was, for good reason, expected to do.

24. Maud (2008, 147–150) presents well-calibrated justification for the rage where Richard W. Emerson is concerned. In a 1951 *Golden Goose*, Emerson wove together statements into one (faked) "symposium" on the poetic career; the

specific placement of Olson's comments made them seem like abrupt and inappropriate remarks insulting William Carlos Williams.

25. In the 1997 essay fronting Olson's *Collected Prose*, Duncan is the one who is cited by Creeley as using a rather vatic "Man" and "Mankind" (Creeley in Olson 1997, xv).

26. Verbal alternatives like "one" and "people" come to the fore in another essay on *Maximus* from 1962 (Creeley 1989, 111).

27. That kind of nonstandard comma (after "man") is incredibly common in Creeley's prose. Although here it does make females seem to be an afterthought, it is more likely to be based on stuttering breath/thought relationships overall.

28. Hence my critical pun on Olson's "Letter 27" (Olson 1983, *Maximus* 185) ("Polis / is this") becomes the subhead of this section.

29. Martin Duberman observes that although Olson had served in a Democratic administration, at the height of McCarthyite witch hunts he disengaged from politics and "all semblance of [his] direct engagement with social issues vanished" (Duberman 1972, 399).

30. Olson had been assistant chief of the foreign language section of the Office of War Information during the administration of Franklin Delano Roosevelt (Billitteri 2009, 120).

31. In VIII: 224–225, Olson is excited by and approving of Pound's "Postscript" to de Gourmont about the brain being a clot of seminal fluid and Pound as a penile power. This reminder from Susan Wells is pertinent, however: "A penis that has become a metaphor for male entitlement is no longer a penis" (Wells 2010, 162).

32. Sometimes male and female creativity. Olson's argument about "the revolution I am responsible for" concerns "the identity of a person and his expression" and "art [as] the only morality" (Olson 1989a, 106, 13 June 1952). This letter denounces a political climate in which "the Right and the Left are synonymous." He affirms a third way, "'Our class'—the non-class—the a-class—the expressers solely, now have the responsibility to restore expression to such prime place" as a response to the "spectatorism" or passivity of both "capitalism and communism" (Olson 1989a, 98, 102–103, 13 June 1952).

33. This may simply be Olson's way of taking away from Lawrence the idea of the phallic as ontological inspiration beyond politics.

34. For "Compulsory Heterosexuality," the article preceding *Guys Like Us*, Michael Davidson interviewed Professor Nancy Armstrong, now a distinguished scholar of the novel (Davidson 1995, 204). I also talked to Armstrong (13 April 2009) about her exclusion from the Olson classroom at SUNY-Buffalo. She was told to sit in the hall, where there were chairs for this segregation; she lasted one day in the class. Speaking about Black Mountain College, Michael Rumaker repeatedly ruminates on and analyzes Olson's articulation of superiority to women, moments of "taunting," and "short temper" with women, the failure to treat

female students as equal participants, and the losses and abrasions that resulted (Rumaker 2003, 134, 155, also 443–445). Charles Boer mentions Olson's rejection of women students at the University of Connecticut by playing on their (stereotyped?) conventionalist expectations—using blasts of in-class profanity—but apparently he became disappointed when "the prettiest" left (Boer 1975, 53–54).

35. This comment has a notable history. One of Marjorie Perloff's first published essays announced a cordial resistance to Olson's poetics on the grounds that he offered nothing new—the claims he made had already been stated by Pound in the Fenollosa materials (Perloff 1973). Olsonites found this essay extremely contentious and seemed astonished that Perloff would dare to make such an argument. She reflected on this more than twenty years after the original essay, answering a sudden new rebuttal to or attack on her former observations by Ralph Maud, who spoke directly to this 1973 essay twenty-two years later: "I now understand my original animosity (and its current residue) as having everything to do with Olson's patriarchal stance." She indicates that Olson's inability to see "that the woman poet or artist might be an equal" made it difficult to see through the cult and the "pure adulation the Olsonites gave their hero" to any appreciation of his originality in poetics, which she now is more inclined to credit (Perloff 1995, 36, 34). This is a model of temperate framing of the issues also raised here.

36. "The very dichotomy man/woman as an opposition between two rival entities may be understood as belonging to metaphysics" (Kristeva 1986, 209).

37. To discuss this, one would need to analyze the irritant of Olson's 1954 critique of "Sages ou Mages" in "Against Wisdom as Such" and Duncan's rejection of this aspersion of mysticism for the calling of poet (Olson 1997, 260–264; Duncan 2011, 278). In such a literary history Robin Blaser (and his relationship with Olson) would figure significantly, and the complex relation that Duncan had with Denise Levertov would be an essential part. For some beginnings, see Rifkin 2000; Keenaghan 2009; and Mossin 2010.

38. The H.D. Book was conceived to honor H.D. by "[t]rying to win her her just literary place," said Duncan (Duncan 2004, 286).

7. Wieners and Creeley after Olson

1. This was a multiauthored collective project of essays and poetic research involving serious intellectual and community commitment. When it began, the contributors included no women essayists/researchers. The Wieners pamphlet was #3. Twenty-nine topics were assigned, written, and published, the bulk of them in the 1970s. Three women were later invited to contribute by the Institute of Further Studies: Joanne Kyger (1989); Alice Notley (1990); and Lisa Jarnot (2002), who was asked to take over the topic of Edward Dorn after his death in 1999. Albert Glover, the surviving member of this coordinating committee, is the source of this information, Charles Olson Centenary Conference, Simon Fraser University, June 2010.

2. Reprinted as "Women" in Wieners 1988, 98–102, dated "Jaunary [*sic*] 8, 1972." In this context, the work is like a prose poem.

3. John Wieners has a 1956 poem about two men who committed suicide, addressed to "Hart Crane, Harry Crosby . . . ," which sums up the sense of need for male company among vulnerable men: "don't run out on me, / stay with me with me, men, / build up my shoulderblades. / Let me carry what you threw away." A paraphrase of the whole: give me the strength to endure male vulnerability (Wieners 1988, 21).

4. John Wilkinson's intent consideration of *Cultural Affairs in Boston* and Wieners as a "drag-queen poet" examines his related poetic performances of stars and fanzine materials but not this particular text (Wilkinson 2007, 244).

5. This event was held just after the trip that Wieners and Olson took to the Spoleto (Italy) Festival of Two Worlds in the summer of 1965, which Wieners's *WOMAN* (1972) in part memorializes.

6. Creeley speaks, for example, about voiding the bowels and of being in that moment, one often unspoken, if certainly important (Clark 1993, 110). In *If I Were Writing This*, a poem beginning with a dream of Allen Ginsberg, Creeley gives an intimate description of urination—informational, sympathetic, and exacting, with an extra meditation on the quondam difficulties of urinating in a public facility (Creeley 2003, 46).

7. I am using words from the essay on Whitman in *On Earth* and from the poem "Shimmer" (Creeley 2006, 59–85, 26, 27).

8. The power of "the hole" for understanding Creeley might be indicated by the fact that Michael Davidson (also for the 2006 Creeley conference and independently of my essay) wrote a consideration of "the hole," focusing on rage. He tracks Creeley's "fits of rage" in his early and mid-career to "the limits of the masculine roles that constrain him" (Davidson 2010, 71, 73).

9. His mother, Genevieve Jules Creeley (1887–1972), a beloved sister, Helen, and a housekeeper, Theresa Turner, were all quite important to him. An aunt (Bernice) who wrote comic poems was another female figure (Clark 1993, 28).

10. Freud [1924] 1957. To bring those little girl escapees into line, incidentally, ideology (including narrative) and domination are used insistently instead. Thus their normative gender identity as brought under the regime of patriarchy is more unstable than that (theorized; projected) for little boys.

11. Creeley is very clear about the difficulty (he repeats this in several interviews) of thereupon learning how to be a man (see the 1973 interview with Lewis MacAdams in Creeley 1993, 81). Sometimes this sense of the company of women is an enormous power in Creeley; sometimes he felt, or claimed to have felt, bereft of the knowledge of his own gender, a situation with which he sometimes played, as in this gnomic late quatrain called "Sign" that begins with and is generated by puns on the name of a diversified worldwide corporation: "'SIEMENS' not / semen's, and I don't / see men's—and I don't / know what it means" (Creeley 1998b, 55).

12. Creeley uses the word "elation" while discussing this poem in a 1991 New College talk (Clark 1993, 111).

13. Without ruining the poem with clumsy identifications, let me raise the possibility that the poem depicts a teasing scene of female masturbation which had the effect of a promissory note for the speaker's own curiosity and desire: a "there" he wants to get to and an act he wants to "follow" (Creeley 1982, 387, 388). It is also plausible that the poem depicts or imagines a mutual act of proto-intercourse between a boy and a woman.

14. Creeley criticizes this poem a little in 1991—he says "I suddenly realized I had changed in my experience of the world. At sixty-four, I no longer believed that the significant disposition of humanness was willed. I'd written, 'The choice is simply, / I will—as mind is a finger, / pointing, as wonder / a place to be'" (Clark 1993, 111). It is significant that his critique is about the force of will, not about the sexual and sublime mythic narrative.

15. The agent of the oedipal threat here is a female figure, not, as in the Freudian account, the paternal figure of the law. Of course, if all men undergo oedipal crises, then, in this reading, all men should be poets. If only male poets undergo this enhanced crisis, then the argument is circular—one is proving only that male poets became male poets.

16. In her study of *Our Bodies, Ourselves*, Susan Wells notes that describing the vagina as a permanent "hole" is neither objective nor neutral but an ideologically resonant rhetorical choice because, strictly speaking, it is inaccurate—the walls of the vagina normally touch (Wells 2010, 154).

17. As Charles Bernstein has pointed out, Creeley "explored regions of male sexuality, aggression, anger, frustration, futility, loss and disorientation (as well as tenderness and love) in a way rarely, if ever, articulated in American poetry" (Bernstein 2005, 374).

18. After all, men do not have to like ideologies of masculinity and manhood any better than women like ideologies of femininity and womanhood. It is just that those male, or maler, stances can (but do not automatically) generate more social benefit—even to very nice men who try personally to repudiate that benefit.

19. In football, conversion means to add one or two points to the original six-point touchdown.

20. On this, see the argument in "Marble Paper" (DuPlessis 2006a, 104–107) about the difficulty the lyric has in animating the voices of the "other." At the end of *Pieces*, I/her is the central relation, and it occurs as much in fantasy as in reality. "I could fashion another / were I to lose her. / Such is thought" (Creeley 1982, 445). This may be chilling, but it is not dishonest.

21. It seems debatable whether a phallic vision of sexuality would be abandoned by virtue of male penetrability; not enough possibilities and contradictions are being allowed for. No system of sexuality is this either/or, as any glance at gay male pornography should indicate.

22. The poem alludes explicitly to a celebrity death in 1921; the truth of the story is in debate. A Hollywood starlet, Virginia Rappe, died of a ruptured bladder after perhaps having being raped by movie star Roscoe (Fatty) Arbuckle at a drunken party—or perhaps not. The rape with a bottle was a rumor that was not even brought up in court, but it became folklore, as the presence of the story in Creeley's youth attests.

23. The poem may well constitute a rethinking of a 1954 statement by the younger Creeley in "A Note on Franz Kline" from the *Black Mountain Review* (Winter 1954): "There is nothing quite so abrupt and even pleasant as rape—ask any woman" (Creeley 1954, 23). This statement was cut in the Kline essay as published in Creeley's *Collected Essays* (Creeley 1989, 381–382). Clayton Eshleman called my attention to this discrepancy.

24. Including hands and feet: one might say that in this poem the poet is trying to bring all body parts—whether anus, or penis, or foot—to the same questions of pleasure, beyond taboo.

25. As for intentionality, about this *oo/o* and the *j/ch* sound, I can only repeat what Creeley himself stated: the echoing of sound is something he simply does in poetry, not necessarily "literally conscious" but by habit, as one might drive a car, as a "resource, in my own abilities now as a poet, to be able to do [this echoing of sound] without thinking twice" (Creeley 1985, 43).

Bibliography

Adams, Rachel, and David Savran, eds. 2002. *The Masculinity Studies Reader.* Oxford: Blackwell.

Adorno, Theodor W. 1991. *Notes to Literature.* Vol. 1. Rolf Tiedemann, ed. Trans. Shierry Weber Nicholsen. New York: Columbia UP.

———. 1992. *Notes to Literature.* Vol. 2. Rolf Tiedemann, ed. Trans. Shierry Weber Nicholsen. New York: Columbia UP.

Allen, Donald, ed. 1960. *The New American Poetry.* New York: Grove P.

Anzaldúa, Gloria. 1987. *Borderlands/La Frontera: The New Mestiza.* San Francisco: Spinsters/Aunt Lute.

Babbitt, Irving. 1910. *The New Laokoon: An Essay on the Confusion of the Arts.* Boston: Houghton Mifflin.

Badenhausen, Richard. 2004. *T. S. Eliot and the Art of Collaboration.* Cambridge: Cambridge UP.

Barreca, Regina, and Deborah Denenholz Morse, eds. 1997. *The Erotics of Instruction.* Hanover and London: UP of New England.

Barthes, Roland. 1975. *The Pleasure of the Text.* Trans. Richard Miller. New York: Hill & Wang.

Battersby, Christine. 1990. *Gender and Genius: Towards a Feminist Aesthetics.* Bloomington: Indiana UP.

Beach, Christopher. 1992. *ABC of Influence: Ezra Pound and the Remaking of American Poetic Tradition.* Berkeley: U of California P.

Bederman, Gail. 1995. *Manliness and Civilization: A Cultural History of Gender and Race in the United States, 1880–1917.* Chicago: U of Chicago P.

Bedient, Calvin. 1986. *He Do The Police in Different Voices: The Waste Land and Its Protagonist.* Chicago: U of Chicago P.

Berger, James. 1999. *After the End: Representations of Post-Apocalypse.* Minneapolis: U of Minnesota P.

Berger, Maurice, Brian Wallis, and Simon Watson, eds. 1995. *Constructing Masculinity.* New York: Routledge.

Bernheimer, Charles. 1992. "Penile Reference in Phallic Theory." *differences: a Journal of Feminist Cultural Studies* 4.1 (Spring): 116–132.

Bernstein, Charles. 1986. "Undone Business" (1984). In *Content's Dream: Essays 1975–1984.* Los Angeles: Sun & Moon P: 321–339.

———. 1996. "Introjective Verse." *Chain* 3.1 (Spring): 23–25.

———. 1999. *My Way: Speeches and Poems.* Chicago: U of Chicago P.

———. 2005. "Hero of the Local: Robert Creeley and the Persistence of American Poetry." *Textual Practice* 19.3: 373–377.

Bersani, Leo. 1988. "Is the Rectum a Grave?" In *AIDS: Cultural Analysis, Cultural Activism*. Douglas Crimp, ed. Cambridge, MA: MIT P: 197–222.

Bhabha, Homi K. 1995. "Are You a Man or a Mouse?" In *Constructing Masculinity*. Maurice Berger, Brian Wallis, and Simon Watson, eds. New York: Routledge: 57–65.

Billitteri, Carla. 2009. *Language and the Renewal of Society in Walt Whitman, Laura (Riding) Jackson, and Charles Olson: The American Cratylus*. New York: Palgrave Macmillan.

Bloom, Harold. 1973. *The Anxiety of Influence*. Oxford: Oxford UP.

Boer, Charles. 1975. *Charles Olson in Connecticut*. Chicago: Swallow P.

Boldereff, Frances M. 1968. *Hermes to His Son Thoth: Being Joyce's Use of Giordano Bruno in Finnegans Wake*. Woodward, PA: Classic Non-Fiction Library.

———. 1999. *Charles Olson and Frances Boldereff: A Modern Correspondence*. Ralph Maud and Sharon Thesen, eds. Middletown, CT: Wesleyan UP.

Boone, Joseph A., and Michael Cadden, eds. 1990. *Engendering Men: The Question of Male Feminist Criticism*. New York: Routledge.

Bourdieu, Pierre. 1996. *The Rules of Art: Genesis and Structure of the Literary Field*. Trans. Susan Emanuel. Stanford: Stanford UP.

Boyarin, Daniel. 1994. *A Radical Jew: Paul and the Politics of Identity*. Berkeley: U of California P.

———. 1997. *Unheroic Conduct: The Rise of Heterosexuality and the Invention of the Jewish Man*. Berkeley: U of California P.

———. 2002. "What Does a Jew Want? or, The Political Meaning of the Phallus." In Adams and Savran, eds., 2002: 274–291.

Boyarin, Daniel, Daniel Itzkovitz, and Ann Pellegrini, eds. 2003. *Queer Theory and the Jewish Question*. New York: Columbia UP.

Breines, Wini. 1992. *Young, White, and Miserable: Growing Up Female in the Fifties*. Boston: Beacon Press.

Brod, Harry. 2002. "Studying Masculinities as Superordinate Studies." In Gardiner, ed., 2002b: 161–175.

Brod, Harry, and Michael Kaufman, eds. 1994. *Theorizing Masculinities*. Thousand Oaks, CA: Sage Publishers.

Brook, Susan Mary. 2007. *Literature and Cultural Criticism of the 1950s: The Feeling Male Body*. New York: Palgrave Macmillan.

Brown, Wendy. 1988. *Manhood and Politics: A Feminist Reading in Political Theory*. Totowa, NJ: Rowman & Littlefield, Publishers.

Buck-Morss, Susan. 1992. "Aesthetics and Anaesthetics: Walter Benjamin's Artwork Essay Reconsidered." *October* 62 (Autumn): 3–41.

Burgin, Victor, James Donald, and Cora Kaplan, eds. 1989. *Formations of Fantasy*. London: Routledge.

Burke, Carolyn. 1985a. "The New Poetry and the New Woman: Mina Loy." In Middlebrook and Yalom, eds., 1985: 37–57.

———. 1985b. "Supposed Persons: Modernist Poetry and the Female Subject." *Feminist Studies* 7.1: 131–148.

———. 1990. "Mina Loy." In B. Scott, ed., 1990: 230–238.

———. 1996. *Becoming Modern: The Life of Mina Loy*. New York: Farrar, Straus & Giroux.

Bush, Ronald. 1990. "Ezra Pound." In B. Scott, ed., 1990: 353–359.

———. 1991. "Excavating the Ideological Fault Lines of Modernism: Editing Ezra Pound's *Cantos*." In George Bornstein, ed. *Representing Modernist Texts: Editing as Interpretation*. Ann Arbor: U of Michigan P: 67–98.

Butler, Judith. 2004. *Undoing Gender*. New York: Routledge.

Butterick, George F. 1980. *A Guide to the Maximus Poems of Charles Olson*. Berkeley: U of California P.

Cheyette, Bryan, and Laura Marcus, eds. 1998. *Modernity, Culture, and "the Jew."* Stanford, CA: Stanford UP.

Churchill, Suzanne W. 2005. "Outing T. S. Eliot." *Criticism* 47.1 (Winter): 7–30.

Cixous, Hélène. 1980. "The Laugh of the Medusa." In *New French Feminisms*. Elaine Marks and Isabelle de Courtivron, eds. Amherst: U of Massachusetts P: 245–264.

Claridge, Laura, and Elizabeth Langland, eds. 1990. *Out of Bounds: Male Writers and Gender(ed) Criticism*. Amherst: U of Massachusetts P.

Clark, Suzanne. 2000. *Cold Warriors: Manliness on Trial in the Rhetoric of the West*. Carbondale: Southern Illinois UP.

Clark, Tom. 1991. *Charles Olson: The Allegory of a Poet's Life*. New York: W. W. Norton.

———, ed. 1993. *Robert Creeley and the Genius of the American Common Place*. New York: New Directions.

Clover, Joshua. *The Totality for Kids*. 2006. Berkeley: U of California P.

Connell, R. W. 1994. "Psychoanalysis on Masculinity." In *Theorizing Masculinities*, Harry Brod and Michael Kaufman, eds. Thousand Oaks, CA: Sage Publications: 11–38.

———. 2002a. "The History of Masculinity." In Adams and Savran, eds., 2002: 245–261.

———. 2002b. "Long and Winding Road: An Outsider's View of U.S. Masculinity and Feminism." In Gardiner, ed., 2002b: 193–209.

———. 2005. *Masculinities*. Berkeley: U of California P.

Corber, Robert J. 1997. *Homosexuality in Cold War America: Resistance and the Crisis of Masculinity*. Durham: Duke UP.

Craciun, Adriana. 2008. "Romantic Poetry, Sexuality, Gender." In *The Cambridge Companion to British Romantic Poetry*. James Chandler and Maureen N. McLane, eds. Cambridge: Cambridge UP: 155–177.

Creeley, Robert. 1954. "A Note on Franz Kline." *Black Mountain Review* (Winter): 23–24.

———. 1962. *For Love, Poems 1950–1960*. New York: Charles Scribner's Sons.

———. 1980–1987. *Charles Olson & Robert Creeley: The Complete Correspondence*. George F. Butterick, ed. 8 vols. Santa Barbara: Black Sparrow P. Vols. 1 and 2, 1980; vol. 3, 1981; vol. 4, 1982; vol. 5, 1983; vol. 6, 1985; vols. 7 and 8, 1987.

———. 1982. *The Collected Poems of Robert Creeley: 1945–1975*. Berkeley: U of California P.

———. 1984. "Dove Sta Memoria." In Terrell, ed., 1984: 199–222.

———. 1985. [Note regarding the anthologized poem "For My Mother"; transcription from a taped commentary in answer to questions, May 1983.] In *45 Contemporary Poems: The Creative Process*. Alberta T. Turner, ed. New York: Longman: 38–43.

———. 1989. *The Collected Essays of Robert Creeley*. Berkeley: U of California P.

———. 1990. *Autobiography*. Madras and New York: Hanuman Books.

———. 1990/1996. *Charles Olson & Robert Creeley: The Complete Correspondence*. Vols. 9–10, completed by Richard Blevins, ed. Santa Barbara: Black Sparrow P. Vol. 9, 1990; vol. 10, 1996.

———. 1991. "Creeley Talks to Charles Bernstein's Poetics Seminar: The Focus Is on Gender Issues." SUNY–Buffalo, Feb. 28, 1991. PennSound. http://writing.upenn.edu/pennsound/x/Creeley.html.

———. 1993. *Tales Out of School: Selected Interviews*. Ann Arbor: U of Michigan P.

———. 1998a. *Life & Death*. New York: New Directions.

———. 1998b. *So There: Poems 1976–1983*. New York: New Directions.

———. 2001. *Just in Time: Poems 1984–1994*. New York: New Directions.

———. 2002. "20 Questions with Robert Creeley." *Milk Magazine* 4 (Oct.). http://www.milkmag.org/20QCreeley.htm.

———. 2003. *If I Were Writing This*. New York: New Directions.

———. 2004. Interview with Leonard Schwartz (conducted Nov. 24, 2003). *Jacket* 25 (Feb.). http://jacketmagazine.com/25/creeley-iv.html.

———. 2006. *On Earth: Last Poems and an Essay*. Berkeley: U of California P.

Davidson, Harriet. 1994. "Improper Desire: Reading *The Waste Land*." In Moody, ed., 1994: 121–131.

Davidson, Michael. 1989. *The San Francisco Renaissance: Poetics and Community at Mid-Century*. Cambridge: Cambridge UP.

———. 1995. "Compulsory Homosociality: Charles Olson, Jack Spicer, and the Gender of Poetics." In *Cruising the Performative: Interventions into the Representation of Ethnicity, Nationality, and Sexuality*. Sue-Ellen Case, Philip Brett, and Susan Leigh Foster, eds. Bloomington: Indiana UP: 197–216.

———. 1997. *Ghostlier Demarcations: Modern Poetry and the Material Word*. Berkeley: U of California P.

———. 2004. *Guys Like Us: Citing Masculinity in Cold War Poetics.* Chicago: U of Chicago P.

———. 2010. "The Repeated Insistence: Creeley's Rage." In Fredman and McCaffery, eds., 2010: 69–88.

Davis, Alex, and Lee E. Jenkins. 2007. *The Cambridge Companion to Modernist Poetry.* Cambridge: Cambridge UP.

Dean, Tim. 2004. "T. S. Eliot: Famous Clairvoyante." In Laity and Gish, eds., 2004: 43–65.

de Beauvoir, Simone. 1953. *The Second Sex* (French original 1949). New York: Bantam Books.

DeKoven, Marianne. 1989. "Male Signature, Female Aesthetic: The Gender Politics of Experimental Writing." In *Breaking the Sequence: Women's Experimental Fiction.* Ed. Ellen Friedman and Miriam Fuchs. Princeton: Princeton UP: 72–81.

———. 1999. "Modernism and Gender." In Levenson, ed., 1999: 174–193.

de Lauretis, Teresa. 1987. *Technologies of Gender: Essays on Theory, Film, and Fiction.* Bloomington: Indiana UP.

Denning, Michael. 1996. *The Cultural Front: The Laboring of American Culture in the Twentieth Century.* London and New York: Verso.

Densmore, Dana. [1998] 2007. "A Year of Living Dangerously: 1968." In DuPlessis and Snitow, eds., [1998] 2007: 71–89.

Dettmar, Kevin J. H., and Stephen Watt, eds. 1996. *Marketing Modernisms: Self-Promotion, Canonization, Rereading.* Ann Arbor: U of Michigan P.

Dewey, Anne Day. 2007. *Beyond Maximus: The Construction of Public Voice in Black Mountain Poetry.* Stanford, CA: Stanford UP.

Dictionary of Literary Biography (on Ralph Cheever Dunning). n.d. www.bookrags.com/biography/ralph-cheever-dunning-dlb/.

Donadey, Anne, with Françoise Lionnet. 2007. "Feminisms, Genders, Sexualities." In *Introduction to Scholarship in Modern Languages and Literatures.* David G. Nicholls, ed. New York: Modern Language Association of America: 225–244.

Duberman, Martin. 1972. *Black Mountain: An Exploration in Community.* New York: E. P. Dutton.

Dubois, Page. 1995. *Sappho Is Burning.* Chicago: U of Chicago P.

Dunbar, Roxanne. [1998] 2007. "Outlaw Woman: Chapters from a Feminist Memoir-in-Progress." In DuPlessis and Snitow, eds., [1998] 2007: 90–114.

Duncan, Robert. 1949. "The Venice Poem." In *Poems 1948–49.* Berkeley: Berkeley Miscellany Editions: 21–52.

———. 1980. "An Interview with Robert Duncan by Ekbert Faas." *boundary2* 8.2: 1–19.

———. 1995. "Projective Project: Charles Olson." Robert Bertholf, ed. *Sulfur* 36 (Spring): 25–43.

——. 2004. *The Letters of Robert Duncan and Denise Levertov*. Robert J. Bertholf and Albert Gelpi, eds. Stanford: Stanford UP.

——. 2011. *The H.D. Book*. Michael Boughn and Victor Coleman, eds. Berkeley: U of California P.

Duncan, Robert, Allen Ginsberg, and Charles Olson. 1993. "Duende, Muse, and Angel." *Sulfur* 33 (Fall): 83–98.

Dunning, Ralph Cheever. 1925. Poems [*The Four Winds*]. *Poetry* 26.1 (April): 1–13.

DuPlessis, Rachel Blau. [1990] 2006. *The Pink Guitar: Writing as Feminist Practice*. Tuscaloosa: U of Alabama P, 2006.

——. 2001. *Genders, Races, and Religious Cultures in Modern American Poetry, 1908–1934*. Cambridge: Cambridge UP.

——. 2006a. *Blue Studios: Poetry and Its Cultural Work*. Tuscaloosa: U of Alabama P.

——. 2006b. "*A Test of Poetry* and Conviction" [essay on Louis Zukofsky]. *Jacket Magazine* 30 (July). http://jacketmagazine.com/30/index.shtml.

DuPlessis, Rachel Blau, and Peter Quartermain, eds. 1999. *The Objectivist Nexus: Essays in Cultural Poetics*. Tuscaloosa: U of Alabama P.

DuPlessis, Rachel Blau, and Ann Snitow, eds. [1998] 2007. *The Feminist Memoir Project: Voices from Women's Liberation*. New Brunswick: Rutgers UP.

Dworkin, Craig. 2008. *Parse*. Berkeley: Atelos.

Easthope, Antony. 1983. *Poetry as Discourse*. London: Methuen.

——. [1986] 1990. *What a Man's Gotta Do: The Masculine Myth in Popular Culture*. Boston: Unwin Hyman.

Edelman, Lee. 1994. *Homographesis: Essays in Gay Literary and Cultural Theory*. New York: Routledge.

Ehrenreich, Barbara. 1983. *The Hearts of Men: American Dreams and the Flight from Commitment*. New York: Doubleday Anchor.

Eliot, T. S. [1917] 1953. "Eeldrop and Appleplex." In *The Little Review Anthology*. Margaret Anderson, ed. New York: Hermitage House: 102–109.

——. 1934. *After Strange Gods: A Primer of Modern Heresy*. New York: Harcourt Brace.

——. 1963a. *Collected Poems, 1909–1962*. London: Faber & Faber.

——. 1963b. "Ezra Pound." In *Ezra Pound: A Collection of Critical Essays*. Walter Sutton, ed. Englewood Cliffs, NJ: Prentice-Hall: 17–25.

——. 1971. *The Waste Land: A Facsimile and Transcript of the Original Drafts, Including the Annotations of Ezra Pound*. Ed. Valerie Eliot. New York: Harcourt Brace Jovanovich.

——. 1988. *The Letters of T. S. Eliot, Volume I, 1898–1922*. Ed. Valerie Eliot. New York: Harcourt Brace Jovanovich.

——. 1996. *Inventions of the March Hare: Poems 1909–1917*. Ed. Christopher Ricks. New York: Harcourt Brace.

Ellmann, Maud. 1987. *The Poetics of Impersonality: T. S. Eliot and Ezra Pound.* Cambridge, MA: Harvard UP.

Enloe, Cynthia. 1993. *The Morning After: Sexual Politics at the End of the Cold War.* Berkeley: U of California P.

Epstein, Andrew. 2006. *Beautiful Enemies: Friendship and Postwar American Poetry.* New York: Oxford UP.

Faas, Ekbert, with Maria Trombacco. 2001. *Robert Creeley: A Biography.* Hanover: UP of New England.

Fabian, Ann. 1993. "Making a Commodity of Truth: Speculations on the Career of Bernarr Macfadden." *American Literary History* 5.1 (Spring): 51–76.

Felski, Rita. 1989. *Beyond Feminist Aesthetics: Feminist Literature and Social Change.* Cambridge, MA: Harvard UP.

Fetterley, Judith. 1978. *The Resisting Reader: A Feminist Approach to American Fiction.* Bloomington: Indiana UP.

Fredman, Stephen. 2010. *Contextual Practice: Assemblage and the Erotic in Postwar Poetry and Art.* Stanford: Stanford UP.

Fredman, Stephen, and Steve McCaffery, eds. 2010. *Form, Power, and Person in Robert Creeley's Life and Work.* Iowa City: U of Iowa P.

Freud, Sigmund. [1912] 1963. "The Dynamics of the Transference." In *Therapy and Technique.* Philip Rieff, ed. New York: Collier Books: 105–115.

———. [1924] 1957. "The Passing of the Oedipus-Complex." In *Collected Papers.* Vol. 2. London: Hogarth P: 269–276.

Friedlander, Ben. 2010. "Letter to the Romans." In Miller and Morris, eds., 2010: 418–438.

Gallop, Jane. 1988. *Thinking through the Body.* New York: Columbia UP.

Gardiner, Judith Kegan. 2002a. "Introduction." In Gardiner, ed., 2002b: 1–29.

———, ed. 2002b. *Masculinity Studies and Feminist Theory: New Directions.* New York: Columbia UP.

Gilbert, Sandra, and Susan Gubar. 1988. *No Man's Land: The Place of the Woman Writer in the Twentieth Century, Volume 1: The War of the Words.* New Haven: Yale UP.

———. 1989. *No Man's Land: The Place of the Woman Writer in the Twentieth Century, Volume 2: Sexchanges.* New Haven: Yale UP.

———. 1994. *No Man's Land: The Place of the Woman Writer in the Twentieth Century, Volume 3: Letters from the Front.* New Haven: Yale UP.

Ginsberg, Allen. [1956] 2006. *Howl.* Barry Miles, ed. New York: Harper Perennial Classics.

———. 1984. *Collected Poems 1947–1980.* New York: Harper & Row, Publishers.

———. n.d. FBI**Narcotics Bureau**CIA files. "Exemplary Shockers & Smoking Typewriters, 1968–1970." Selections from FBI, Narcotics Bureau, and CIA Files. "Xerox Government Files of the Grand Master Plan for Disrupting Political Minorities & Specific Instances Exemplifying These

Conspiracies." Photocopied typescript in possession of the author (from Allen Ginsberg).

Gordon, Lyndall. 1999. *T. S. Eliot: An Imperfect Life*. New York: W. W. Norton.

Gourmont, Rémy de. 1922. *The Natural Philosophy of Love*. Trans. with a postscript by Ezra Pound. New York: Boni & Liveright.

Graves, Robert. [1948] 1978. *The White Goddess: A Historical Grammar of Poetic Myth*. New York: Octagon Books, Farrar, Straus & Giroux.

Gregson, Ian. 1999. *The Male Image: Representations of Masculinity in Postwar Poetry*. New York: St. Martin's.

Grieve-Carlson, Gary, ed. 2007. *Olson's Prose*. Newcastle: Cambridge Scholars Publishing.

Griffin, Susan. 1978. *Woman and Nature: The Roaring inside Her*. New York: Harper & Row.

Grosz, Elizabeth, and Elspeth Probyn, eds. 1995. *Sexy Bodies: The Strange Carnalities of Feminism*. London: Routledge.

Halberstam, David. 1993. *The Fifties*. New York: Villard Books.

Halberstam, Judith. 1998. *Female Masculinity*. Durham: Duke UP.

———. 2002. "The Good, the Bad, and the Ugly: Men, Women, and Masculinity." In Gardiner, ed., 2002b: 344–367.

Halpern, Rob. 2010. "Becoming a Patient of History: George Oppen's Domesticity and the Relocation of Politics." George Oppen Memorial Lecture, San Francisco. Typescript dated 11 December 2010.

Handelman, Susan A. 1982. *The Slayers of Moses: The Emergence of Rabbinic Interpretation in Modern Literary Theory*. Albany: SUNY P.

Hatlen, Burton. 1997. "From Modernism to Postmodernism: Zukofsky's 'A'-12." In Scroggins, ed., 1997: 214–229.

Heilbrun, Carolyn G. 1973. *Toward a Recognition of Androgyny*. New York: Knopf.

Heuving, Jeanne. n.d. "The Transmutation of Love in Twentieth Century Poetry" (manuscript).

Hokanson, Robert O'Brien. 1990. "'Projecting' Like a Man: Charles Olson and the Poetics of Gender." *Sagetrieb* 9.1–2 (Spring–Fall): 169–183.

Hopkins, David. 2007. *Dada's Boys: Masculinity after Duchamp*. New Haven: Yale UP.

Howe, Fanny. 1985. "Artobiography." In Perelman, ed., 1985: 192–206.

Howe, Susan. 1989. "Since a Dialogue We Are." *Acts* 10: 166–173.

Hulme, T. E. 1955. *Further Speculations*. Samuel Hynes, ed. Minneapolis: U of Minnesota P.

Hunt, William R. 1989. *Body Love: The Amazing Career of Bernarr Macfadden*. Bowling Green, OH: Bowling Green State U Popular P.

Huyssen, Andreas. 1986. *After the Great Divide: Modernism, Mass Culture, Postmodernism*. Bloomington: Indiana UP.

Jakobson, Roman. 1987. "What Is Poetry?" In *Language in Literature*. Krystyna Pomorska and Stephen Rudy, eds. Cambridge: Harvard UP: 368–378.

Jardine, Alice. 1987. "Men in Feminism: Odor di Uomo or Compagnons de Route?" In Jardine and Smith, eds., 1987: 54–61.

Jardine, Alice, and Paul Smith, eds. 1987. *Men in Feminism*. New York: Methuen.

Jarnot, Lisa. 1996. *Some Other Kind of Mission*. Providence: Burning Deck.

Jehlen, Myra. 1990. "Gender." In *Critical Terms for Literary Study*. Frank Lentricchia and Thomas McLaughlin, eds. Chicago: U of Chicago P: 263–273.

Johnson, Barbara. 1987. *A World of Difference*. Baltimore: Johns Hopkins UP.

———. 1998. *The Feminist Difference: Literature, Psychoanalysis, Race, and Gender*. Cambridge, MA: Harvard UP.

Johnson, David K. 2004. *The Lavender Scare: The Cold War Persecution of Gays and Lesbians in the Federal Government*. Chicago: U of Chicago P.

Kasson, John F. 2001. *Houdini, Tarzan, and the Perfect Man: The White Male Body and the Challenge of Modernity in America*. New York: Hill & Wang.

Katz, Vincent, ed. 2002. *Black Mountain College: Experiment in Art*. Cambridge, MA: MIT P.

Keenaghan, Eric. 2009. *Queering Cold War Poetry: Ethics of Vulnerability in Cuba and the United States*. Columbus: Ohio State UP.

Kimmel, Michael S. 1994. "Foreword." In Brod and Kaufman 1994: vii–ix.

———. 2002. "Foreword." In Gardiner, ed., 2002b: ix–xi.

———. 2005. *The History of Men: Essays on the History of American and British Masculinities*. Albany: SUNY P.

Koestenbaum, Wayne. 1989. *Double Talk: The Erotics of Male Literary Collaboration*. New York: Routledge.

Korsmeyer, Carolyn. 2004. *Gender and Aesthetics: An Introduction*. New York: Routledge.

Kristeva, Julia. 1986. *The Kristeva Reader*. Toril Moi, ed. Oxford: Basil Blackwell.

Laity, Cassandra. 1996. *H.D. and the Victorian Fin de Siècle: Gender, Modernism, Decadence*. Cambridge: Cambridge UP.

Laity, Cassandra, and Nancy K. Gish, eds. 2004. *Gender, Desire, and Sexuality in T. S. Eliot*. Cambridge: Cambridge UP.

Lamos, Colleen. 1998. *Deviant Modernism: Sexual and Textual Errancy in T. S. Eliot, James Joyce, and Marcel Proust*. Cambridge: Cambridge UP.

Laughlin, James. 1987. *Pound as Wuz: Essays and Lectures on Ezra Pound*. St. Paul: Graywolf P.

Lawrence, D. H. [1929] 1973. *The Escaped Cock*. Gerald M. Lacy, ed. Los Angeles: Black Sparrow P.

Leja, Michael. 1995. *Reframing Abstract Expressionism: Subjectivity and Painting in the 1940s*. New Haven: Yale UP.

Lentricchia, Frank. 1987. "Patriarchy against Itself—The Young Manhood of Wallace Stevens." *Critical Inquiry* 13.4 (Summer): 742–786.

Levenson, Michael. 1984. *A Genealogy of Modernism: A Study of English Literary Doctrine 1908–1922*. Cambridge: Cambridge UP.

———, ed. 1999. *The Cambridge Companion to Modernism*. Cambridge: Cambridge UP.

Levertov, Denise. 2004. *The Letters of Robert Duncan and Denise Levertov*. Robert J. Bertholf and Albert Gelpi, eds. Stanford: Stanford UP.

Linett, Maren Tova. 2007. *Modernism, Feminism, and Jewishness*. Cambridge: Cambridge UP.

Litz, A. Walton, and Lawrence Rainey. 2000. "Ezra Pound." In *The Cambridge History of Literary Criticism, Vol. 7, Modernism and the New Criticism*. A. Walton Litz, Louis Menand, and Lawrence Rainey, eds. Cambridge: Cambridge UP: 57–92.

Longenbach, James. 1999. "Modern Poetry." In Levenson, ed., 1999: 100–129.

Lopez, Tony. 2006. *Meaning Performance: Essays on Poetry*. Cambridge: Salt Publishing.

Loy, Mina. 1996. *The Lost Lunar Baedeker*. Selected and ed. Roger L. Conover. New York: Farrar, Straus & Giroux.

Lyon, Janet. 1999. *Manifestoes: Provocations of the Modern*. Ithaca: Cornell UP.

Macey, David. 1992. "Phallus." In *Feminism and Psychoanalysis: A Critical Dictionary*. Elizabeth Wright, ed. Oxford: Blackwell 1992: 318–320.

Macleod, Joseph Gordon. 1930a. *The Ecliptic*. London: Faber & Faber.

———. 1930b. "Leo: Sign from 'The Ecliptic.'" *Criterion* 9.37 (July): 671–674.

Maud, Ralph. 1995. "A Challenge to Marjorie Perloff." *Minutes of the Charles Olson Society* 7 (March) (no pagination).

———. 1996. *Charles Olson's Reading: A Biography*. Carbondale: Southern Illinois UP, 1996.

———. 2008. *Charles Olson at the Harbor: A Biography*. Vancouver: Talonbooks.

Maxwell, Catherine. 2001. *The Female Sublime from Milton to Swinburne: Bearing Blindness*. Manchester: Manchester UP.

May, Elaine Tyler. 1989. "Explosive Issues: Sex, Women, and the Bomb." In Lary May, ed., 1989: 154–170.

May, Lary, ed. 1989. *Recasting America: Culture and Politics in the Age of Cold War*. Chicago: U of Chicago P.

Mayer, Bernadette. 1984. *Utopia*. New York: United Artists Books.

McCoy, Bob. 2000. *QUACK! Tales of Medical Fraud: From the Museum of Questionable Medical Devices*. Santa Monica: Santa Monica P.

McDonald, Gail. 1993. *Learning to Be Modern: Pound, Eliot, and the American University*. Oxford: Oxford UP.

Melville, Herman. 1947. *Collected Poems of Herman Melville*. Howard P. Vincent, ed. Chicago: Packard.

Mencken, H. L. 1923. *The American Language: An Inquiry into the Development of English in the United States*. New York: Alfred A. Knopf.

Middlebrook, Diane, and Marilyn Yalom, eds. 1985. *Coming to Light: American Women Poets in the Twentieth Century*. Ann Arbor: U of Michigan P.

Middleton, Peter. 1991. "Silent Inscription of Gender: Recent Men's Poetry." *fragmente* 4 (Autumn/Winter): 66–76.

———. 1992. *The Inward Gaze: Masculinity and Subjectivity in Modern Culture*. London: Routledge.

———. 2010a. "Conclusion: The History and Interpretation of Modernist Poetry." In Middleton and Marsh, eds., 2010: 179–201.

———. 2010b. "Scenes of Instruction: Creeley's Reflexive Poetics." In Fredman and McCaffery, eds., 2010: 159–180.

Middleton, Peter, and Nicky Marsh, eds. 2010. *Teaching Modernist Poetry*. Houndmills: Palgrave Macmillan.

Miller, Cristanne. 2007. "Gender, Sexuality and the Modernist Poem." In Davis and Jenkins, eds., 2007: 68–84.

Miller, Douglas T., and Marion Nowak. 1977. *The Fifties: The Way We Really Were*. Garden City, NY: Doubleday.

Miller, James E., Jr. 1977. *T. S. Eliot's Personal Waste Land: Exorcism of the Demons*. University Park: Pennsylvania State UP.

Miller, Stephen Paul, and Daniel Morris, eds. 2010. *Radical Poetics and Secular Jewish Culture*. Tuscaloosa: U of Alabama P.

Milne, Drew. 2010. "Politics and Modernist Poetics." In Middleton and Marsh, eds., 2010: 25–44.

Modelski, Tania. 1991. *Feminism without Women: Culture and Criticism in a "Postfeminist" Age*. New York: Routledge.

Monroe, Harriet. 1931a. ["Announcement."] *Poetry: A Magazine of Verse* 37.4 (January): 231.

———. 1931b. "The Arrogance of Youth." *Poetry: A Magazine of Verse* 37.6 (March): 328–333.

———. 1931c. "News Notes." *Poetry: A Magazine of Verse* 37.4 (January): 231–235.

Moody, A. David, ed. 1994. *The Cambridge Companion to T. S. Eliot*. Cambridge: Cambridge UP.

———. 2007. *Ezra Pound: Poet, Vol. 1, The Young Genius, 1885–1920*. Oxford and New York: Oxford UP.

Moore, Marianne. 1924. *Observations*. New York: Dial P.

———. 1986. *The Complete Prose of Marianne Moore*. Patricia C. Willis, ed. New York: Viking.

———. 1997. *The Selected Letters of Marianne Moore*. Bonnie Costello, ed., with Celeste Goodridge and Cristanne Miller. New York: Alfred Knopf.

Morgan, Thaïs, ed. 1994. *Men Writing the Feminine: Literature, Theory, and the Question of Genders*. Albany: SUNY P.

Morrison, Toni. 1992. *Playing in the Dark: Whiteness and the Literary Imagination*. Cambridge, MA: Harvard UP.

Mossin, Andrew. 2005. "'In Thicket': Charles Olson, Frances Boldereff, Robert Creeley and the Crisis of Masculinity at Mid-Century." *jml: Journal of Modern Literature* 28.4 (Summer): 13–40.

———. 2007. "'In Thicket': Charles Olson, Frances Boldereff, Robert Creeley and the Crisis of Masculinity at Mid-Century." In Grieve-Carlson, ed., 2007: 16–46.

———. 2010. *Male Subjectivity and Poetic Form in "New American" Poetry*. New York: Palgrave Macmillan.

Nelson, Cary. 1996. "The Fate of Gender in Modern American Poetry." In Dettmar and Watt, eds., 1996: 321–360.

Nelson, Maggie. 2007. *Women, the New York School, and Other True Abstractions*. Iowa City: U of Iowa P.

Ngai, Sianne. 2001. "Moody Subjects/Projectile Objects: Anxiety and Intellectual Displacement in Hitchcock, Heidegger, and Melville." *Qui Parle: Literature, Philosophy, Visual Arts, History* 12.2 (Spring/Summer): 15–55.

Nicholls, David G., ed. 2007. *Introduction to Scholarship in Modern Language and Literatures*. 3rd ed. New York: MLA Publications.

Nicholls, Peter. 1994. "'A Consciousness Disjunct': Sex and the Writer in Ezra Pound's 'Hugh Selwyn Mauberley.'" *Journal of American Studies* 28.1 (April): 61–75.

———. 2001. "'Arid Clarity': Ezra Pound, Mina Loy, and Jules Laforgue." *HOW2* 1.5 (March 2001). http://www.asu.edu/pipercwcenter/how2journal/archive/online_archive/v1_5_2001/current/in-conference/mina-loy/nicholls.html.

———. 2007. "The Poetics of Modernism." In Davis and Jenkins, eds., 2007: 51–67.

———. 2008. [Review of A. David Moody, *Ezra Pound: Poet*, vol. 1, 1885–1920. Oxford: Oxford UP, 2007.] *Modernism/Modernity* 15.3 (September): 571–573.

———. 2010. "The Elusive Allusion: Poetry and Exegesis." In Middleton and Marsh, eds., 2010: 10–24.

North, Michael. 1994. *The Dialect of Modernism: Race, Language, and Twentieth-Century Literature*. Oxford: Oxford UP.

———. 1999. *Reading 1922: A Return to the Scene of the Modern*. New York: Oxford UP.

Notley, Alice. 1980. *Dr. Williams' Heiresses*. San Francisco: Tuumba P.

Olson, Charles. 1947. *Call Me Ishmael: A Study of Melville*. San Francisco: City Lights Books.

———. 1966. *Selected Writings*. Robert Creeley, ed. New York: New Directions, 1966.

———. 1975. *Charles Olson & Ezra Pound: An Encounter at St. Elizabeths*. Ed. Catherine Seelye. New York: Grossman Publishers.

———. ca. 1978–1979. *Muthologos: The Collected Lectures & Interviews*. George F. Butterick, ed. Bolinas, CA: Four Seasons Foundation.

——. 1980–1987. *Charles Olson & Robert Creeley: The Complete Correspon-dence*. George F. Butterick, ed. 8 vols. Santa Barbara: Black Sparrow P. Vols. 1 and 2, 1980; vol. 3, 1981; vol. 4, 1982; vol. 5, 1983; vol. 6, 1985; vols. 7 and 8, 1987.

——. 1983. *The Maximus Poems*. Berkeley: U of California P.

——. 1987a. *Charles Olson & Cid Corman: Complete Correspondence, 1950–1964*. 2 vols. George Evans, ed. Orono, ME: National Poetry Foundation.

——. 1987b. *The Collected Poems of Charles Olson, Excluding the Maximus Poems*. George F. Butterick, ed. Berkeley: U of California P.

——. 1989a. *Letters for Origin, 1950–1956*. Albert Glover, ed. New York: Para-gon House.

——. 1989b. *A Nation of Nothing But Poetry: Supplementary Poems*. George F. Butterick, ed. Santa Rosa: Black Sparrow P.

——. 1990. *In Love, in Sorrow: The Complete Correspondence of Charles Olson and Edward Dahlberg*. Paul Christensen, ed. New York: Paragon House.

——. 1990/1996. *Charles Olson & Robert Creeley: The Complete Correspon-dence*. Vols. 9–10, completed by Richard Blevins, ed. Santa Barbara: Black Sparrow P. Vol. 9, 1990; vol. 10, 1996.

——. 1993. *Selected Poems*. Robert Creeley, ed. Berkeley: U of California P.

——. 1997. *Collected Prose*. Donald Allen and Benjamin Friedlander, eds. In-troduction by Robert Creeley. Berkeley: U of California P.

——. 1999. *Charles Olson and Frances Boldereff: A Modern Correspondence*. Ralph Maud and Sharon Thesen, eds. Middletown, CT: Wesleyan UP.

——. 2000. *Selected Letters*. Ralph Maud, ed. Berkeley: U of California P.

——. 2003. *Poet to Publisher: Charles Olson's Correspondence with Donald Allen*. Ralph Maud, ed. Vancouver: Talonbooks.

Orton, Fred, and Griselda Pollock. 1996. *Avant-Gardes and Partisans Reviewed*. Manchester: Manchester UP.

Pateman, Carole. 1989. *The Disorder of Women: Democracy, Feminism and Politi-cal Theory*. Stanford: Stanford UP.

——. 2002. "The Fraternal Social Contract." In Adams and Savran, eds., 2002: 118–134.

Perelman, Bob. 1984. "'A'-24." In *The L=A=N=G=U=A=G=E Book*. Bruce An-drews and Charles Bernstein, eds. Carbondale: Southern Illinois UP: 292–293.

——, ed. 1985. *Writing/Talks*. Carbondale: Southern Illinois UP.

——. 1994. *The Trouble with Genius: Reading Pound, Joyce, Stein, and Zukofsky*. Berkeley: U of California P.

Perelman, Bob, et al. 1978. Performances of Zukofsky's "A"-24, June and Novem-ber 1978. http://writing.upenn.edu/pennsound/x/Zukofsky.php.

Perloff, Marjorie. 1973. "Charles Olson and the 'Inferior Predecessors': 'Projec-tive Verse' Revisited." *ELH* 40.2 (Summer): 285–306.

———. 1995. "[Response to Ralph Maud, April 16, 1995.]" *Minutes of the Charles Olson Society* #8 (May [June?]): 34–36.

Pfeil, Fred. 1995. *White Guys: Studies in Postmodern Domination & Difference.* London: Verso.

Poggi, Christine. 1997. "Dreams of Metallized Flesh: Futurism and the Masculine Body." *Modernism/Modernity* 4.3 (September): 19–43.

Pollock, Griselda. 1993. "The Politics of Theory: Generations and Geographies: Feminist Theory and the Histories of Art History." *Genders* 17 (Fall): 97–120.

———. 1999. *Differencing the Canon: Feminist Desire and the Writing of Art's Histories.* London: Routledge.

Pound, Ezra. [1916] 1917. *Lustra, with Earlier Poems.* New York: Alfred A. Knopf.

———. [1920] 1967. *Instigations.* Freeport, NY: Books for Libraries P.

———. [1921] 1958. "Postscript to *The Natural Philosophy of Love* by Rémy de Gourmont." In *Pavannes and Divigations.* New York: New Directions: 203–214.

———. 1924. "A Communication." *1924: A Magazine of the Arts* 3 (Sept./Nov.): 97–98.

———. 1925. "Mr. Dunning's Poetry." *Poetry* 26.6 (September): 339–345.

———. [1926] [1950?]. *Personae: The Collected Shorter Poems of Ezra Pound.* New York: New Directions.

———. 1932a. "Harold Monro." *Criterion* 11 (July): 581–592.

———, ed. 1932b. *Profile: An Anthology Collected in MCMXXXI.* Milan: John Scheiwiller.

———. [1938] 1966. *Guide to Kulchur.* London: Peter Owen.

———. [1948] 2003. *The Pisan Cantos.* Richard Sieburth, ed. New York: New Directions.

———. 1950. *The Letters of Ezra Pound 1907–1941.* D. D. Paige, ed. New York: Harcourt, Brace & World.

———. 1954. *Literary Essays of Ezra Pound.* London: Faber & Faber.

———. 1968. *Drafts & Fragments of Cantos CX–CXVII.* New York: New Directions.

———. 1973. *Selected Prose, 1909–1965.* William Cookson, ed. New York: New Directions.

———. 1985. *Pound/Lewis: The Letters of Ezra Pound and Wyndham Lewis.* Timothy Materer, ed. New York: New Directions.

———. 1987. *Pound/Zukofsky: Selected Letters of Ezra Pound and Louis Zukofsky.* Barry Ahearn, ed. New York: New Directions.

———. 1988. *Pound/The Little Review: The Letters of Ezra Pound to Margaret Anderson: The Little Review Correspondence.* Thomas L. Scott, Melvin J. Friedman, and Jackson R. Bryer, eds. New York: New Directions.

———. 1991. *The Selected Letters of Ezra Pound to John Quinn, 1915–1924.* Timothy Materer, ed. Durham: Duke UP.

———. 1996a. *The Cantos of Ezra Pound.* New York: New Directions.

———. 1996b. *Pound/Williams: Selected Letters of Ezra Pound and William Carlos Williams.* Hugh Witemeyer, ed. New York: New Directions.

Probyn, Elspeth. 1993. *Sexing the Self: Gendered Positions in Cultural Studies.* London: Routledge.

Quartermain, Peter. 1992. *Disjunctive Poetics: From Gertrude Stein and Louis Zukofsky to Susan Howe.* Cambridge: Cambridge UP.

Rainey, Lawrence. 1999. "The Cultural Economy of Modernism." In Levenson, ed., 1999: 33–69.

———, ed. 2005. *The Annotated Waste Land with Eliot's Contemporary Prose.* New Haven: Yale UP.

———. 2007. "Pound or Eliot: Whose Era?" In Davis and Jenkins, eds., 2007: 87–113.

Retallack, Joan. 2003. *The Poethical Wager.* Berkeley: U of California P.

Rifkin, Libbie. 2000. *Career Moves: Olson, Creeley, Zukofsky, Berrigan and the American Avant-Garde.* Madison: U of Wisconsin P.

———. 2010. "Reconsidering the Company of Love: Creeley between Olson and Levertov." In Fredman and McCaffery, eds., 2010: 143–158.

Riviere, Joan. [1929] 1989. "Womanliness as a Masquerade." In Burgin et al., eds., 1989: 35–44.

Robertson, Ritchie. 1998. "Historicizing Weininger: The Nineteenth-Century German Image of the Feminized Jew." In Cheyette and Marcus, eds., 1998: 23–39.

Ross, Andrew. 1986. *The Failure of Modernism: Symptoms of American Poetry.* New York: Columbia UP.

Rubin, Gayle S. 1975. "The Traffic in Women: Notes on the 'Political Economy' of Sex." In *Toward an Anthropology of Women.* Rayna Rapp Reiter, ed. New York: Monthly Review P: 157–210.

Rumaker, Michael. 2003. *Black Mountain Days.* Asheville, NC: Black Mountain P.

Said, Edward. 1983. *The World, the Text, and the Critic.* Cambridge: Harvard UP.

———. 1993. *Culture and Imperialism.* New York: Alfred A. Knopf.

Satiricus, Doctor. 1920. *Doddering Daddies and the Wimpus.* Norfolk, VA: Sunshine Publishers.

Savran, David. 1992. *Communists, Cowboys, and Queers: The Politics of Masculinity in the Work of Arthur Miller and Tennessee Williams.* Minneapolis: U of Minnesota P.

———. 1998. *Taking It Like a Man: White Masculinity, Masochism, and Contemporary American Culture.* Princeton, NJ: Princeton UP.

Schwenger, Peter. 1989. "The Masculine Mode." In Showalter, ed., 1989: 101–112.

Scott, Bonnie Kime, ed. 1990. *The Gender of Modernism: A Critical Anthology.* Bloomington: Indiana UP.

Scott, Peter Dale. 1990. "Pound in 'The Waste Land,' Eliot in *The Cantos.*" *Paideuma* 19.3 (Winter): 99–114.

Scroggins, Mark, ed. 1997. *Upper Limit Music: The Writing of Louis Zukofsky.* Tuscaloosa: U of Alabama P.

———. 1998. *Louis Zukofsky and the Poetry of Knowledge.* Tuscaloosa: U of Alabama P.

———. 2007a. *The Poem of a Life: A Biography of Louis Zukofsky.* Emeryville, CA: Shoemaker, Hoard.

———. 2007b. "US Modernism II: The Other Tradition—Williams, Zukofsky, and Olson." In Davis and Jenkins, eds., 2007: 181–194.

Sedgwick, Eve Kosofsky. 1985. *Between Men: English Literature and Male Homosocial Desire.* New York: Columbia UP.

———. 1990. *Epistemology of the Closet.* Berkeley: U of California P.

———. 1993. *Tendencies.* Durham: Duke UP.

Segal, Lynne. 1990. *Slow Motion: Changing Masculinities, Changing Men.* London: Virago P.

———. 1999. *Why Feminism?* New York: Columbia UP.

———. 2001. "Back to the Boys? Temptations of the Good Gender Theorist." *Textual Practice* 15.2: 231–250.

Seymour-Jones, Carole. 2001. *Painted Shadow: A Life of Vivienne Eliot.* New York: Doubleday.

Shaw, Lytle. 2006. *Frank O'Hara: The Poetics of Coterie.* Iowa City: U of Iowa P.

Shklovsky, Victor. 1989. "From Art as Technique." In *Modern Literary Theory: A Reader.* Philip Rice and Patricia Waugh, eds. London: Edward Arnold: 16–21.

Showalter, Elaine, ed. 1989. *Speaking of Gender.* New York: Routledge.

Shreiber, Maeera Y. 2007. *Singing in a Strange Land: A Jewish American Poetics.* Stanford: Stanford UP.

Solomon-Godeau, Abigail. 1995. "Male Trouble." In Berger et al., eds., 1995: 69–76.

Spahr, Juliana. 2000. *Power Sonnets.* Brooklyn: Subpress Self-Publish or Perish.

Spicer, Jack. 2008. *My Vocabulary Did This to Me: The Collected Poetry of Jack Spicer.* Peter Gizzi and Kevin Killian, eds. Middletown, CT: Wesleyan UP.

Spivak, Gayatri Chakravorty. 1987. *In Other Worlds: Essays in Cultural Politics.* New York: Methuen.

———. 1993. "An Interview with Gayatri Chakravorty Spivak." Interviewed by Sara Danius and Stefan Jonsson. *boundary2* 20.2 (Summer): 24–50.

Stanley, Sandra Kumamoto. 1994. *Louis Zukofsky and the Transformation of a Modern American Poetics.* Berkeley: U of California P.

Stecopoulos, Harry, and Michael Uebel, eds. 1997. *Race and the Subject of Masculinities.* Durham: Duke UP.

Stein, Gertrude. [1927] 1980. "Patriarchal Poetry." In *The Yale Gertrude Stein.* Richard Kostelanetz, ed. New Haven: Yale UP: 106–146.

———. 1933. *The Autobiography of Alice B. Toklas.* In Stein [1946] 1962: 1–237.

———. [1935] 1985. *Lectures in America.* New York: Random House.

———. [1946] 1962. *Selected Writings of Gertrude Stein*. Carl Van Vechten, ed. New York: Modern Library.

Stillinger, Jack. 1991. *Multiple Authorship and the Myth of Solitary Genius*. New York: Oxford UP.

Stimpson, Catharine R. 1973–1974. "Charles Olson: Some Preliminary Images." *boundary 2* 2.1–2 (Fall–Winter): 151–172.

Suleiman, Susan. 1990. *Subversive Intent: Gender, Politics, and the Avant-Garde*. Cambridge, MA: Harvard UP.

Susman, Warren, with Edward Griffin. "Did Success Spoil the United States? Dual Representations in Postwar America." In L. May, ed., 1989: 19–37.

Sutton, Walter, ed. 1963. *Ezra Pound: A Collection of Critical Essays*. Englewood Cliffs, NJ: Prentice-Hall.

Terrell, Carroll F., ed. 1984. *Robert Creeley: The Poet's Workshop*. Orono, ME: National Poetry Foundation.

Thomas, Calvin. 1996. *Male Matters: Masculinity, Anxiety and the Male Body on the Line*. Urbana: U of Illinois P.

Thomas, Calvin, ed., with Joseph O. Aimone and Catherine A. F. MacGillivray. 2000. *Straight with a Twist: Queer Theory and the Subject of Heterosexuality*. Urbana: U of Illinois P.

Tickner, Lisa. 1994. "Men's Work? Masculinity and Modernism." In *Visual Culture: Images and Interpretations*. Norman Bryson, Michael Ann Holly, and Keith Moxley, eds. Hanover: Wesleyan UP: 42–82.

Tuma, Keith. 1998. *Fishing by Obstinate Isles: Modern and Postmodern British Poetry and American Readers*. Evanston, IL: Northwestern UP.

Urban Dictionary. n.d. www.urbandictionary.com.

von Hallberg, Robert. 1978. *Charles Olson: The Scholar's Art*. Cambridge, MA: Harvard UP.

Waldby, Catherine. 1995. "Destruction: Boundary Erotics and Refigurations of the Heterosexual Male Body." In Grosz and Probyn, eds., 1995: 266–277.

Waldman, Anne. 1993/1997. *Iovis*. Books I and II. Minneapolis: Coffee House P.

Watten, Barrett. 1985. *Total Syntax*. Carbondale: Southern Illinois UP.

———. 1998. "What I See in 'How I Became Hetty Jones.'" *Poetics Journal* 10 (June): 98–121.

———. 1999. "Career Anti-Triumphalism" [review of Libbie Rifkin, *Career Moves*]. *Sagetrieb: A Journal Devoted to Poets in the Imagist/Objectivist Tradition* 18.1 (Spring [pub. 2001]): 149–161.

———. 2000. "The Lost America of Love: A Genealogy." *Genre* 33 (Fall–Winter): 278–318.

———. 2003. *The Constructivist Moment: From Material Text to Cultural Poetics*. Middletown: Wesleyan UP.

Weiner, Hannah. 2007. *Hannah Weiner's Open House*. Patrick F. Durgin, ed. [Chicago]: Kenning Editions.

Weininger, Otto. [1903] 2005. *Sex and Character: An Investigation of Fundamental Principles*. Daniel Steuer, ed. Bloomington: Indiana UP.

Wellman, Donald. 2007. "Olson and Subjectivity: 'Projective Verse' and the Uncertainties of Sex." In Grieve-Carlson, ed., 2007: 47–61.

Wells, Susan. 2010. *Our Bodies, Ourselves and the Work of Writing*. Stanford: Stanford UP.

Whyte, William H. 1956. *The Organization Man*. Garden City, NY: Doubleday.

Wiegman, Robyn. "Unmaking: Men and Masculinity in Feminist Theory." In Gardiner, ed., 2002b: 31–59.

Wieners, John. 1972. *WOMAN*. A Curriculum of the Soul, #3. Canton, NY: Institute of Further Studies.

———. 1988. *Cultural Affairs in Boston: Poetry and Prose, 1956–1985*. Preface by Robert Creeley. Santa Rosa: Black Sparrow P.

Wilkinson, John. 2007. *The Lyric Touch*. Cambridge: Salt Publishing.

Williams, William Carlos. 1951. *The Autobiography of William Carlos Williams*. New York: New Directions.

———. 1996. *Pound/Williams: Selected Letters of Ezra Pound and William Carlos Williams*. Hugh Witemeyer, ed. New York: New Directions.

———. 2003. *The Correspondence of William Carlos Williams & Louis Zukofsky*. Barry Ahearn, ed. Middletown, CT: Wesleyan UP.

"The Wimpus Fraud." 1926. *Journal of the American Medical Association* 87.18 (30 October), 1497. jama.ama-assn.org/content/87/18/1497.full.pdf.

Woods, Tim. 2002. *The Poetic of the Limit: Ethics and Politics in Modern and Contemporary American Poetry*. New York: Palgrave.

Woolf, Virginia. [1929] 1957. *A Room of One's Own*. New York: Harcourt, Brace & World.

———. [1942] 1970. "Professions for Women" (1931). In *The Death of the Moth and Other Essays*. New York: Harcourt Brace Jovanovich: 235–242.

Wordsworth, William. 1974. *The Prose Works of William Wordsworth*. W. J. B. Owen and Jane Worthington Smyser, eds. Vol. 1. Oxford: Clarendon P.

Zukofsky, Louis. 1927. "Preface." *Exile* 3: 8.

———, ed. 1932. *An "Objectivists" Anthology*. Le Beausset/New York: TO Publishers.

———. [1967] 2000. *Prepositions+: The Collected Critical Essays*. Additional prose edited and introduced by Mark Scroggins. Middletown, CT: Wesleyan UP.

———. 1969. "Louis Zukofsky Interviewed by L. S. Dembo (1968)." *Contemporary Literature* 10.2 (Spring): 203–219.

———. 1978a. *"A."* Berkeley: U of California P.

———. 1987b. *Pound/Zukofsky: Selected Letters of Ezra Pound and Louis Zukofsky*. Barry Ahearn, ed. New York: New Directions.

———. 1991. *Complete Short Poetry*. Baltimore: Johns Hopkins UP.

———. 2003. *The Correspondence of William Carlos Williams and Louis Zukofsky*. Barry Ahearn, ed. Middletown, CT: Wesleyan UP.

———. 2006. *Louis Zukofsky: Selected Poems*. Charles Bernstein, ed. New York: Library of America.

Index

Contemporary North American Poetry Series

Industrial Poetics: Demo Tracks for a Mobile Culture
By Joe Amato

What Are Poets For? An Anthropology of Contemporary Poetry and Poetics
By Gerald L. Bruns

Postliterary America: From Bagel Shop Jazz to Micropoetries
By Maria Damon

*Purple Passages: Pound, Eliot, Zukofsky, Olson, Creeley, and
the Ends of Patriarchal Poetry*
By Rachel Blau DuPlessis

On Mount Vision: Forms of the Sacred in Contemporary American Poetry
By Norman Finkelstein

Form, Power, and Person in Robert Creeley's Life and Work
By Stephen Fredman and Steven McCaffery

Jorie Graham: Essays on the Poetry
Edited by Thomas Gardner
University of Wisconsin Press, 2005

Gary Snyder and the Pacific Rim: Creating Countercultural Community
By Timothy Gray

Urban Pastoral: Natural Currents in the New York School
By Timothy Gray

Racial Things, Racial Forms: Objecthood in Avant-Garde Asian American Poetry
By Joseph Jonghyun Jeon

We Saw the Light: Conversations between the New American Cinema and Poetry
By Daniel Kane

History, Memory, and the Literary Left: Modern American Poetry, 1935–1968
By John Lowney

Paracritical Hinge: Essays, Talks, Notes, Interviews
By Nathaniel Mackey
University of Wisconsin Press, 2004

Behind the Lines: War Resistance Poetry on the American Homefront
By Philip Metres

Hold-Outs: The Los Angeles Poetry Renaissance, 1948–1992
By Bill Mohr

Frank O'Hara: The Poetics of Coterie
By Lytle Shaw

Renegade Poetics: Black Aesthetics and Formal Innovation in African American Poetry
By Evie Shockley

Radical Vernacular: Lorine Niedecker and the Poetics of Place
Edited by Elizabeth Willis